LEGENDARY LOCALS

OF

WALLA WALLA

WASHINGTON

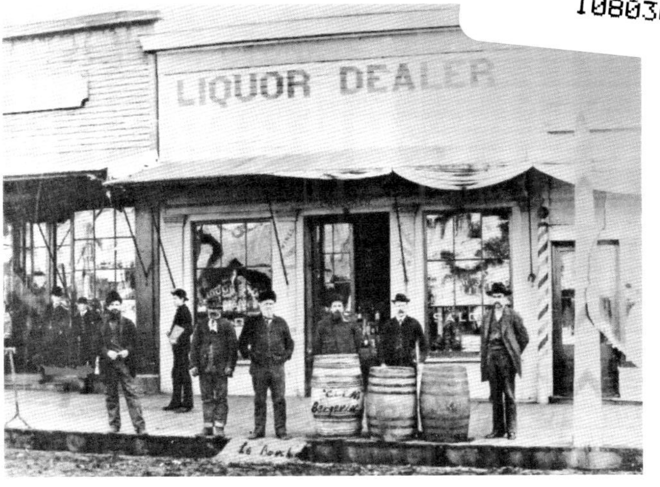

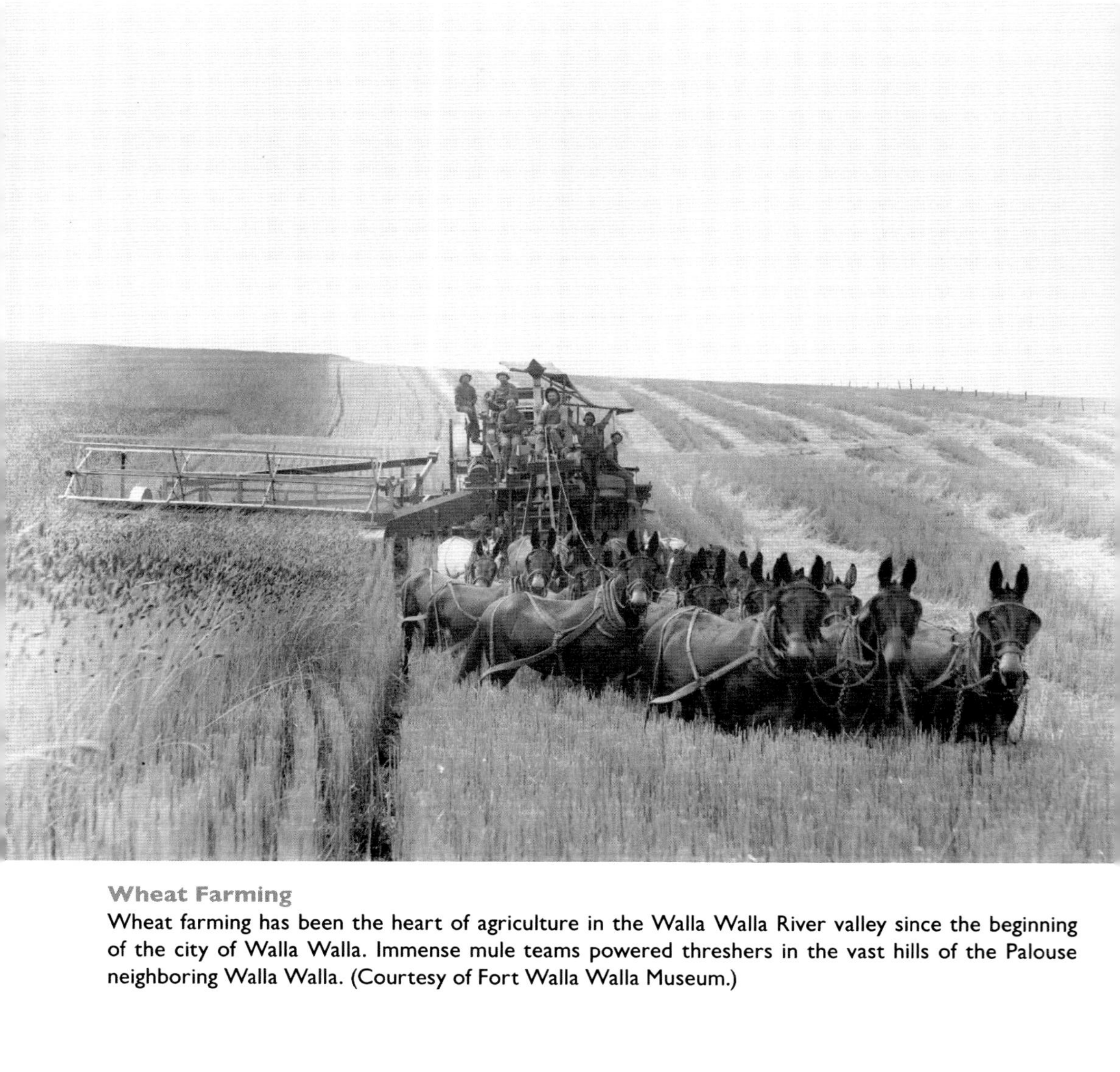

Wheat Farming
Wheat farming has been the heart of agriculture in the Walla Walla River valley since the beginning of the city of Walla Walla. Immense mule teams powered threshers in the vast hills of the Palouse neighboring Walla Walla. (Courtesy of Fort Walla Walla Museum.)

Page 1: Clem Bergevin at Le Boucher's Saloon
Clem Bergevin (third from right) is pictured in front of Le Boucher's saloon in the early days of Walla Walla. The saloon dates back to when the frontier town catered to miners on their way to the gold fields in Idaho and beyond. The saloon was destroyed in the great fire of 1887. (Courtesy of Claro Bergevin.)

LEGENDARY LOCALS

OF

WALLA WALLA

WASHINGTON

DIANE B. REED

LEGENDARY LOCALS

ISBN 978-1-4671-0117-2

Legendary Locals is an imprint of Arcadia Publishing
Charleston, South Carolina

Printed in the United States of America

Library of Congress Control Number: 2013944360

For all general information, please contact Arcadia Publishing:
Telephone 843-853-2070
Fax 843-853-0044
E-mail sales@arcadiapublishing.com
For customer service and orders:
Toll-Free 1-888-313-2665

Visit us on the Internet at www.arcadiapublishing.com

On the Front Cover: Clockwise from top left:
Gen. Jonathan Mayhew Wainwright, native son (Courtesy of Library of Congress, see page 79), Adam West, actor (Author's collection, see page 92), PioPio-Maksmaks, Walla Walla Indian, son of Peo-Peo-Mox-Mox (Courtesy of Library of Congress, see page 66), Jeannette Hayner, Walla Walla School Board, state legislator, senate majority leader (Courtesy of Washington State Archives, see page 95), Izzy the camel (Colby Kuschatka photograph, see page 121), Tony Criscola, big-league baseball player (Author's collection, see page 83), Yuso Shinbo, Japanese pioneer (Courtesy of Shinbo family, see page 81), Dean Derby, Walla Walla High School and University of Washington athlete, NFL football player, Spring Valley Wines (Greg Lehman photograph, see page 101), Josephine "Dutch Jo" Wolfe (portrayed by Lois Hahn of Fort Walla Walla Museum), madam (Author photograph, see page 33).

On the Back Cover: From left to right:
Clem Bergevin at Le Boucher's saloon (Courtesy of Claro Bergevin, see page 1), wheat farming in the Walla Walla River valley (Courtesy of Fort Walla Walla Museum, see page 2).

CONTENTS

ACKNOWLEDGMENTS

When I was asked to write a book titled *Legendary Locals of Walla Walla*, I quickly realized it would be impossible to recognize all the notable people throughout Walla Walla's long and illustrious history. So this book is in many ways a starting point for your own journey through the history of Walla Walla and the Walla Walla River valley. Enjoy it, and then let it pique your interest to learning more about your own favorite legendary locals. Because there are so many interesting and important figures in Walla Walla's history, I chose remarkable people who represent a wide range of figures—Indian tribes, early explorers, settlers, merchants, manufacturers, artists, musicians, civic leaders, and more. This history ranges from the days before there was a city of Walla Walla and through the area's economic ups and downs to its remarkable renaissance, paving the way for a bright future.

Along my journey, I have been privileged to work with many people who helped me tell this fascinating story. I am especially indebted to James Payne and Laura Schulz at Fort Walla Walla Museum, Bill Huntington of Whitman College and Northwest Archives, Brooke Davey of Walla Walla University Archives, and Joe Drazan of Bygone Walla Walla. They not only assisted me in assembling the images in the book, they also provided feedback, ideas, and encouragement. And thanks to Angie Gibson of Providence St. Mary Medical Center, Jeanne McMenemy of ArtWalla, and all the individuals, organizations, and businesses who shared their photographs and memories of Walla Wallans past and present. Special thanks go to James Payne, Dan Clark, Joe Drazan, and others who reviewed the list of subjects and suggested legendary figures who might be included. Finally, special thanks to my husband, Bruce Henrickson, who ably served as sounding board and copy editor and offered the author much-needed encouragement.

This book belongs to all of you, and to everyone who loves Walla Walla.

INTRODUCTION

Before people settled in the Walla Walla River valley, massive floods scoured today's Columbia River Basin during the Ice Age. Glacial Lake Missoula (near present-day Missoula, Montana), dammed by ice jams, periodically burst and tore through the basin. The floods, which began about 15,300 years ago and ended about 12,700 years ago, carved new channels for the ancient Columbia River, at times forming a lake that covered most of the Walla Walla Valley. When the waters finally receded, the Walla Walla River valley remained.

The first well-documented people who lived near the mouth of the Walla Walla River in the area now known as Wallula appeared between 8,000 and 11,000 years ago. Since then, the Walla Walla River valley served as a crossroads, trading center, and meeting place. Before Lewis and Clark and the early explorers arrived, Indian tribes gathered seasonally at Wallula at the confluence of the Walla Walla River and the mighty Columbia River to greet salmon runs and trade. A short distance up the Walla Walla River was an area rich in mussels and sturgeon, ideal for setting up fish weirs (nets).

So it was not surprising that the British, Canadians, and later, the Americans would choose this meeting place as a location for their trading posts. Later, one of the branches of the Oregon Trail passed through the Walla Walla River valley, a route that took pioneers to Wallula and transportation down the Columbia River.

The establishment of the Whitman Mission in 1836 marked the beginning of the end of traditional life for the Indian tribes in the valley. A devastating outbreak of measles and the subsequent slayings at Whitman Mission in 1847 set in motion the eventual displacement of the Indians, first through the treaty councils of 1855 and 1856 and ultimately by force. Col. Edward J. Steptoe built the first military fort, a temporary blockhouse and stockade constructed in 1856 that was followed by a more substantial fort in what is now downtown Walla Walla. In 1858, a permanent fort was completed on a square mile of land southwest of the city. With the presence of the fort and the expulsion of the tribes, the valley was open for white settlement.

The completion of the Mullan Road in 1862 ensured Walla Walla's role as the preeminent commercial center of the Inland Northwest. Intended as a military road, it became important as a route for miners headed for the goldfields of Idaho and beyond. And it proved to be a conduit for pioneers coming west, some of whom settled in the valley. The city was situated perfectly to take advantage of commerce these groups generated.

Walla Walla was soon affected by two gold rushes, one involving the mineral and the miners, the other embodied by rolling hills of golden wheat. So by the time the mining rush had waned, the city was already enjoying a strong agricultural prosperity. The introduction of orchards, nurseries, livestock, and the first vineyards laid the roots of Walla Walla's agricultural diversity.

The city transformed itself from a frontier town to a prosperous regional center. It quickly developed institutions that would create a well-rounded community—government, newspapers, churches, schools, libraries, hospitals, and colleges. Civic-minded leaders and citizens donated time and money to ensure that Walla Walla would be a community to be proud of. They lobbied the state to establish the territorial prison in the city, and that penitentiary still provides employment for the community. Walla Walla was larger than Seattle until the 1880s and was even suggested as a possible state capital.

Walla Walla continued to prosper into the 20th century. Its economy thrived on a diverse blend of agriculture, canning, manufacturing, and commerce. Immigrants brought a rich cultural, agricultural, and institutional presence. From the first peoples in the valley to the present day, newcomers throughout the years have found a home in the area. French, Italians, Germans, Chinese, Japanese, Latinos, and many other groups and individuals came to Walla Walla for a better life and enriched the city and valley.

The early part of the 20th century saw the construction many landmark buildings in downtown Walla Walla. Baker Boyer Bank, founded in 1869, rose to new heights in 1911 with its seven-story headquarters, a building befitting a prosperous city. In 1928, the president of the bank, W.W. Baker, spearheaded a community fundraising campaign to help finance an equally magnificent building to accommodate visitors, the Marcus Whitman Hotel. Both buildings are still Walla Walla landmarks.

City residents supported two hospitals, a YMCA and YWCA, parks, sports teams, and colleges. The city also embarked on an initiative to create a series of beautiful parks.

At the same time, the fate of Fort Walla Walla was uncertain. The fort closed on September 28, 1910. In 1921, the fort was transferred to the Veterans Bureau (later the Veterans Administration). In 1959, it became a veterans' general medical and surgical facility (now the Jonathan M. Wainwright Memorial VA Medical Center).

The outbreak of World War II brought war to Walla Walla's doorstep both in terms of sacrifices made by its citizens and as home to the US Army Air Force (USAAF) airfield. After the war, the airfield once again became the city's airport. A new military presence came with the establishment of the US Army Corps of Engineers Walla Walla District in 1948.

The opening of Walla Walla Community College in 1966 was a welcome addition to higher education in the valley.

By the 1980s, Walla Walla, especially the downtown, seemed to be experiencing an identity crisis. With the best of intentions, many property owners had modernized their buildings, hiding or destroying historical facades. The arrival of a suburban mall in 1989 threatened the viability of the aging downtown. The formation of the Downtown Walla Walla Foundation sparked a Local Improvement District that helped finance streetscape improvements, encouraged millions of dollars of restoration, and attracted shoppers and visitors to the downtown through promotions, events, and infrastructure improvements.

Today, the Confederated Tribes of the Umatilla Indian Reservation (Walla Walla, Cayuse, and Umatilla) are headquartered in nearby Mission, Oregon. While they maintain their ancient traditions, they have become the largest employer in Umatilla County, Oregon, operating a casino, a hotel, a golf course, technology and energy businesses, and a thriving business park. Their museum at Tamástslikt Cultural Institute highlights the rich culture of the tribes. The tribal department of natural resources is also active in restoring habitat on the Walla Walla River and its tributaries to protect the salmon, a traditional food.

Walla Walla is well known for its wineries. From the first commercial wineries of the 1970s, the wine industry has grown to more than 100 wineries. Visitors and locals enjoy wine at nearby vineyards and downtown tasting rooms and flock to special seasonal events like Fall Release Weekend and Holiday Barrel Tasting.

Walla Walla attracts visitors, retirees, and businesses with its charm, economic diversity, and quality of life. Anchored in its rich history and surrounded by natural beauty and architectural treasures, Walla Walla looks forward to a bright future.

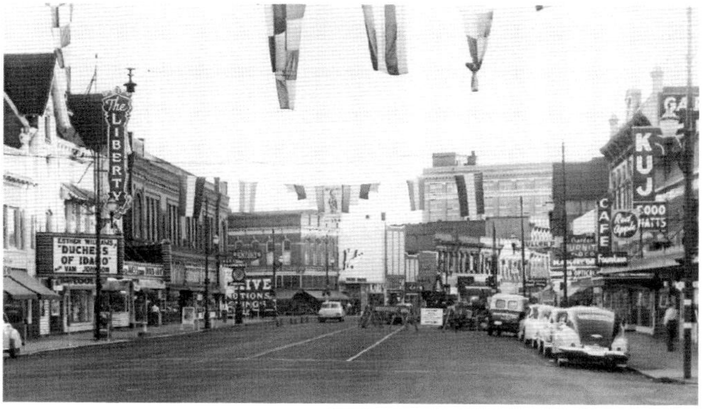

Downtown Scene
Downtown Walla Walla is pictured here in the 1940s. (Courtesy of Joe Drazan.)

CHAPTER ONE

In the Beginning

In the beginning, there was the landscape. The Walla Walla River valley was carved by the Ice Age floods and sculpted by its many waterways. The Indian people gave it the name *Walla Walla*—the place of many waters. The tribes and bands lived in this area for thousands of years before the white man "discovered" it.

For the most part, Indian people welcomed early visitors—including the British and Lewis and Clark—little knowing that the travelers were evaluating the area for their own purposes. The fur trading posts run by the Hudson's Bay Company at the mouth of the Walla Walla River heralded an influx of newcomers.

Among the first newcomers to the valley were the Métis (of mixed French and Indian ancestry). These trappers and traders lived in relative harmony with their Indian neighbors, and the early French pioneers who farmed in the valley were accepted by the tribes as well.

When missionaries Marcus and Narcissa Whitman arrived in the valley, they were initially tolerated. They tried to convert the tribes to their religion but to little avail. But as more settlers streamed into the area and brought diseases for which the Indian people had no defenses, tensions escalated. After a measles outbreak decimated a nearby Cayuse village, the Whitmans were blamed, and they and others at the mission were slain.

Settlers sought to buy land that the tribes understood belonged to no one, and tensions escalated. After the treaty council of 1855 and the ensuing rapid push to move the Indians out of the valley, the tribes engaged in a fierce battle with the Oregon Volunteers from December 7 to 11, 1855, resulting in the death of Chief Peo-Peo-Mox-Mox. A final treaty council was held in 1856, and the Indians were forced out of the Walla Walla Valley and onto reservations.

The influx of white settlers resumed. Out of this period of conflict and change, Walla Walla was poised to become a city.

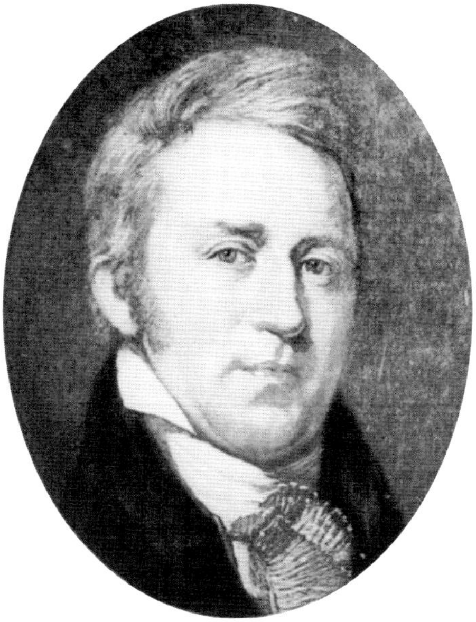

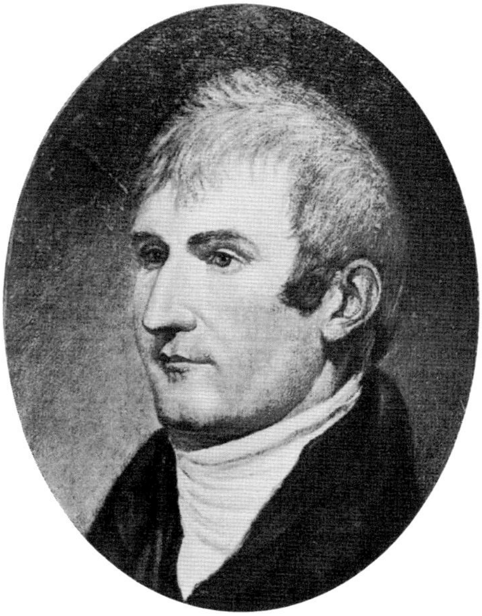

Capt. Meriwether Lewis (Right) and Lt. William Clark (Left), Explorers
Lewis and Clark, their interpreter Sacagawea, and the Corps of Discovery passed the confluence of the Walla Walla and Columbia Rivers on their way west in 1805. They traveled overland through the Walla Walla Valley on their way back from the mouth of the Columbia River in 1806. Although Lewis and Clark's quest to find the Northwest Passage was unsuccessful in locating a viable water route across the American continent, their expedition sought to establish the United States' claim to the Pacific Northwest, which brought settlers to the Walla Walla Valley just a few decades later. (Above, both courtesy of Library of Congress; below, courtesy of Fort Walla Walla Museum.)

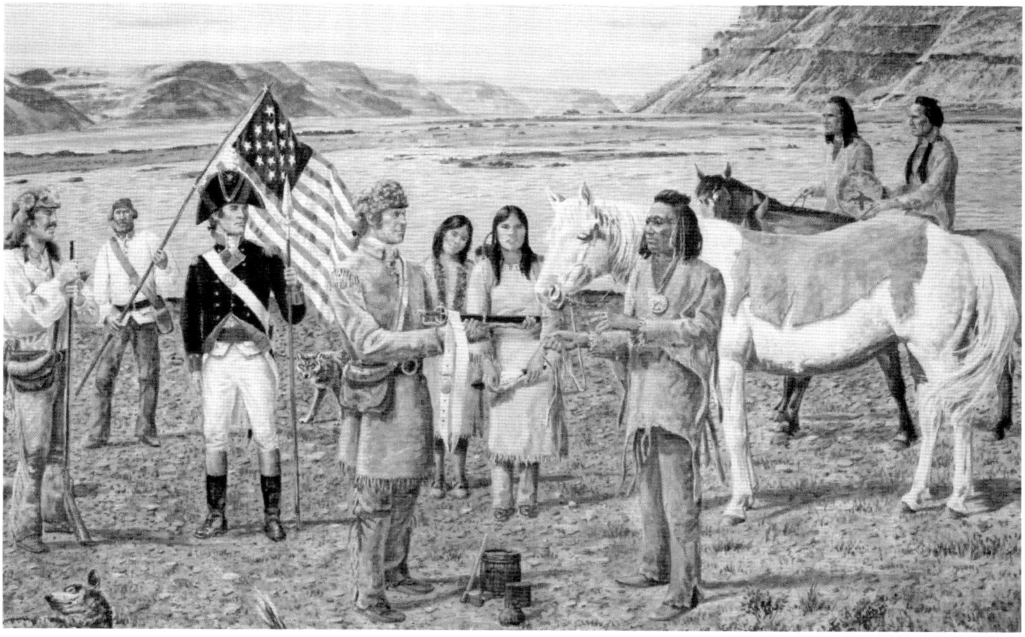

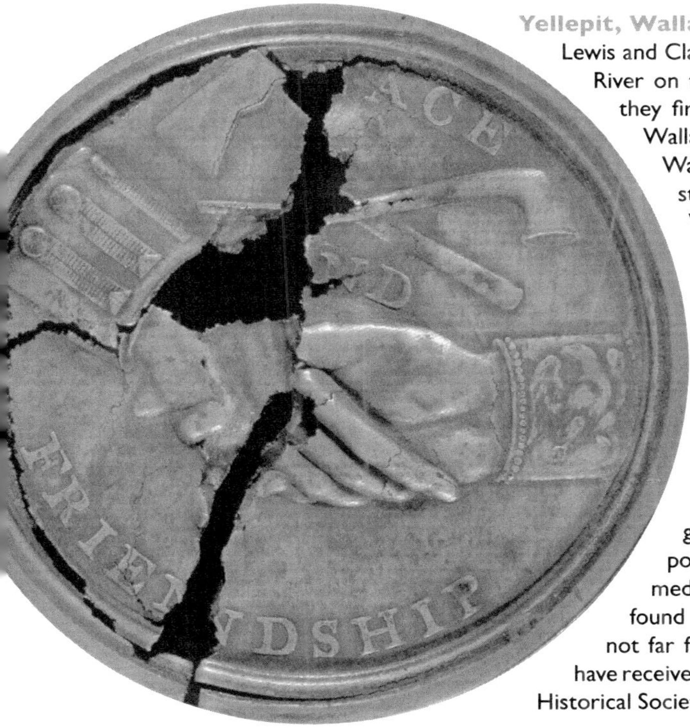

Yellepit, Walla Walla Headman

Lewis and Clark had finally arrived at the Columbia River on their way to the Pacific Ocean when they first encountered a band of the Walla Walla tribe near the mouth of the Walla Walla River. In April 1806, the party also stopped for several days at the Walla Walla Indian village on their return trip. Various gifts were exchanged, and the explorers received a magnificent white stallion from Walla Walla headman Yellepit (depicted in the Norman Adams painting on the opposite page). In return, the headman asked for a copper kettle, but the party did not have any left. So William Clark gave Yellepit his personal sword, and Lewis and Clark gave Yellepit a peace medal bearing a portrait of Thomas Jefferson. The peace medal shown here was, by one account, found on an island near Wallula in the 1880s not far from the location where Yellepit may have received his medal. (Both, courtesy of Oregon Historical Society OrHi 100141, 100142.)

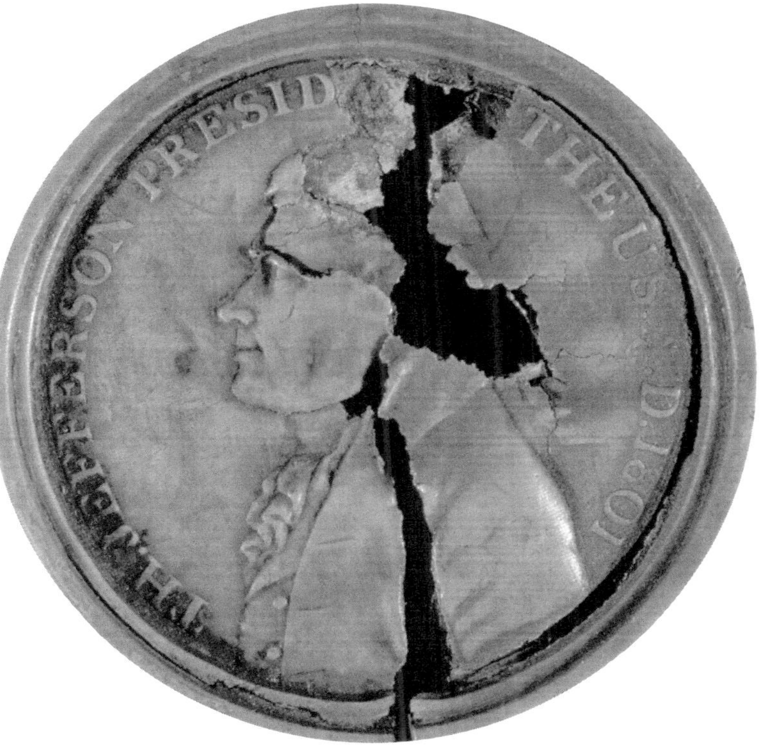

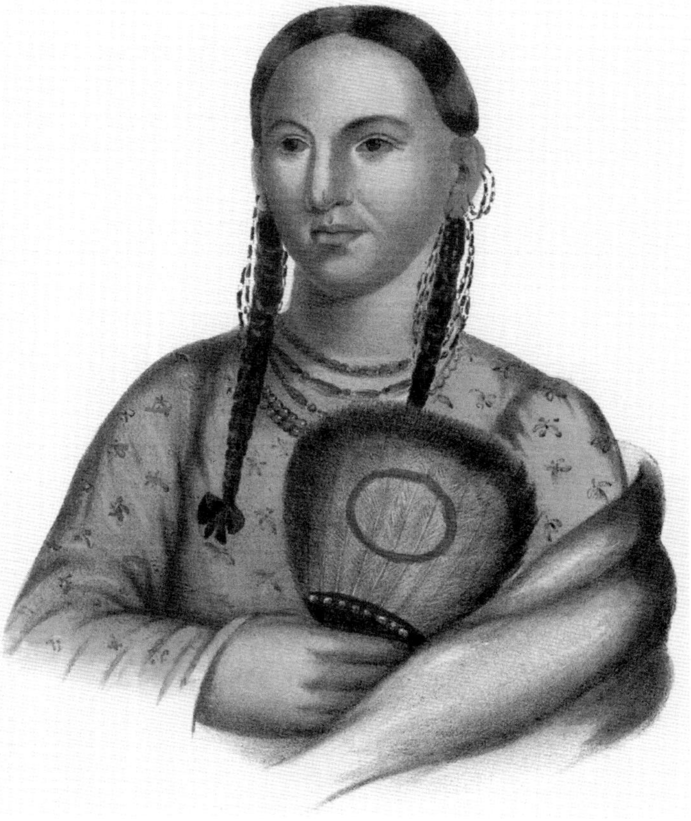

Marie Aioe Dorion, Indian Heroine

Marie Aioe Dorion (1786–1850), a courageous Iowa Indian, accompanied her husband Pierre Dorion when he served as the interpreter to the Astor Expedition (1810–1812), the first fur traders to reach the Columbia River from Montreal. Dorion was the second woman to come overland to the West, though she is not as well known as her predecessor, Sacagawea. Dorion and the Astor party traveled to Fort Astoria near the mouth of the Columbia. In 1813, the Dorions left Fort Astoria with a trapping party, which set up a base of operations at the confluence of the Boise and Snake Rivers in January 1814. At the base camp, Marie was warned about a possible raid on her husband's trapping party, which had gone up the Boise River. With her two sons, she set out to warn him but arrived too late. Only the gravely wounded Giles LeClerc had survived. Marie strapped LeClerc to his horse to make the three-day trip back to the base camp, but he died on the way. When she got to the base camp, she found that everyone there had been slain—she and her two sons were alone in the wilderness. Fearing the raiders would return, Dorion headed northwest to seek refuge with one of the friendlier tribes near the Columbia River, but winter snows stranded her and her sons in the Blue Mountains for almost two months. Desperate, she finally set out alone to seek help and was found by the Walla Walla Indians. They took her to their village and sent scouts who rescued the children. Dorion married again, first to trapper Louis Venier at Fort Okanogan, and after Venier's death, to Jean Toupin, an interpreter at Fort Nez Perce. She died in 1850 in St. Louis, Oregon, where she had been known as "Madame Dorion," and was buried at the log cabin Roman Catholic church there. Dorion is celebrated at Madame Dorion Memorial Park at the confluence of the Walla Walla River and the Columbia River. The park is near the site of Fort Nez Perce, now inundated by Lake Wallula behind McNary Lock and Dam. (Courtesy of State Historical Society of Iowa, Iowa City.)

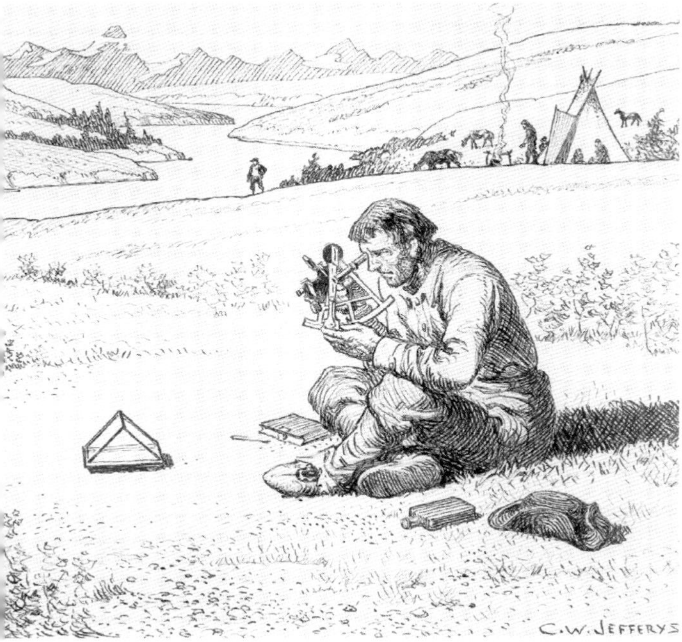

David Thompson, North West Company

In 1811, David Thompson was one of the earliest white people to reach the Walla Walla Valley. Thompson, a surveyor and mapmaker for the British-Canadian North West Company, was the first white person known to navigate the entire length of the Columbia River. On July 9, 1811, he met Yellepit of the Walla Walla Indians, who showed him the peace medal he had received from Lewis and Clark. Thompson promised Yellepit that the North West Company would build a trading post nearby, but it never came to be. (Illustration by Charles William Jefferys, courtesy of Library and Archives Canada C-073573.)

David Douglas, Naturalist

Scottish naturalist David Douglas made three trips to the Northwest between 1825 and 1834 on behalf of the Royal Horticultural Society, collecting and describing more than 200 different species of birds, animals, and plants. He was a regular visitor at the Hudson's Bay Company fort at the confluence of the Walla Walla and Columbia Rivers. In June 1826, he headed into the Blue Mountains in search of alpine plants, a foray he repeated four years later. Many of Douglas's specimens were propagated by the Royal Horticultural Society and introduced into English and European gardens, including one of his namesakes, the Douglas fir. (Courtesy of Oregon Historical Society, CN 019683.)

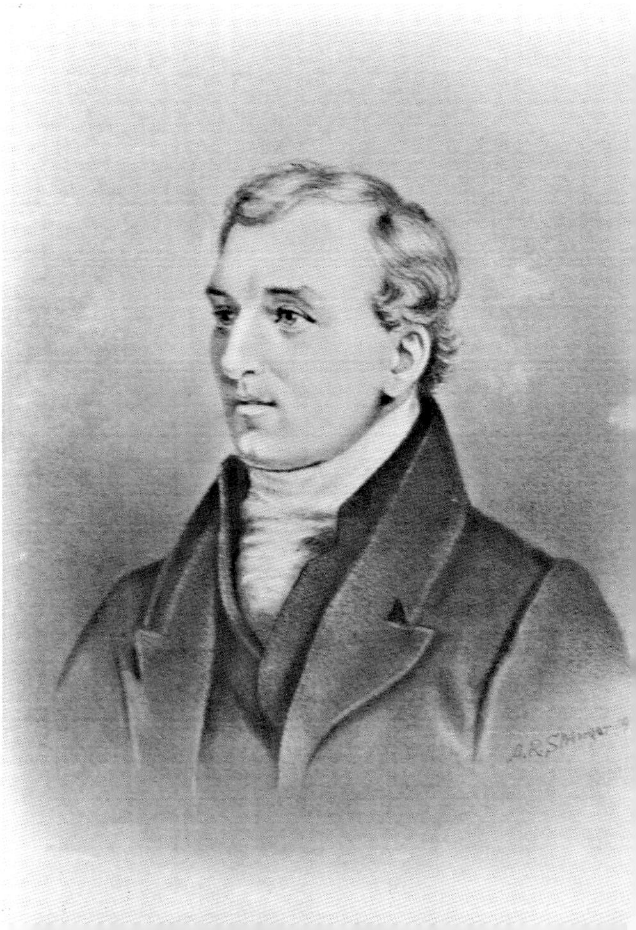

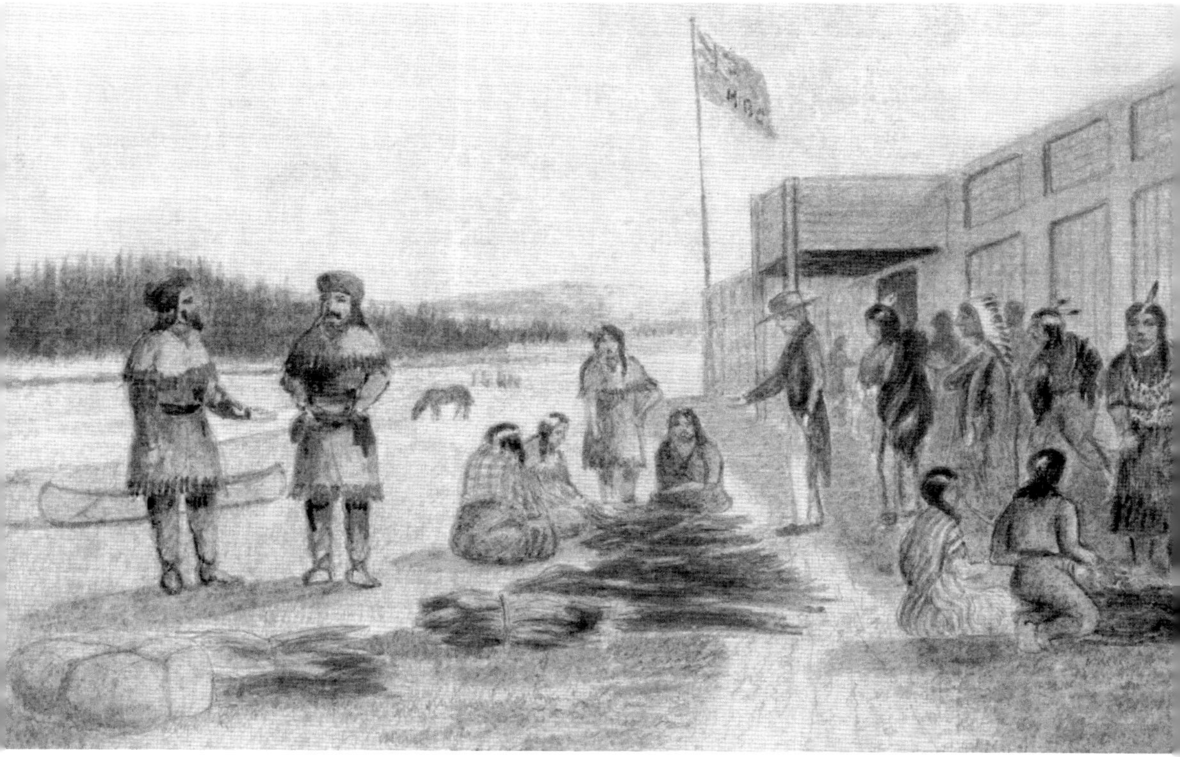

Pierre Pambrun, Hudson's Bay Company Trader
Born in Quebec, Canada, in 1792, Pierre Chrysologue Pambrun ran the Hudson's Bay Company's Fort Walla Walla (shown in this c. 1841 drawing by Joseph Drayton) on the Columbia River at Wallula from 1832 until his death in 1841. Pambrun welcomed notables including Capt. Benjamin Bonneville and Kit Carson, and he helped Marcus and Narcissa Whitman negotiate with the Cayuse Indians for permission to build their mission at Waiilatpu. Pambrun's son Andrew Dominique Pambrun was the chief trader at the fort from 1852 to 1854, and his descendants still live in the valley. (Courtesy of Oregon Historical Society OrHi 964.)

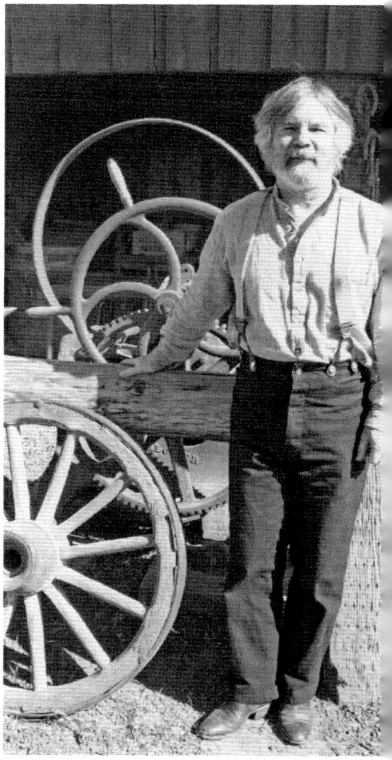

William McBean, Chief Factor of Hudson's Bay Company
William McBean, of British and Indian parentage (Métis), came to Wallula in 1846. He was the chief factor (manager) of the Hudson's Bay Company fort at the mouth of the Walla Walla River at the time of the slayings at the Whitman Mission in 1847. McBean left the area in 1855 at the time of the Indian Wars and later returned with his Indian wife and children, living in Walla Walla until his death in 1872. Here, William McBean is portrayed by Richard Monacelli at Fort Walla Walla Museum. (Author photograph.)

Peo-Peo-Mox-Mox (Yellow Bird), Chief of the Walla Walla Tribe

Peo-Peo-Mox-Mox, also known as Yellow Bird, was the leader of the Walla Walla Indians. He represented the tribe at the Walla Walla Treaty Council called by territorial governor Isaac Stevens on May 29, 1855. He advocated for a separate treaty granting a reservation for the Walla Walla, Cayuse, and Umatilla Indians near their ancestral homelands. In negotiations with Stevens, Peo-Peo-Mox-Mox was assured that the tribes would not have to move to the reservation for several years. However, as soon as the treaty was signed, there was an immediate influx of white settlers into the valley. By December, the 1st Oregon Volunteers had entered the Walla Walla Valley in response to the conflict between settlers and the Indian people. Peo-Peo-Mox-Mox and several others were taken hostage. On December 7, 1855, a battle broke out between the Oregon troops and the tribes. The Walla Wallas, Cayuse, Umatillas, and others defended the Walla Wallas' position near Frenchtown on the Walla Walla River. On the first day of the conflict, the chief and other hostages were killed. The Battle of Walla Walla raged for four days, with the tribes finally fleeing east beyond the Snake River. By 1858, Northwest tribes ceased to resist the incursion of white settlers. Today, the site of the battle is part of the Frenchtown Historic Site east of Touchet. This bronze statue of the chief by sculptor Roger McGee is located at West Rose Street and Third Avenue in Walla Walla. (Author photograph.)

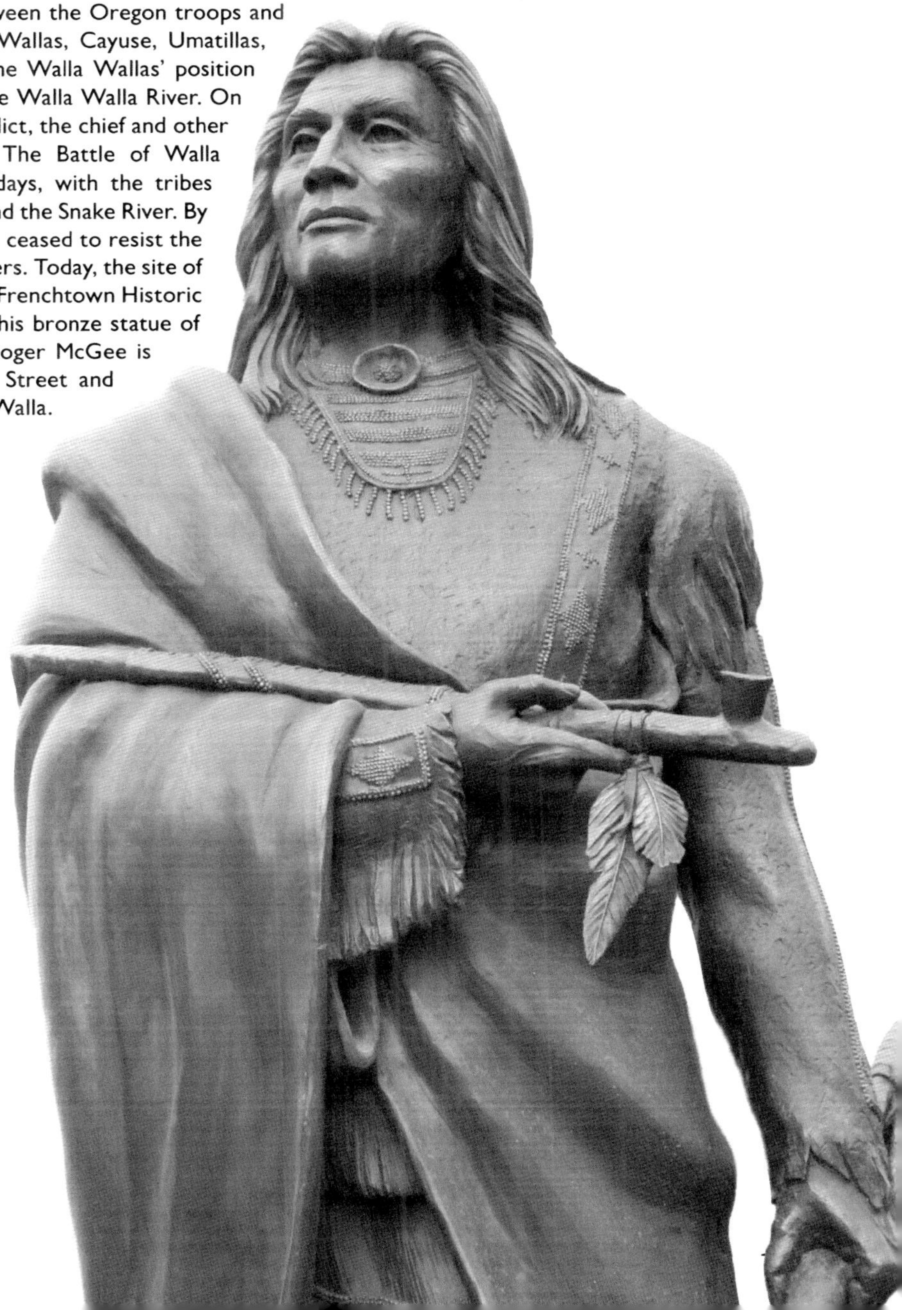

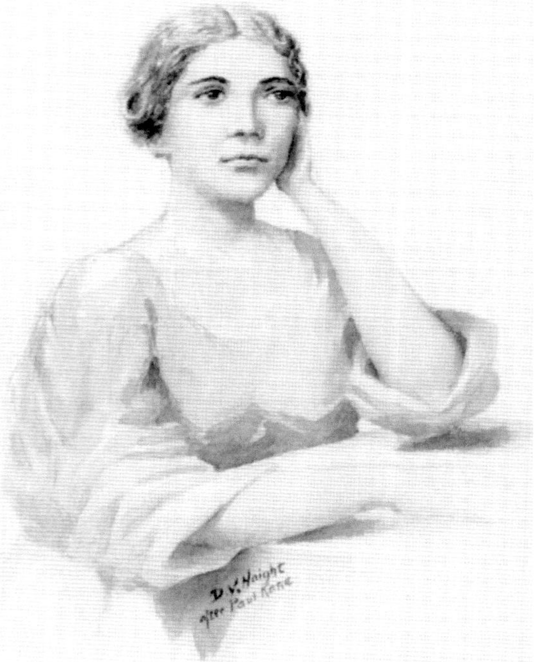

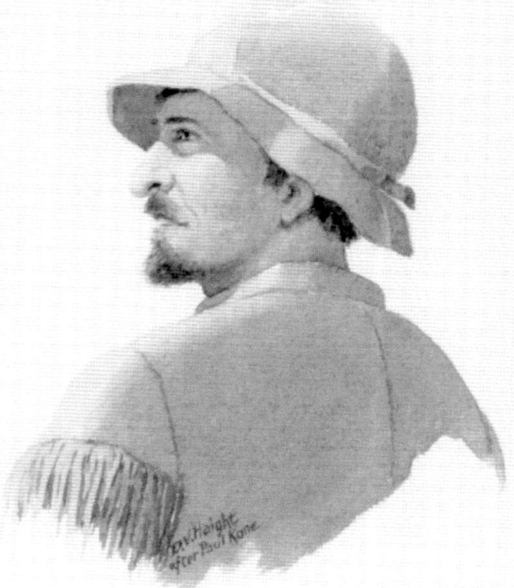

Marcus and Narcissa Whitman, Missionaries
Marcus and Narcissa Whitman came by wagon train to the Walla Walla Valley in 1836 to establish a mission among the Cayuse Indians. They established their mission at Waiilatpu on the Walla Walla River along what would become one of the Oregon Trail routes. The Whitmans had limited success converting the Cayuse. In 1843, Marcus led a wagon train of white settlers from Fort Hall, Idaho, into the valley, and he and Narcissa subsequently set up a boarding school for the pioneer children. The influx of settlers to the area brought tension with the tribes and diseases that Indians succumbed to in significant numbers. A measles epidemic in 1847 decimated the Cayuse. Although the Whitmans did their best to tend to them, half of the tribe died, including most of their children. The tribe accused Marcus Whitman of poisoning them. They considered him to be a white medicine man, and their own medicine men would have been slain for this offense. On November 29, 1847, half a dozen Cayuse warriors killed the Whitmans and 12 other white settlers and destroyed most of the buildings at the mission. (Both, courtesy of National Park Service.)

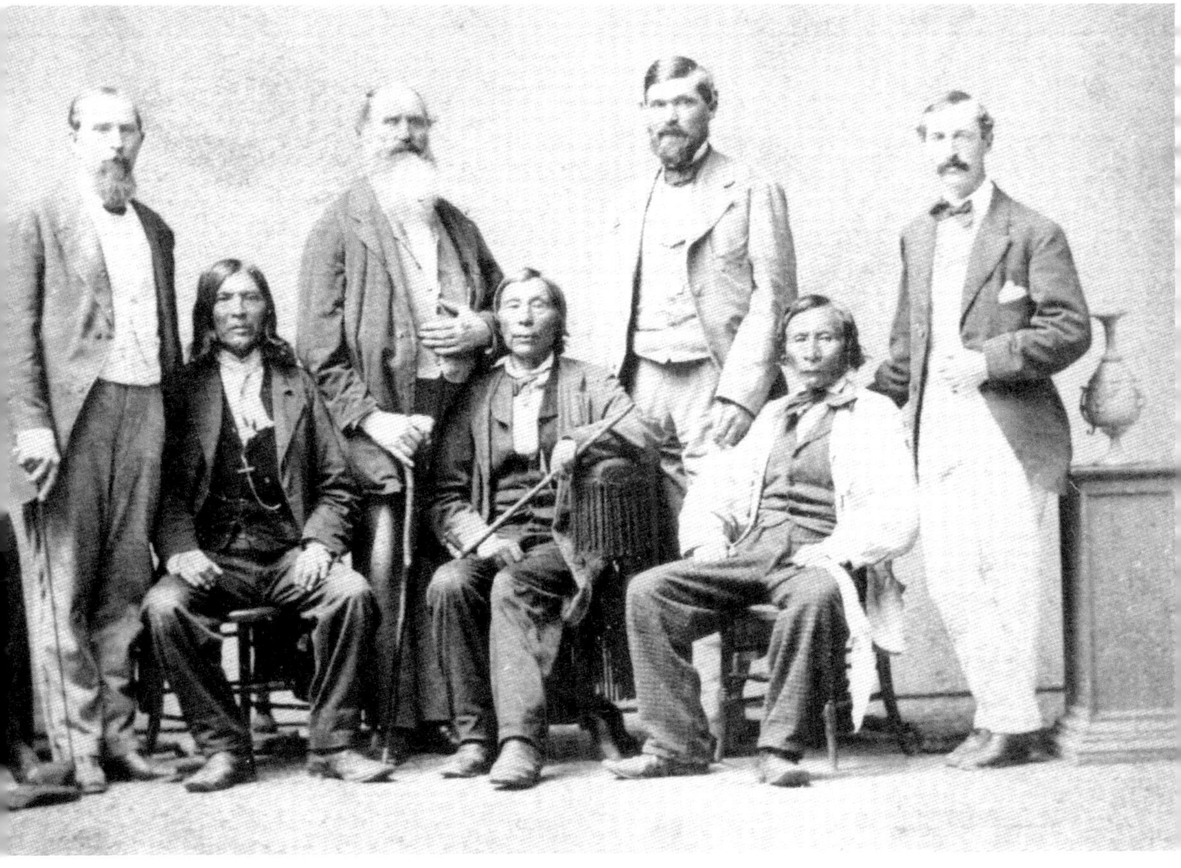

Chief Timothy, Nez Perce Indian Guide

Chief Timothy (1808–1891) of the Nez Perce converted to Christianity and was baptized by Marcus Whitman's colleague Henry Spalding, who had established a mission amid the Nez Perce east of present-day Lewiston, Idaho. After the Whitmans were slain in 1847, Timothy went to Whitman Mission to rescue Spalding's daughter Eliza, who had been at the mission and was being held by the Cayuse. After the 1855 treaty with the tribes brought on unrest, Chief Timothy came to aid of Lt. Col. Edward Steptoe, leading his troops to safety from an attack by Spokane, Palouse, and Coeur d'Alene warriors. In 1863, he was one of the Nez Perce who signed the treaty that ceded most of their lands. Unlike Chief Joseph, he did not take part in the 1877 Nez Perce War. Chief Timothy died in 1891. He is pictured with a Nez Perce delegation to Washington, DC, in 1868. Seated from left to right are Chief Timothy, Chief Lawyer, and Chief Jason. The men standing are not identified. (Courtesy of Manuscripts, Archives, and Special Collections, Washington State University Libraries, McWhorter Collection 70-0251.)

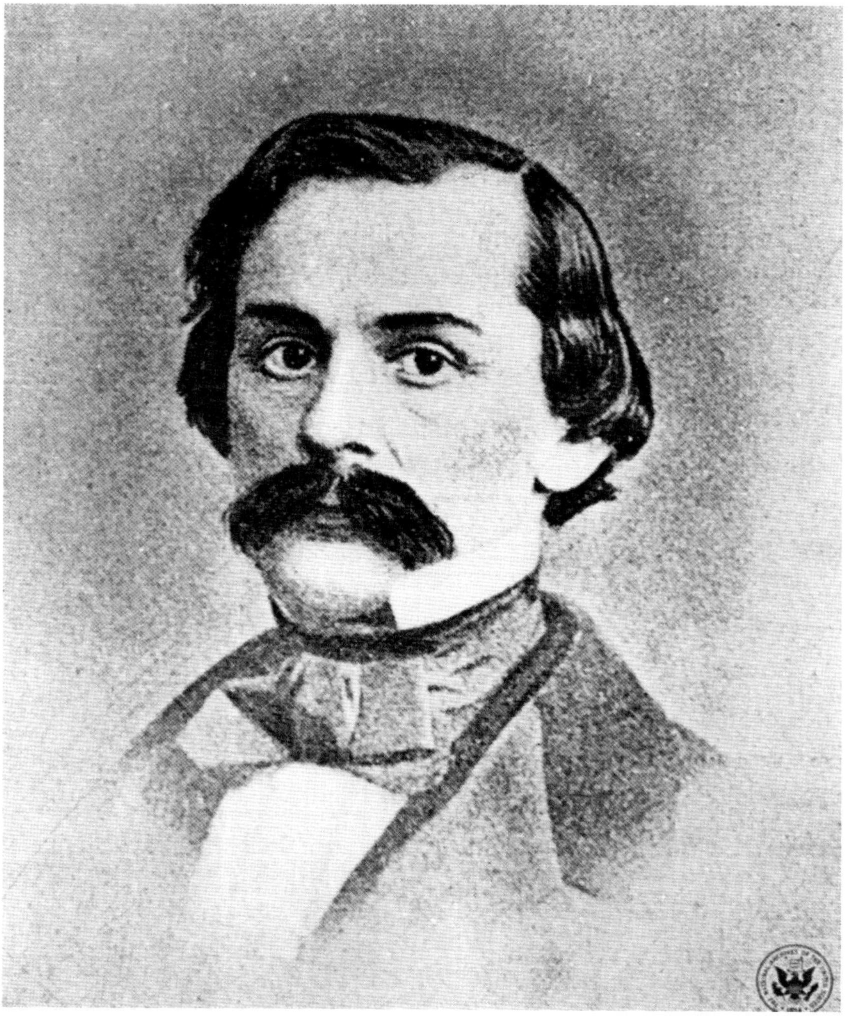

Lt. Col. Edward J. Steptoe, First Commander of Fort Walla Walla

Edward Steptoe (1815–1865) was a West Point–trained officer and Mexican War veteran who spent the last part of his career fighting Indians in the Northwest. During the 1856 treaty council with the tribes in present-day Walla Walla, Lieutenant Colonel Steptoe's men camped along Mill Creek several miles east of the council. After the meeting, Steptoe's men skirmished with a group of Indian warriors who attacked Gov. Isaac Stevens's wagon train as it left. The next day, Steptoe and his men began construction of a stockade and blockhouse. The hurriedly built fortification was the first military Fort Walla Walla. It was replaced a month later by a group of adjacent log structures built under the direction of Steptoe and Col. George Wright. Finally, the first permanent Fort Walla Walla was completed in 1858 on a square mile of land west of the growing town. It was from this post that Steptoe led 158 soldiers north of the Snake River. Although he had been warned not to travel there and his men were not well armed, Steptoe proceeded. On May 17, they were attacked by a large force of Spokane, Palouse, and Coeur d'Alene warriors near present-day Rosalia, Washington. Steptoe's troops took heavy casualties and nearly ran out of ammunition. One of their Nez Perce scouts, Chief Timothy, is said to have helped them escape during the night. Steptoe's defeat led to a major military buildup in the region, which in turn led to increased safety for arriving settlers. (Courtesy of Yakima Valley Museum.)

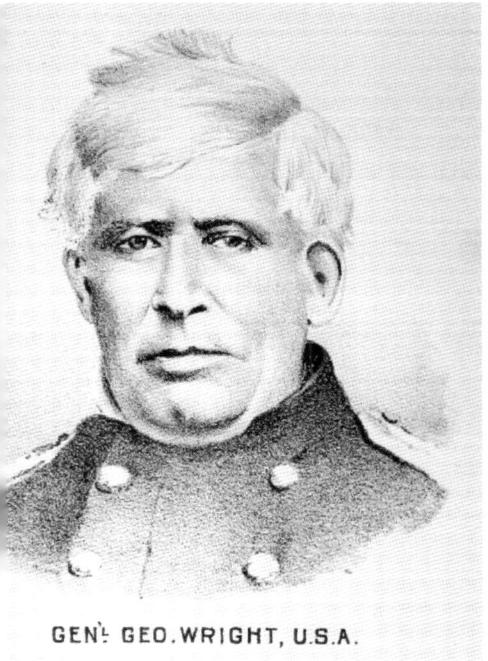

Col. George Wright, Indian Fighter
West Point graduate Col. George Wright (1803–1865) was named colonel of the 9th Infantry Regiment in Washington Territory in 1855. After the attack on Steptoe's troops, Wright led a punitive expedition in September 1858 against the northern tribes. He defeated them at Four Lakes and Spokane Plains, executed a number of Indians, and slaughtered 800 Indian horses. Wright was named brigadier general in 1865. En route to his new command of the Department of the Columbia, he was lost at sea off the California coast. (From *History of the Pacific Northwest, Oregon and Washington*, 1889.)

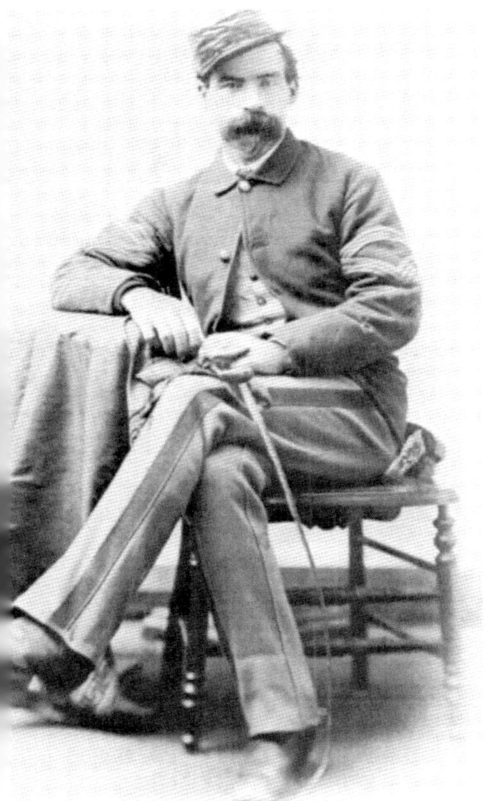

Col. Michael M. McCarthy, Indian Campaign Congressional Medal of Honor Recipient
Michael McCarthy entered the US Army in 1865, becoming a first sergeant of Troop H, 1st US Cavalry. He fought in the Battle of White Bird Canyon in 1876. He and six other men were detailed to hold a key position against the Indians, and when he was forced to fall back, he courageously fought his way back to his command. McCarthy was awarded the Medal of Honor in 1897 for his "extraordinary heroism." McCarthy served as colonel and quartermaster general for the Washington National Guard from 1897 to 1905 and died in 1914. He is buried in Mountain View Cemetery in Walla Walla. (Courtesy of Library of Congress.)

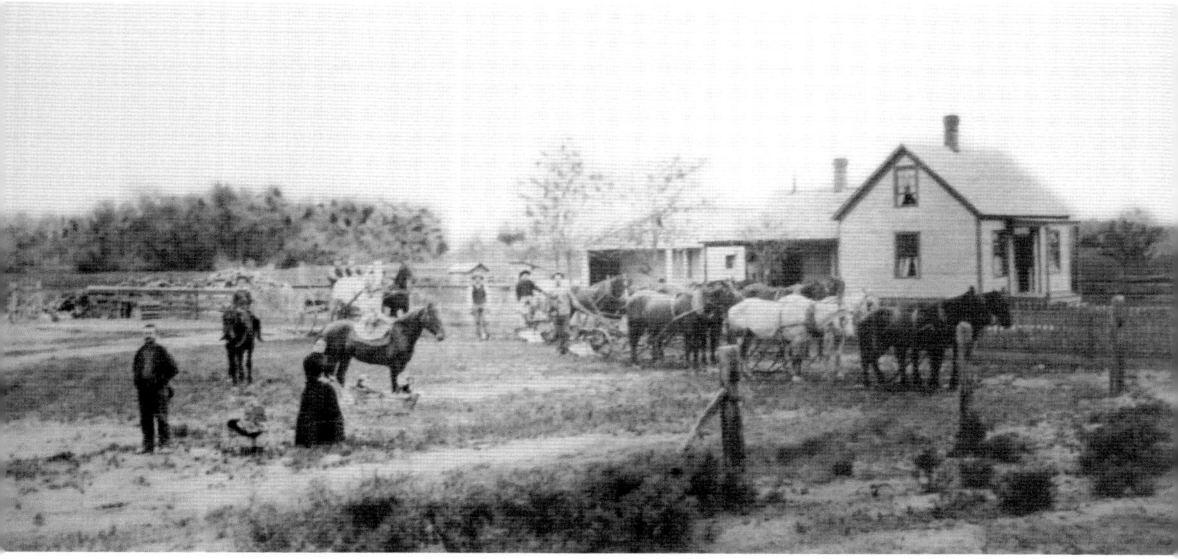

The Bergevin Family, Pioneer French Settlers
Before there was a town of Walla Walla, the Bergevin family was farming the fields of the Walla Walla River valley. They joined a hardy group of French settlers, many of whom were Métis—children of French Canadian fathers and Indian mothers. The Bergevin brothers (Louis, Joseph, Damase, and Clement) established their farm in a settlement called Frenchtown in the 1850s. Descendants of the first Bergevins still farm one of the original homesteads. (Courtesy of Claro Bergevin.)

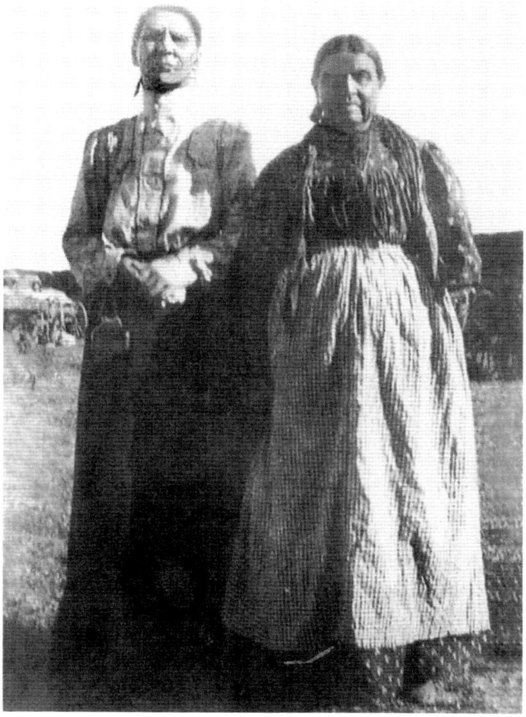

Suzanne Cayouse Dauphin, First Indian Woman Landowner
Suzanne Cayouse Dauphin was born in 1825 on Cayuse lands. In 1840, she married Mathieu Dauphin, a trapper from St. Louis. After Mathieu attended the 1855 treaty council near Walla Walla as an interpreter and witness for the Nez Perce, the Dauphins settled on a 160-acre donation claim near Frenchtown, west of Walla Walla. When Mathieu died in 1867, Suzanne became the first Indian woman recognized as owning land in this region. Suzanne died in 1876 and was buried in St. Rose of Lima cemetery at Frenchtown. She is shown standing to the right of daughter Catherine Dauphin Woodward. Her great-great-granddaughter Judith Fortney portrays Suzanne at Fort Walla Walla Museum. (Courtesy of Judith Fortney.)

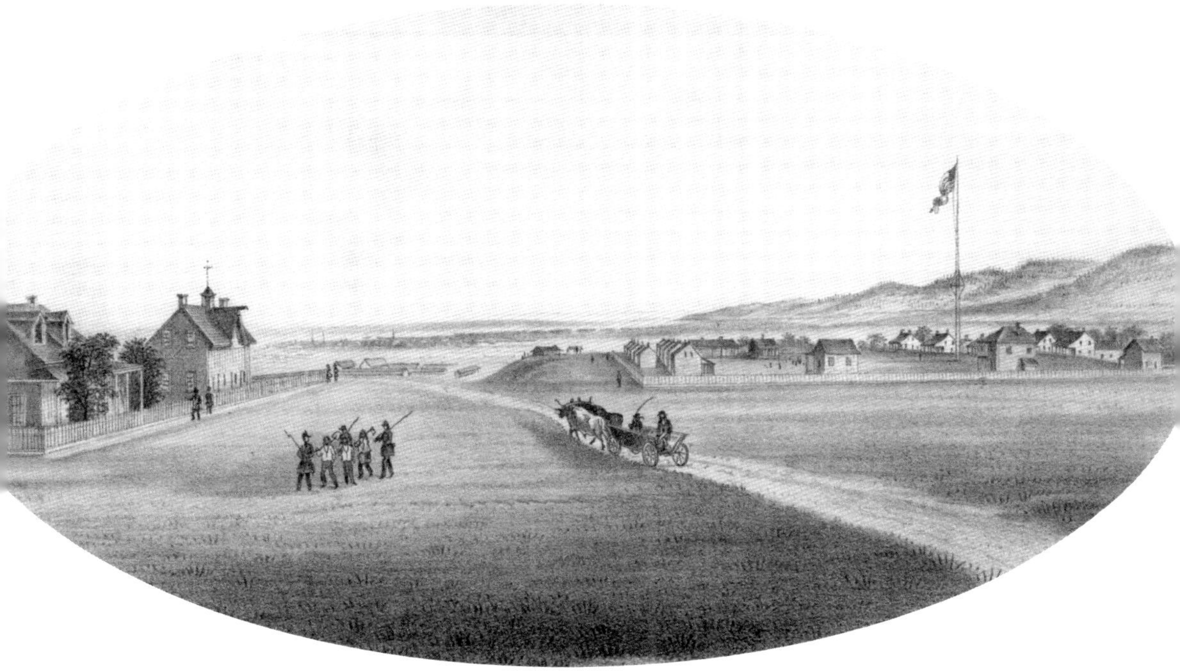

Capt. John Mullan, Builder of the Mullan Road
Capt. John Mullan (1830–1909), a West Point graduate, was assigned to establish a wagon and pack route from the steamship dock on the Columbia River west of Walla Walla to the steamship dock at Fort Benton, Montana, at the headwaters of the Missouri River. Although construction was supposed to begin in 1858, the Mullan Road was not completed until 1862. It was the first engineered wagon road to cross the Continental Divide and reach the Northwest (the drawing by Gustav Sohon, above, from Capt. Mullan's report, shows the road passing through military Fort Walla Walla west of the city). Though it was frequently in such disrepair that only foot travelers and pack animals could follow its course, it was instrumental in the development of the Inland Northwest and Walla Walla. After resigning his commission, Mullan and his wife, Rebecca, came to Walla Walla in 1863 to try their hand at farming, However, Mullan was unsuccessful as a farmer and left to pursue a law career in San Francisco. (Courtesy of Fort Walla Walla Museum.)

Isaac Stevens, Governor of Washington Territory

Isaac Stevens was an ambitious man. A West Point graduate, he served in the Mexican-American War (1846–1847), which secured western territories for the United States. After the war, he returned to the US Army Corps of Engineers but longed for more. When the Washington Territory was formed on March 2, 1853, he petitioned Pres. Franklin Pierce for its governorship. Pierce appointed him governor in addition to giving him the companion job of superintendent of Indian Affairs for the territory. Not satisfied with those roles, Stevens lobbied to lead an 1853 survey of a northern route (passing through Washington Territory) for a transcontinental railway (later the Northern Pacific, 1864). As superintendent of Indian Affairs, he dealt with Indian people and tribal claims to land in the territory. He initiated a series of treaty councils and convened the First Walla Walla Council with the tribes on May 29, 1855. The council—attended by 5,000 Indians—included representatives of the Yakama, Nez Perce, Walla Walla, Umatilla, and Cayuse tribes. Only the Palouse declined to participate. Stevens's goal was to gain title to lands in the territory and open it for white settlement by offering the tribes reservations, money, and the rights to both retain their ancient and well-established hunting and fishing grounds and gather foods traditional to their cultures. Stevens wanted to convince the local tribes to move east to the Nez Perce reservation, but the tribes strongly resisted. Communication among the parties was difficult, resulting in a series of misunderstandings that led to the Battle of Walla Walla just a few months later. A second treaty council in 1856 was followed by an attack on Stevens's wagon train and resulted in the construction of the first military Fort Walla Walla. Stevens left Washington Territory for Washington, DC, in 1857 to serve as a territorial delegate to Congress, never to return. He served as a brigadier general in the Civil War and was killed in action in 1862 at the Battle of Chantilly, Virginia. (Courtesy of Library of Congress.)

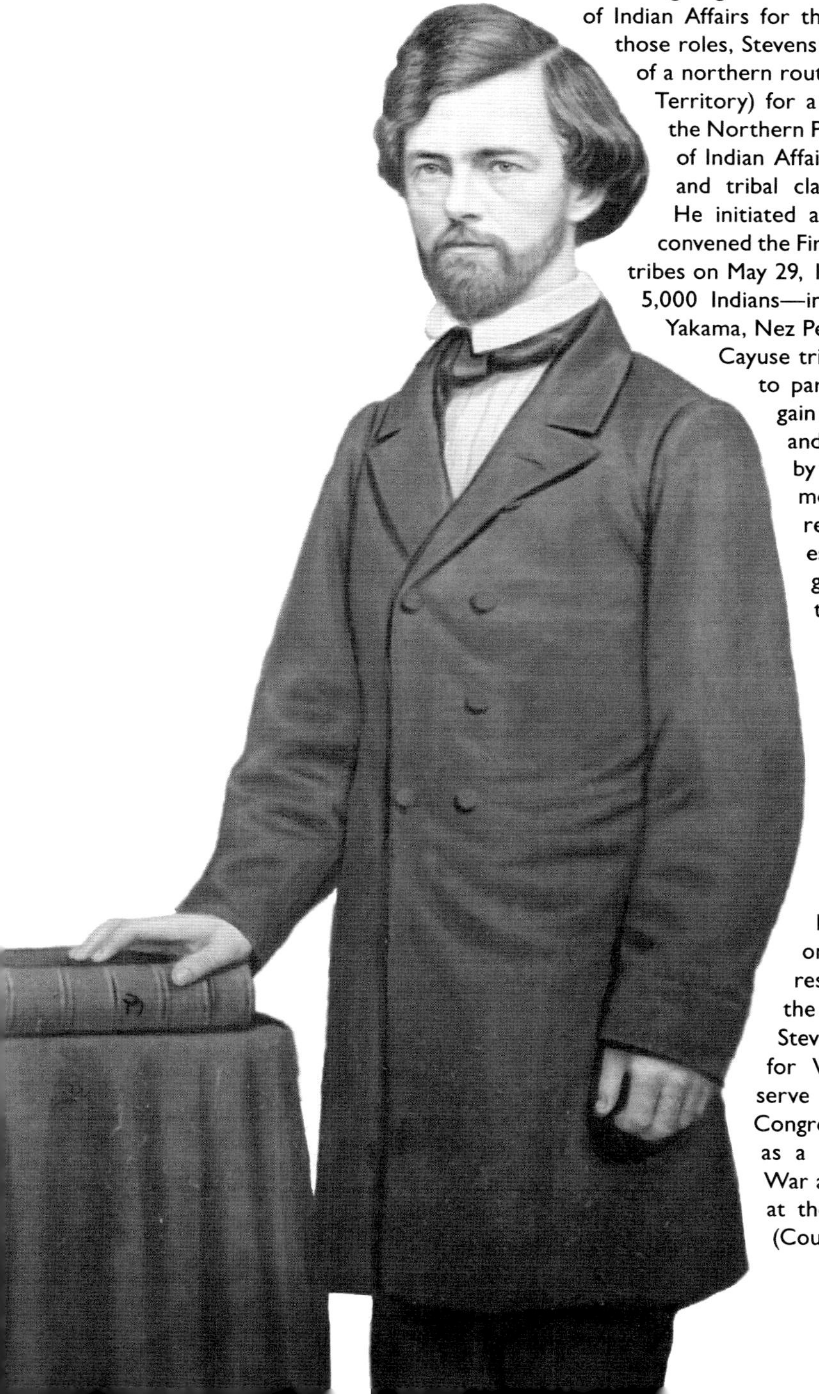

CHAPTER TWO

The Early Days

After the period of conflict between the Indian tribes and settlers was resolved—albeit to the detriment of the tribes—the Walla Walla Valley was ripe for white settlement. The route to the valley for many settlers was a somewhat unlikely one. The construction of a military road between Fort Walla Walla and Fort Benton on the Missouri River, on opposite sides of the Continental Divide, was intended to create an important link between frontier forts in the West. The Mullan Road also became a catalyst for Walla Walla's establishment as the new locus of the Inland Northwest.

Construction of the new road began in 1859, and rough as it was, it attracted settlers interested in moving west. At the same time, it proved to be the main route to and from gold mines in Idaho and British Columbia.

By the time of the road's completion in 1862, Walla Walla was an incorporated city and was already prospering. Although the town had a wild frontier edge to it, the presence of Fort Walla Walla enhanced the safety of its inhabitants. Small merchants prospered and became business leaders, like merchandisers-turned-bankers Dorsey Syng Baker and John Boyer, who founded Baker Boyer Bank. As wheat became the new gold in the valley, grain helped men like mill owner Henry Isaacs make their fortunes and pointed to the future of agriculture in the Walla Walla Valley.

In 1861, the first teacher, Sarah Miner, opened her school, heralding a more family-friendly city. Meanwhile, the first newspaper informed the citizens about the far-off Civil War as well as local happenings. Still, the rough frontier edge of Walla Walla persisted in people like kind-hearted madam Josephine "Dutch Jo" Wolfe.

But change was on the horizon. Agriculture became more important in the valley. A small seminary was founded, destined to become Whitman College. Saloons and brothels gave way to banks and new businesses that catered to the increasingly prosperous residents of Walla Walla.

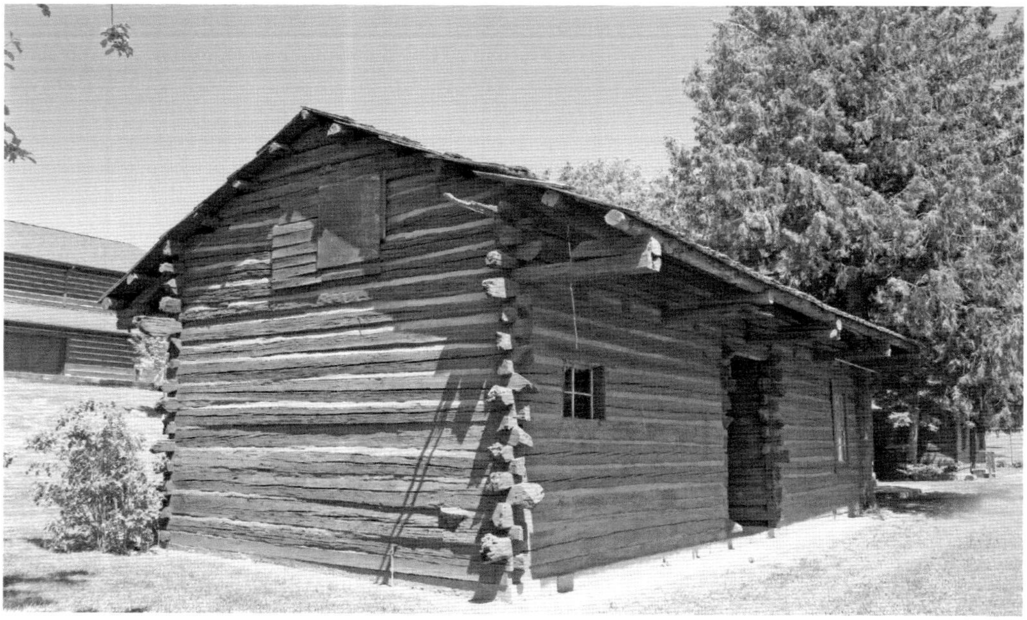

Ransom Clark, Donation Lands Pioneer

Ransom Clark (1809–1859), a member of John C. Frémont's 1843 survey expedition, settled on his Donation Lands in the Walla Walla Valley and began building his log home in 1859. Although he died in 1859, his widow, Lettice, farmed the property until 1861, when she married Almos Reynolds. The double cabin is one of the few remaining pioneer farm homes in the Northwest. The Ransom Clark cabin was donated by the Reynolds family to Fort Walla Walla Museum and moved to the museum's pioneer village in 1969. (Author photograph.)

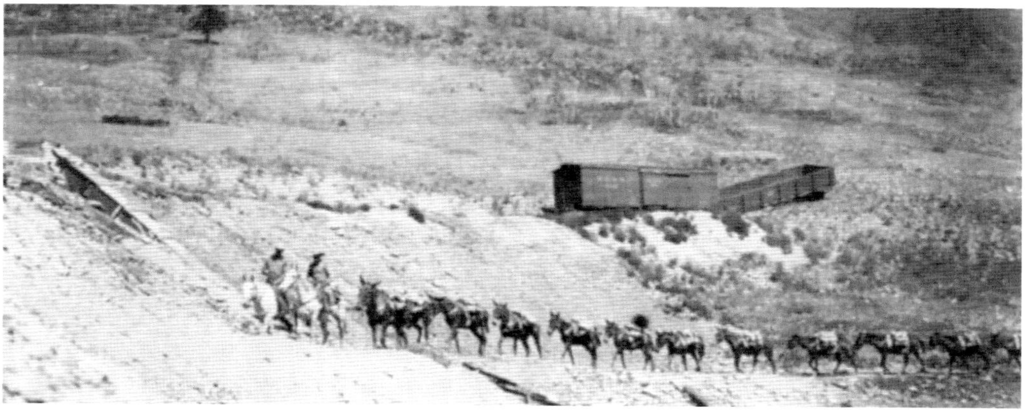

Sebastian Colon, Early Latino Settler

Sebastian Colon came to Walla Walla around 1872, one of the earliest Latinos to arrive in the valley. Born in Spain around 1831, Colon worked in the placer mines of California before coming to Walla Walla. He worked as a freight packer for a number of years, packing the mail between Boise, Idaho, and Walla Walla. After the heyday of packing, Colon opened a restaurant and was nicknamed the "Tamale King" of Walla Walla. He was still living in Walla Walla in 1915, and his restaurant was listed at 10 ½ South First Avenue. (Author's collection.)

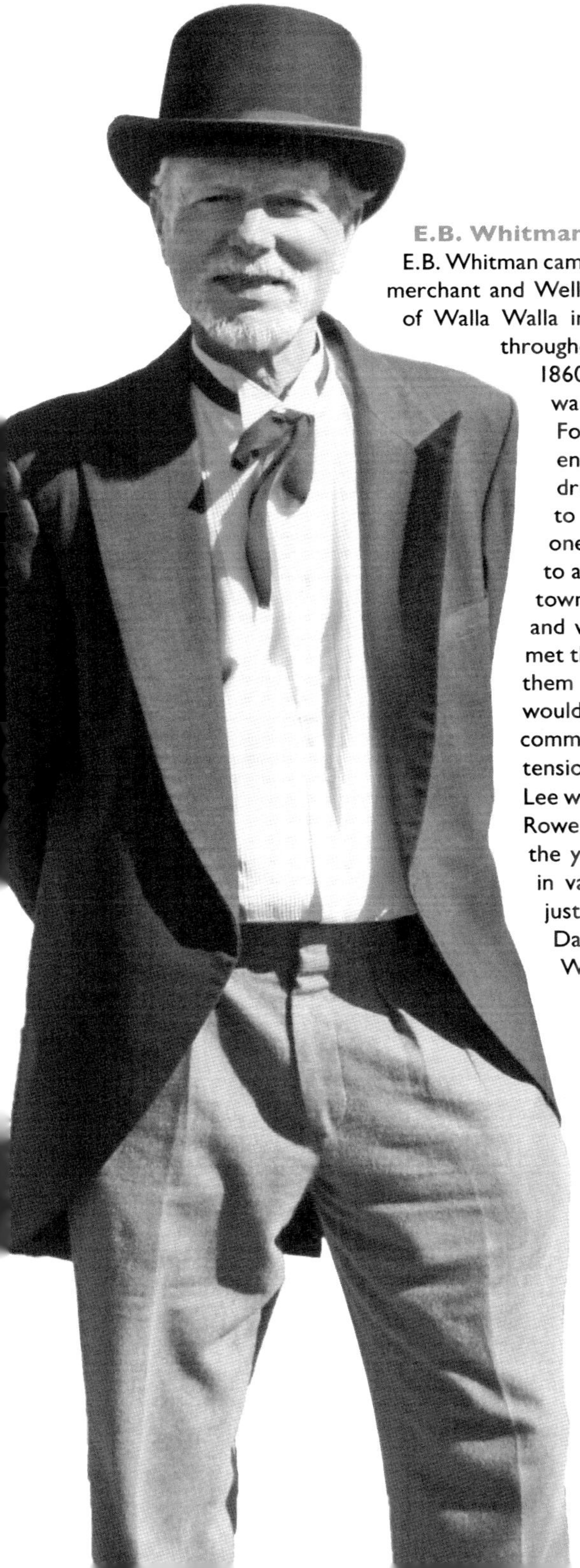

E.B. Whitman, First Mayor of Walla Walla

E.B. Whitman came to Walla Walla in 1859 and became a successful merchant and Wells Fargo agent. He was elected the first mayor of Walla Walla in 1862 and was prominent in the community throughout the rough-and-tumble times of the mid-1860s. On the day of his inauguration in 1862, there was a riot at Robinson's Theatre. Soldiers from Fort Walla Walla attending a performance were enamored with J.B. Robinson's daughter Susie. A drunken soldier staggered up to the stage and tried to grab her, whereupon he was shot and killed by one of the townspeople. When a marshal refused to arrest the perpetrator, the soldiers marched into town, surrounded the sheriff's office, arrested him, and were marching him to the fort when Whitman met the group at the city limits. The mayor convinced them that the civil government—not the fort—would be the law in the town. Lt. Col. Henry Lee, commander of Fort Walla Walla, did not agree. The tension between the fort and the town continued until Lee was reassigned to San Francisco and Capt. G.W.G. Rowell was installed as the new commander. Over the years, Whitman had a successful career serving in various civic capacities, including mayor, sheriff, justice of the peace, and clerk of the school board. Dan Clark portrays E.B. Whitman at Fort Walla Walla Museum. (Author photograph.)

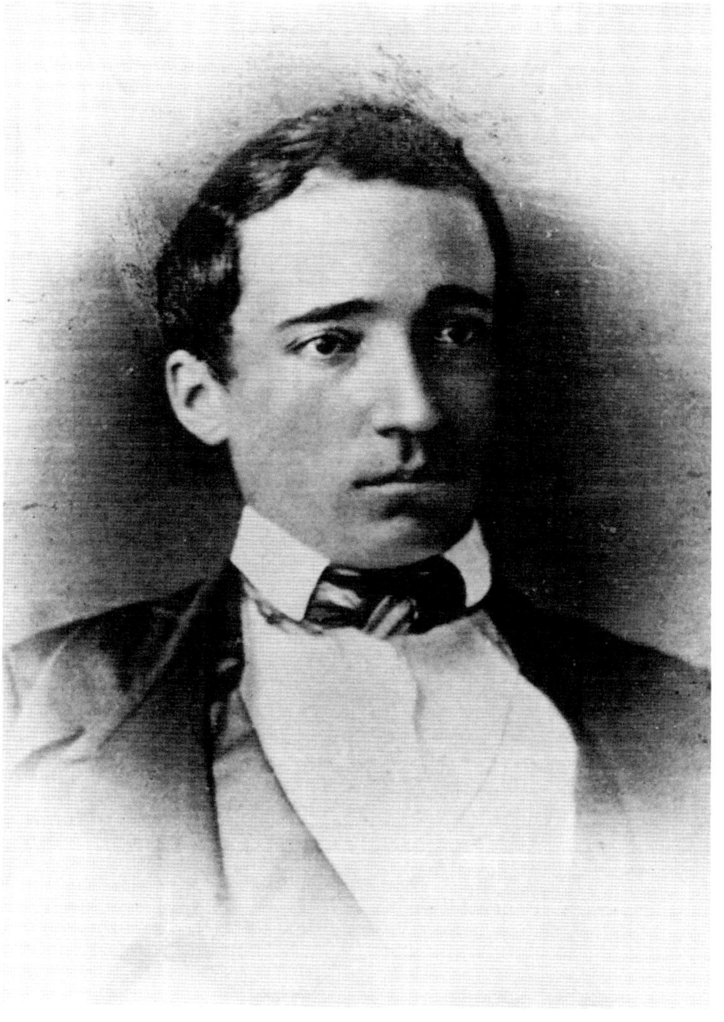

Dr. Dorsey Syng Baker, Cofounder of Baker Boyer Bank and Railway Founder
Dorsey Syng Baker (more commonly known as "D.S.") was born in Illinois in 1823. He graduated from Jefferson Medical College in 1845 and practiced medicine in Des Moines, Iowa, before moving to Portland in 1848. Baker saw immense possibilities in the burgeoning goldfields of California and spent part of 1849 and 1850 there, returning with a large stock of merchandise he turned at a profit. In 1850, Baker married Caroline Tibbetts. Ten years later, they moved to Walla Walla, where he farmed, raised stock, milled flour, and ran a mercantile. With the boom that the town enjoyed thanks to its role as a supply center for the Idaho gold mines, he opened a store with his brother-in-law John Boyer (who was married to Baker's sister Sarah). The partners' honest reputation for holding the miners' funds led to their expansion into banking services. Baker Boyer Bank was formally established in 1869. Seeing the need for transportation from the Columbia River to Walla Walla, Baker funded the construction of the Walla Walla & Columbia River Railroad (locally known as the "Baker Railway"), which operated from 1872 until 1875. The railroad was subsequently sold to the Union Pacific. Dorsey Baker died in 1888. The Baker Boyer Bank is still headquartered in Walla Walla in a magnificent, seven-story 1911 building, which was erected on the same site as the original bank. For a brief time, it was the tallest building west of the Mississippi. (Courtesy of Whitman College and Northwest Archives.)

John F. Boyer, Cofounder of Baker Boyer Bank

John F. Boyer was born in Kentucky in 1824 and moved to Ohio and Indiana before going to Arkansas to work as a clerk in a general store. In 1849, he traveled to California and had enough luck in the gold fields to become a merchant in Sonora, California. In 1853, he married Sarah Elizabeth Baker (Dorsey Syng Baker's sister), and in 1859, the couple moved to Walla Walla. John became Dorsey Syng Baker's partner in a merchandising business. He had a reputation for honesty and affability, and many of the miners who frequented the store entrusted their gold to him, sometimes leaving thousands of dollars at the store for safekeeping. Eventually, the partners decided to sell their merchandising business, and in 1869, they founded Baker Boyer Bank, the first bank in what would become the state of Washington. Boyer concentrated on the bank, while Baker focused on building the Walla Walla & Columbia River Railroad and other enterprises. When the bank received its national charter, Boyer was elected its first president, a position he held until his death in 1897. Boyer was involved in a number of civic pursuits as well, serving as treasurer of Walla Walla County for 12 years and as receiver of the US Land Office in 1872. A close friend and supporter of Cushing Eells and the founders of Whitman College, he was generous with contributions and his time. (Courtesy of Whitman College and Northwest Archives.)

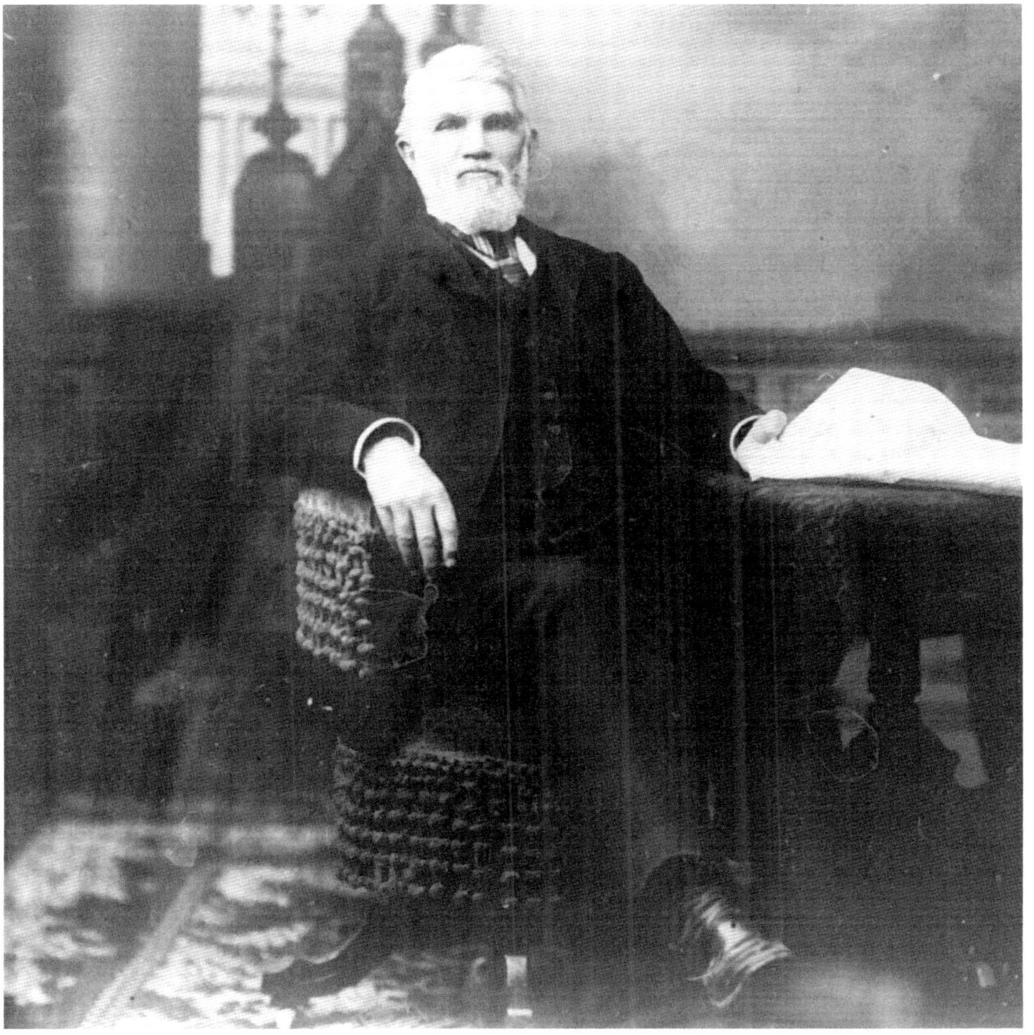

Henry P. Isaacs, North Pacific Flour Mills Founder, State Legislator

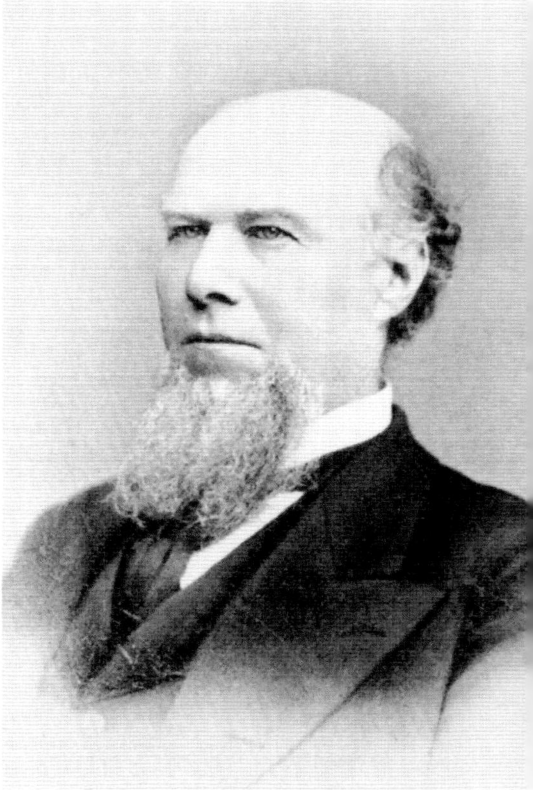

Henry P. Isaacs was born in Philadelphia, Pennsylvania, in 1822. He and his brother Josh followed the Gold Rush to California in 1849, then moved to the Pacific Northwest, where they became successful merchants and millers. In 1858, Isaacs had a store in The Dalles, Oregon. Seeing opportunities in Walla Walla, he sent William McWhirk to open a store there. In 1862, Isaacs moved to Walla Walla with his wife, Lucie, and built North Pacific Flour Mills in Walla Walla and in nearby Prescott (below). In 1867, Isaacs moved to Boise, building the War Eagle Mills and opening a store. He also financed the Middleton Mills, in which his brother was a partner. By 1874, Isaacs was back in Walla Walla, and he served in the Washington Territory Legislature from 1885 to 1886. During that session, he was instrumental in getting the territory to establish a penitentiary at Walla Walla. His wife, Lucie Fulton Isaacs, was a force in her own right. An early suffragist, philanthropist, and supporter of the arts, she also wrote poetry and essays. Henry Isaacs died in Walla Walla in 1900. (Right, courtesy of Fort Walla Walla Museum; below, courtesy of Whitman College and Northwest Archives.)

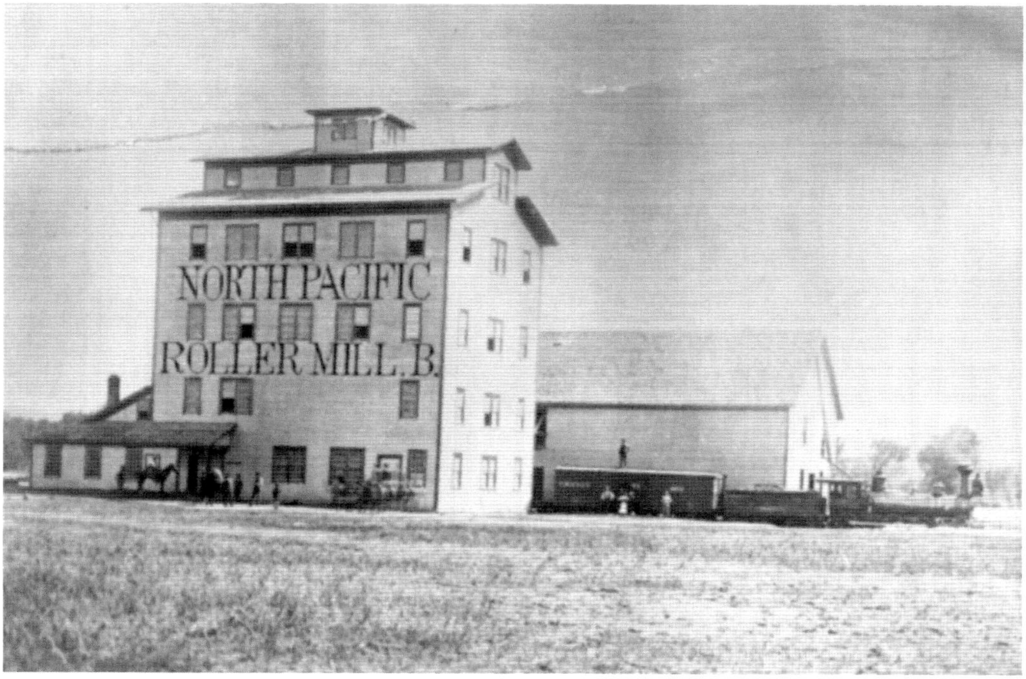

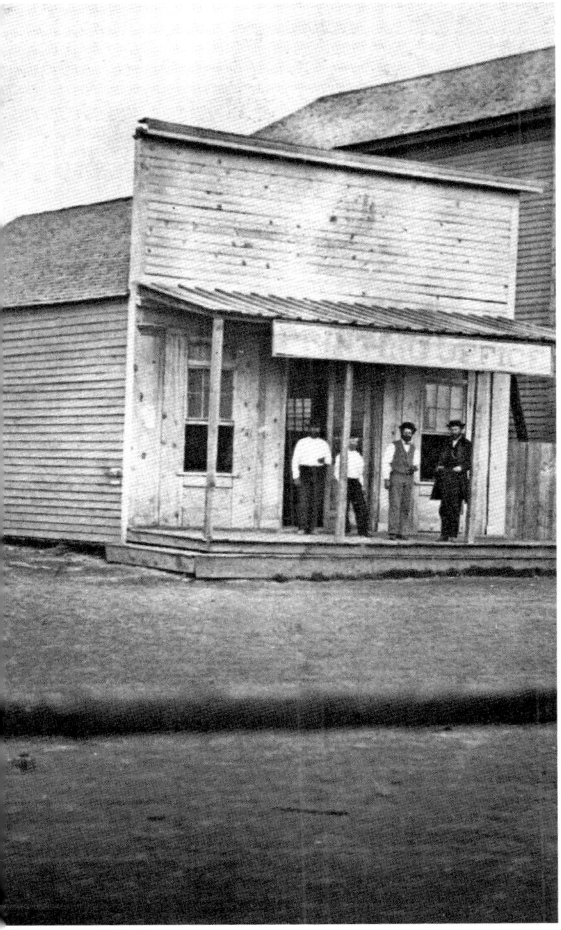

William N. and R.B. Smith, Publishers of the *Washington Statesman*
Walla Walla's first newspaper, the *Washington Statesman*, was established and began publication on November 29, 1861. Brothers William and R.B. Smith put out the four-page newspaper; in 1864, they changed the name of the paper to the *Walla Walla Statesman*, whose motto, "The Constitution and the Union," reflected their ongoing support for the Union cause. In 1865, William Newell took over the newspaper. In 1878, it became the first daily newspaper in eastern Washington, and in 1903, it was renamed the *Evening Statesman*. In 1907, the newspaper was consolidated with the *Walla Walla Union*. (Courtesy of Whitman College and Northwest Archives.)

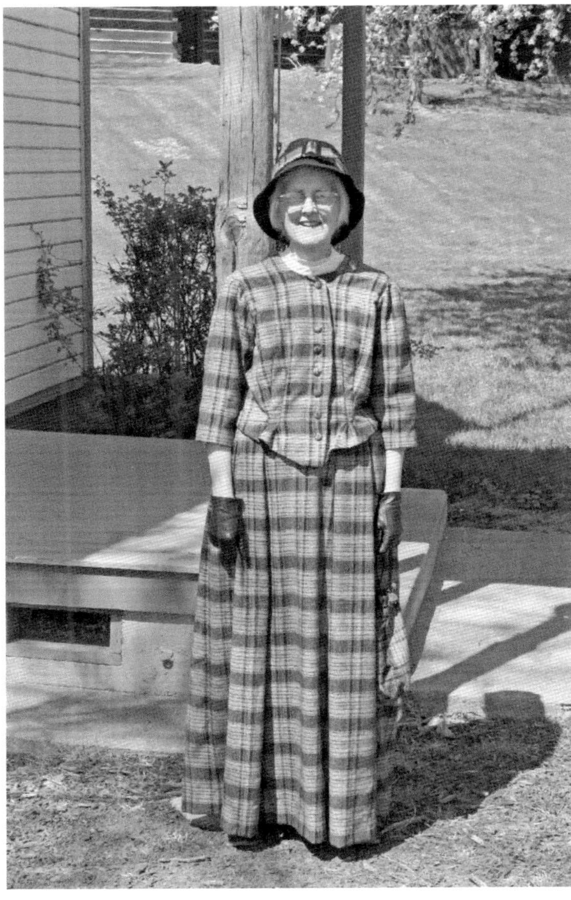

Sarah Miner, First Walla Walla Schoolteacher
In 1861, Sarah Miner and her husband, A.J., came to Walla Walla, where A.J. opened a planing mill. Sarah started a private school in the winter of 1861–1862. *Early Schools of Washington Territory*, by Angie Bowden, described her as "a lovely, cultured woman, who had the finest house plants in town." Sarah Miner is portrayed by Barbara Daniel at Fort Walla Walla Museum. (Author photograph.)

Cushing Eells, Founder of Whitman Seminary

Cushing Eells was born in Blandford, Massachusetts, in 1810. In 1834, Eells graduated from Williams College and entered East Windsor Theological Institute, graduating in 1837. In 1838, he and new wife Myra left to be missionaries to the Indians in Oregon. The Eellses and their party arrived at Waiilatpu in the Walla Walla Valley in late summer and went on to the Spokane area, where they worked among the Spokane Indians. After the deaths of Marcus and Narcissa Whitman, the Eellses were escorted by the military to Oregon. Eells spent 14 years in Forest Grove, Oregon, founding the Tualatin Academy (now Pacific University). When the Walla Walla Valley was reopened, Eells decided to build a school in honor of Marcus and Narcissa Whitman. In December 1859, the territorial legislature granted a charter to Whitman Seminary. The first classes were held at Waiilatpu, but in the summer of 1866, the first building of the Whitman Seminary was built on a site in Walla Walla provided by Dr. Dorsey Syng Baker. Eells (standing in front of the school) served simultaneously as the first principal of Whitman Seminary and as superintendent of schools for Walla Walla County. In 1883, a new charter was issued naming the school Whitman College. Eells continued to do missionary work and was actively involved with the college until his death in 1893; he willed much of his property to the college. (Courtesy of Whitman College and Northwest Archives.)

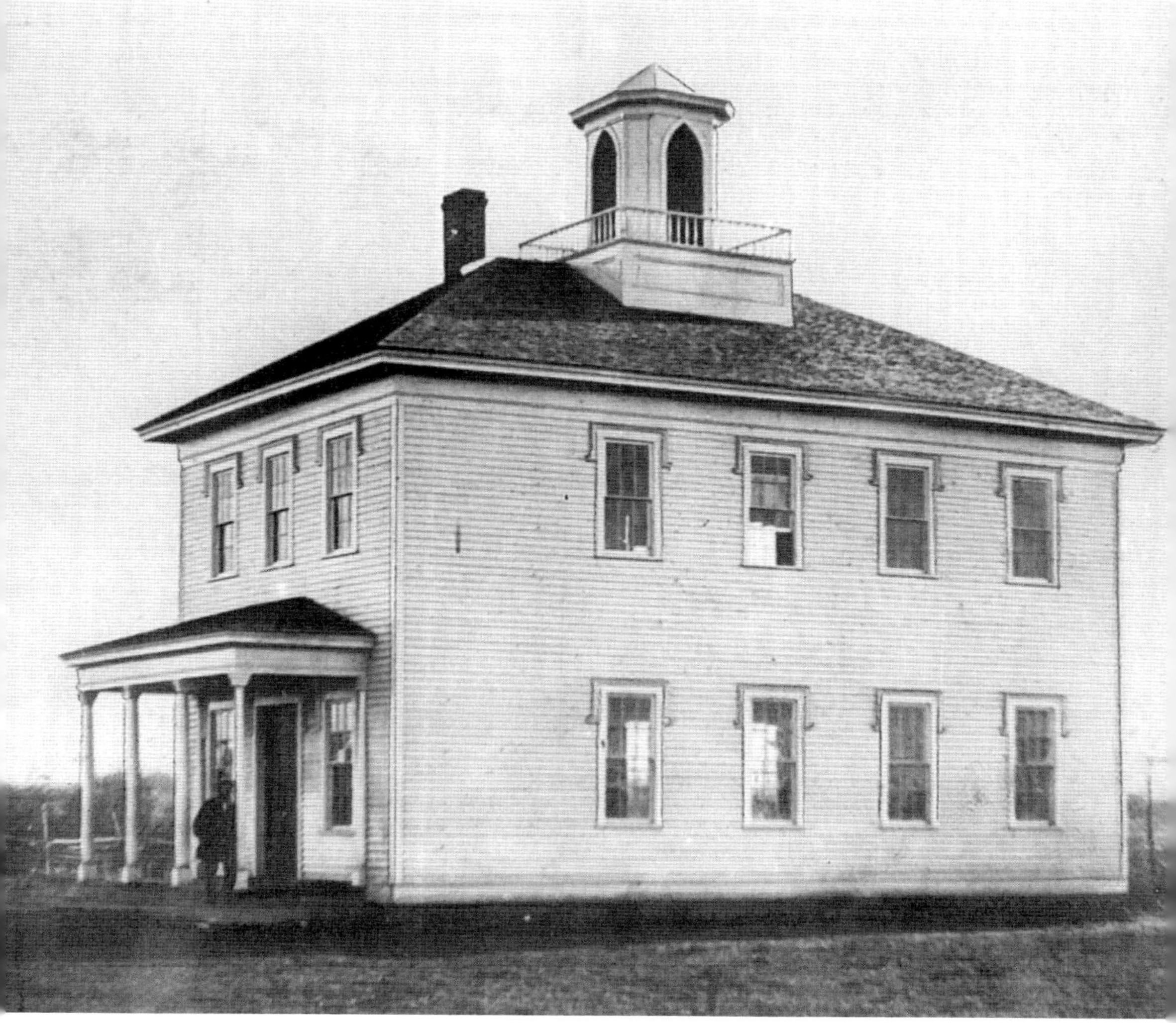

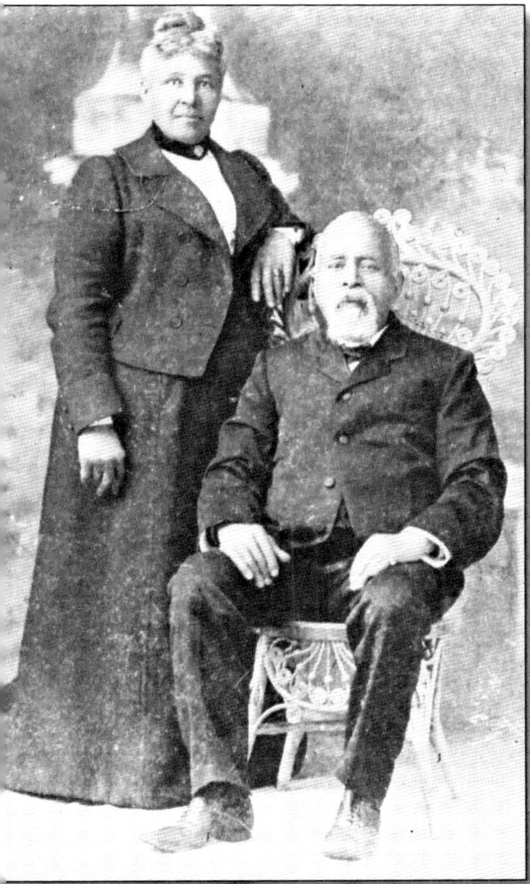

Richard Bogle, African American Barber, Rancher, and Bank Cofounder

Born in the West Indies in 1835, Richard Bogle moved to New York City in 1847 and to the Oregon Territory in 1851. After apprenticing with a barber in Yreka, California, he opened a barbershop in Roseburg, Oregon. In 1863, Bogle married America Waldo, and the couple moved to Walla Walla. He tried his hand at mining and later opened a barbershop. The Bogles were also successful ranchers, which allowed Richard to provide capital as one of the founders of the Walla Walla Savings & Loan Association. (Courtesy of Oregon Historical Society, OrHi12649.)

Jacob Betz, Betz's Star Brewery

In 1869, Gustav Joseph opened a brewery, which he sold to George Seisser in 1872. Jacob Betz, a brewer from San Francisco, joined the brewery in 1874 and bought it in 1875. By 1896, he was producing 10,000 barrels a year and bottling beer. In 1902, he built a large brewery downtown. In 1904, he sold half his interest in the brewery, which bore the Betz name until it merged with Stahl Brewing & Malting in 1910. Betz served as councilman from 1891 to 1895 and as mayor from 1896 to 1900; he died in 1912. (From *History of the Pacific Northwest: Oregon and Washington*, 1889.)

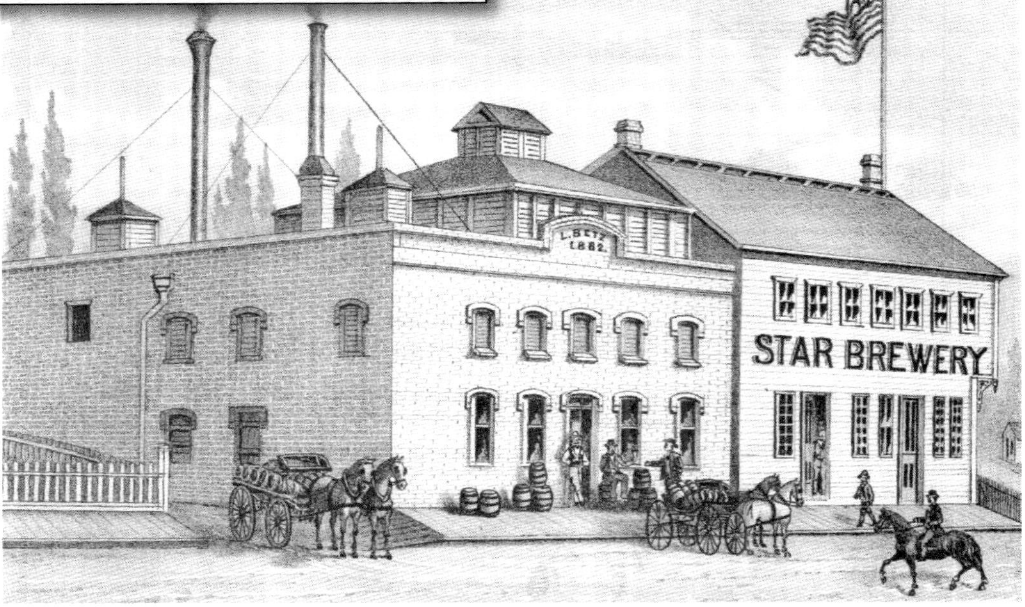

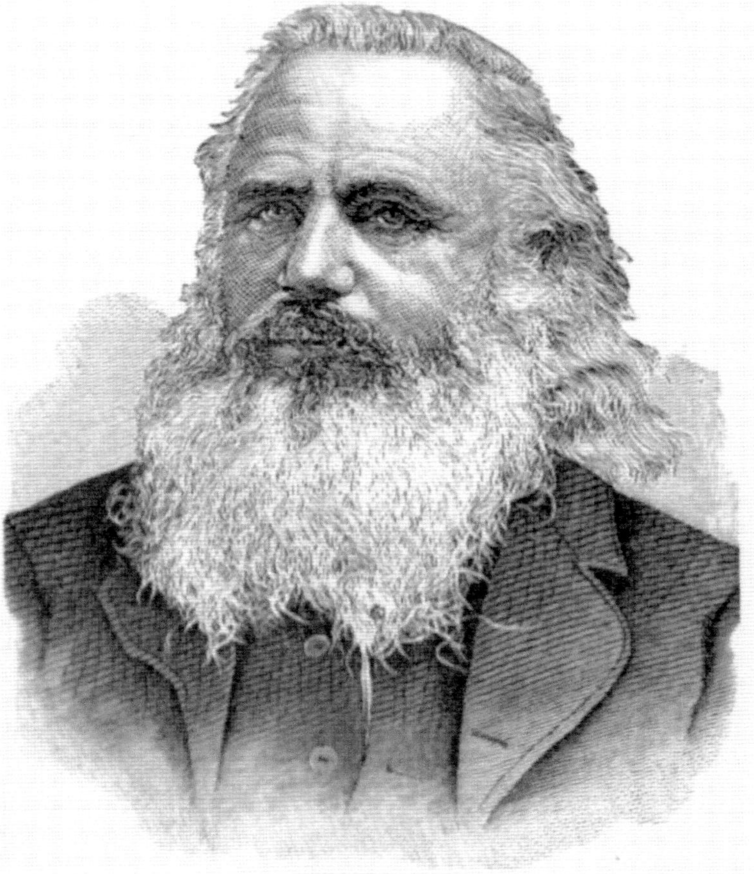

WILLIAM W. DAVIES.

William W. Davies, Leader of the Kingdom of Heaven Mormon Sect

East of Walla Walla, a rough road named the Mormon Grade and a remote cemetery are all that are left of a Mormon splinter group known as the Kingdom of Heaven, which lasted from 1867 to 1881. The group was led by William W. Davies. Although raised as a Methodist, Davies converted to Mormonism, and in 1854, he moved to Utah Territory to join the Church of Jesus Christ of Latter-day Saints, which was establishing a community there. By 1857, he had shifted his allegiance to Joseph Morris, who led a Mormon faction known as the Morrisites. In 1862, Morris was killed in a skirmish with the Utah territorial militia, dubbed the "Morrisite War." After Morris's death, bands of his followers scattered, with some, including Davies, fleeing to Deer Lodge, Montana. There, Davies had a number of revelations telling him that he should establish the Kingdom of Heaven in Walla Walla. He and 40 followers moved to an 80-acre commune just east of town. Davies, who believed in reincarnation, told his followers that he was the archangel Michael and that he had previously lived as Adam, Abraham, and David. When his son Arthur was born in 1868, he informed them the child was the reincarnation of Jesus Christ. The child, dubbed the "Walla Walla Jesus," attracted more followers, doubling the size of the community. A year later, Davies asserted that his second son was God the Father. Disillusionment had set in by 1880, when both of his sons died of diphtheria. The remaining 43 members of the community sued Davies, who was forced to sell the property. Davies died November 25, 1906, and is buried in a hilltop cemetery that overlooks his former "kingdom." (From Frank T. Gilbert's *Historic Sketches of Walla Walla, Whitman, Columbia, and Garfield Counties, Washington Territory, and Umatilla County, Oregon*, 1882.)

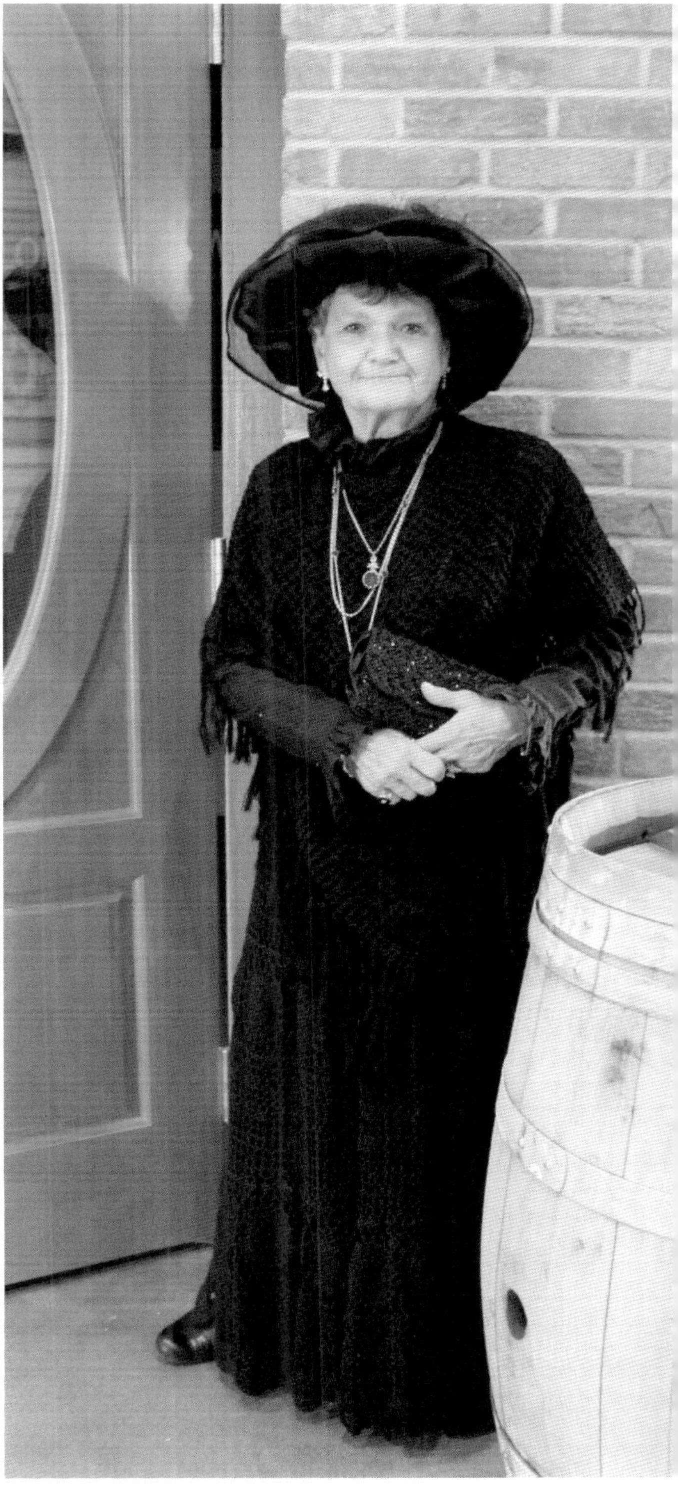

Josephine "Dutch Jo" Wolfe, Madam
Josephine Wolfe, nicknamed "Dutch Jo," arrived in Walla Walla around 1860, shortly after her husband was shot and killed in a card game in San Francisco. She hoped to capitalize on the town's reputation as a supply center for the goldfields of Idaho and Montana. She became well known as the savvy proprietress of two of Walla Walla's houses of ill repute: the Coast House and the Hotel State. The hotel had a second-floor walkway to the adjacent fire station; there was even a fire alarm in the hotel in case any of the men were "visiting" when a fire broke out. Wolfe's establishments were popular with local officials, army officers, and miners back from the goldfields. On one occasion, her establishment was quarantined, and the mayor, a doctor, and several priests were caught inside. For two weeks, the town was run by orders dropped in a basket over the side of the second story. Wolfe was also a public benefactress, giving generously to the Catholic Church and the Stubblefield Orphanage and providing for needy firemen. She paid for the firefighter's statue at Mountain View Cemetery. Wolfe and several of her "girls" are buried in the same cemetery. Before she died, Wolfe arranged to have all photographs of her destroyed. Today, her character is portrayed by Lois Hahn (seen here) at Fort Walla Walla Museum. (Author photograph.)

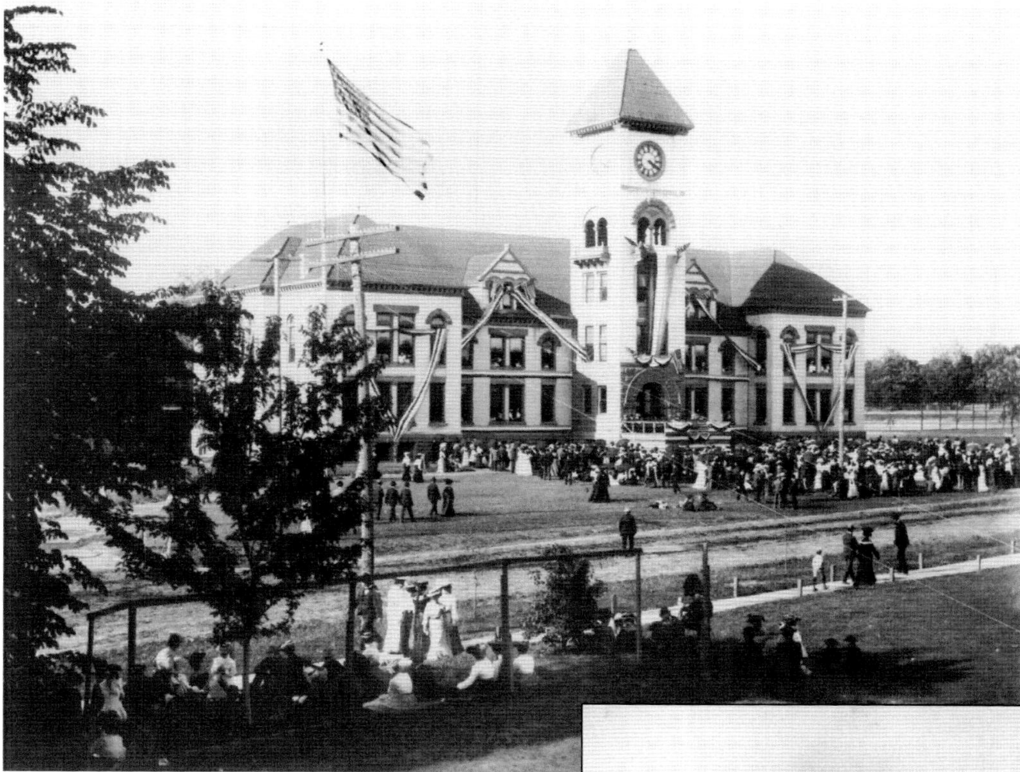

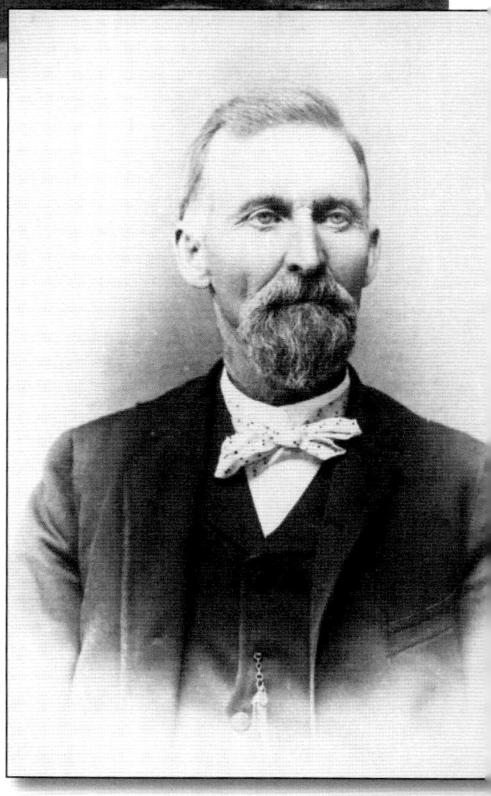

Norman Francis Butler,
Builder of Early Walla Walla Buildings

Norman Francis Butler was born in Maine in 1829. He was apprenticed to a carpenter but left Maine in 1849 and sailed around Cape Horn to California to try his luck at gold mining. By 1861, he had moved to the Walla Walla Valley, where he started a planing mill with John Dovall. He established a contracting business and built a number of buildings in town as well as some of the early buildings at Fort Walla Walla. He built four of the first five buildings on the Whitman College campus, including Memorial Hall (shown on the occasion of a visit from Pres. Theodore Roosevelt in 1903), Billings, Reynolds, and the gymnasium. Butler is noted for contributing all of his salary (except $1 a day) toward the construction of the Whitman College buildings. In 1865, he married Rebecca Boggs. The couple had three children—Belle, Ed, and Stella. Rebecca died in 1885, and Norman died in 1913. The family home, designed and built by Butler around 1882, is at 207 East Cherry Street. It is in the Queen Anne style and is listed in the National Register of Historic Places. (Both, courtesy of Whitman College and Northwest Archives.)

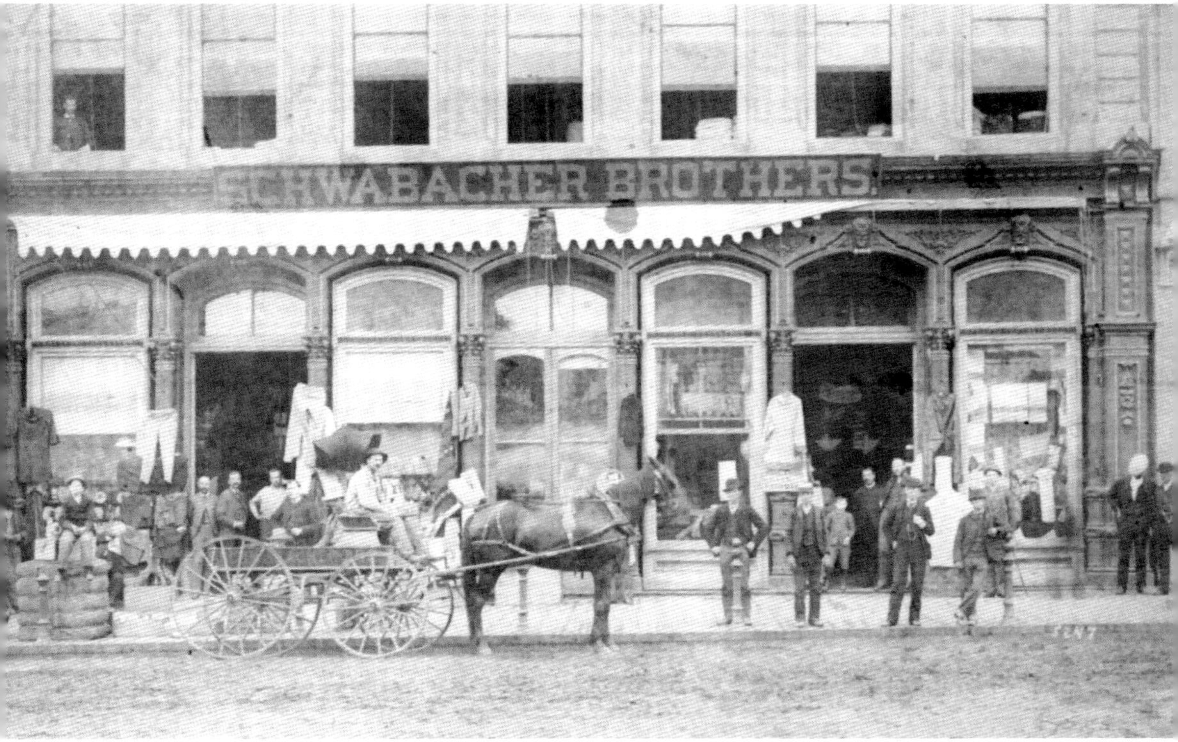

Schwabacher Brothers, Jewish Merchants

Leaving Europe, where anti-Semitism was on the rise in the mid-19th century, Louis Schwabacher emigrated from Germany with the encouragement of his uncle Isaac Bloch of San Francisco. Louis started in business in Mississippi. In 1858, he went to California. After traveling to Washington Territory in 1859, he saw great business opportunities and sent for his brothers Abraham and Sigmund. With the 1860 discovery of gold in eastern Washington Territory (now part of Idaho), Walla Walla quickly established itself as a hub for miners. The Schwabachers took advantage of the market and in September 1860 opened their mercantile full of mining provisions in Walla Walla. When the mining boom ended, the brothers adapted their inventory to serve the growing agricultural market. In 1876, the Schwabachers constructed one of the first brick buildings in the growing community at the corner of Third Avenue and Main Street (above). The local newspaper described it as "the finest building north of San Francisco, its front resplendent with massive iron columns and arches. The interior was 16 feet high, painted white. Its six iron pillars were painted and gilded. In the northwest corner, there was a glass space of 12x16 elevated with a fireplace where Mr. Sigmund Schwabacher could observe and direct the activities." Although Sigmund Schwabacher returned to San Francisco in the 1880s, the store continued. Sigmund died in 1900, and in 1910, the family sold their Walla Walla store to Gardner & Co., which operated it as a department store until it closed in 1980. (Courtesy of Whitman College and Northwest Archives.)

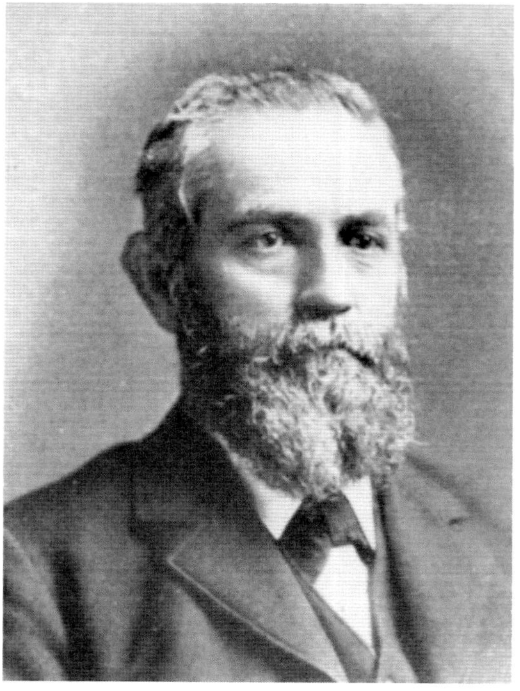

Philip Ritz, Orchardist

Philip Ritz was born in Pennsylvania around 1827. Encouraged by the success of pioneer orchardist A.B. Roberts, Ritz brought fruit trees from Corvallis, Oregon, and established a nursery south of Walla Walla in 1861. By 1872, Ritz is said to have had a stock of one million trees, and he was destined to become the leading orchardist in Washington State. He also planted vineyards comprising 21 grape varieties. Ever the entrepreneur, Ritz employed a number of salesmen who sold trees all over the Northwest. In 1881, the new town of Ritzville, Washington, was named in his honor, in part because he had planted trees along the Northern Pacific Railroad in the area. At the time of his death in 1889, he had one of the largest nurseries in the Northwest. In 1895, his widow, Catharine Snodgrass Ritz, completed their elaborate Victorian mansion (based on a house in Portland, Oregon) on Plaza Way, still a private residence. (Left, courtesy of Joe Drazan; below, author photograph.)

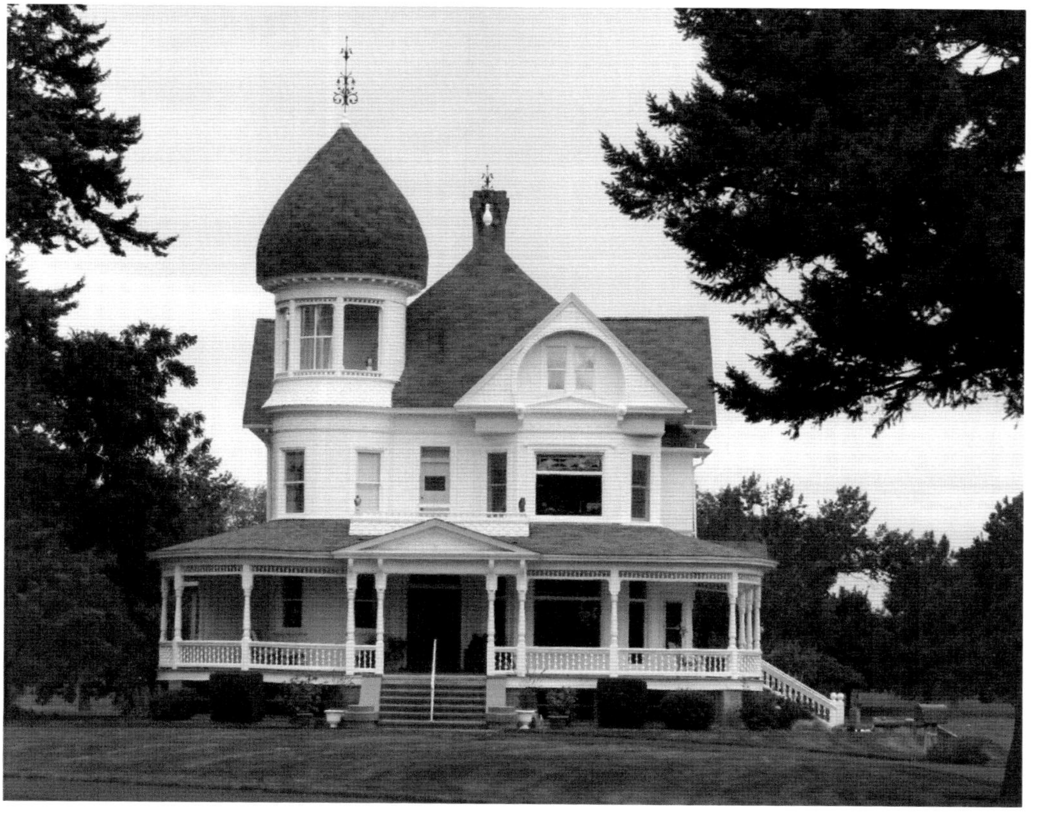

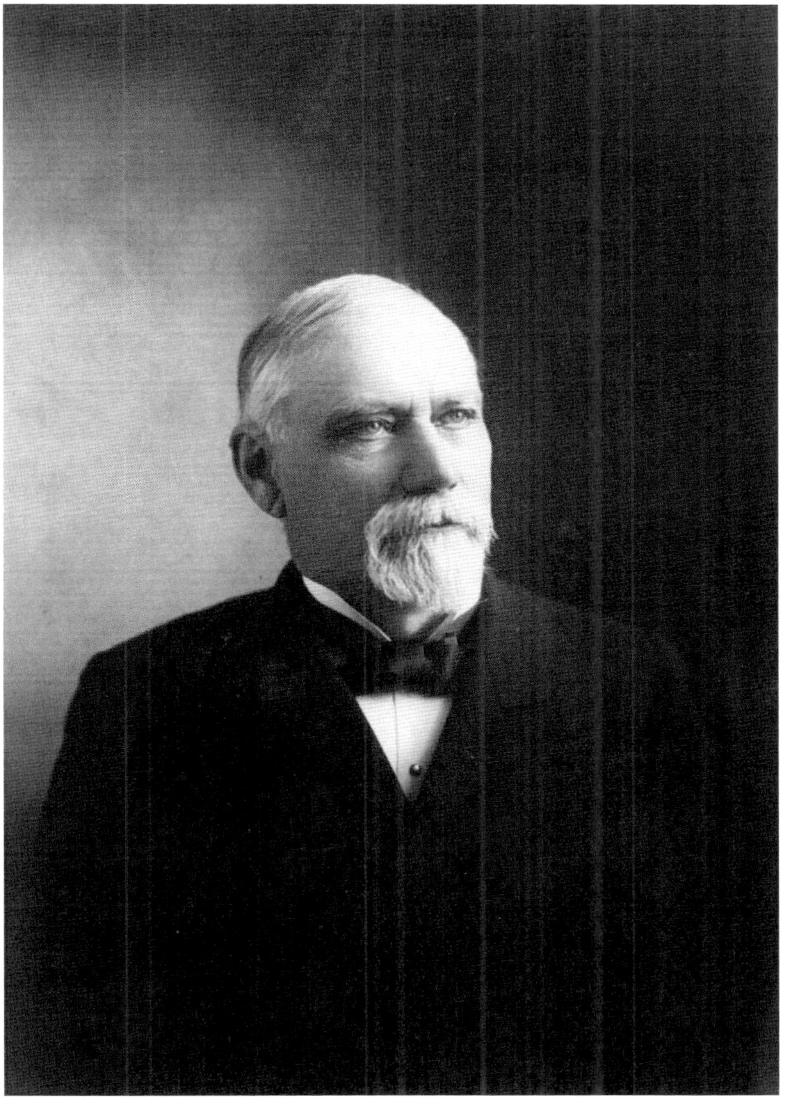

Miles C. Moore, Last Governor of Washington Territory
Miles Conway Moore, born in Rix Mills, Ohio, in 1845, came to Walla Walla in 1863 and took a job as a store clerk. By 1869, he partnered with H.E. Johnson & Company to form Paine Brothers & Moore, selling general merchandise and farm supplies. From 1878 to 1879, Moore served as a member of the Walla Walla City Council, and he was elected mayor in 1878. Moore, who married Mary Baker (daughter of banker Dorsey Baker), became a prominent member of the Walla Walla community. He was appointed territorial governor of Washington by Pres. Benjamin Harrison, becoming the last to hold the office before statehood. His term only lasted for seven months, as Washington became a state on November 11, 1889. After his term as territorial governor, Moore served as vice president and, subsequently, president of Baker Boyer Bank and was elected president of Whitman College's board of overseers. He died in 1919 and is buried at Mountain View Cemetery in Walla Walla. Moore's home still stands at 720 Bryant Avenue in Walla Walla and is listed in the National Register of Historic Places. (Courtesy of Whitman College and Northwest Archives.)

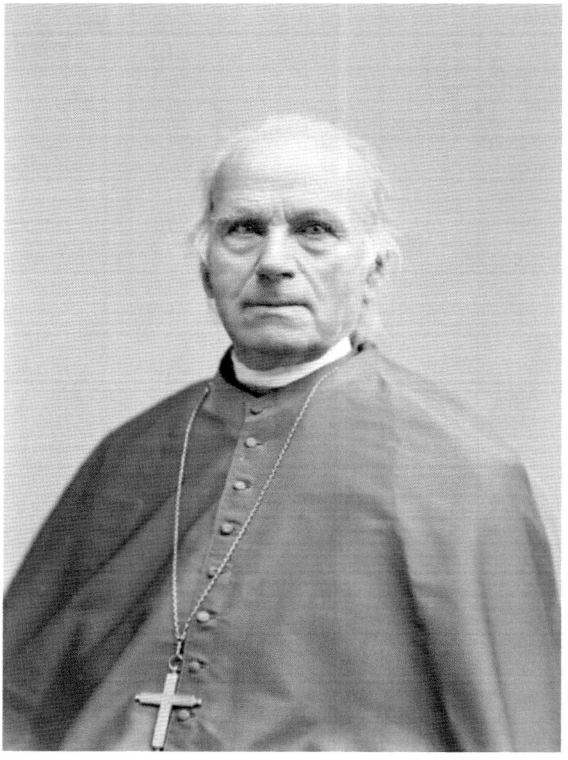

Rev. A.M.A. Blanchet, First Bishop of the Diocese of Walla Walla
Efforts to establish the Catholic Church in the region began in 1846 with the appointment of Augustin Blanchet as bishop of Walla Walla. The Whitman Massacre delayed the establishment of the church until the late 1850s, when Fr. Toussaint Mesplie started St. Patrick's Church. The rudimentary church had no floor and little seating. Mesplie conducted the first mass in the early 1860s, and by 1863, a new building was constructed. St. Vincent's Academy was added in 1864. A larger church was built in 1865, and in 1881, the present church building was completed. (Courtesy of Providence St. Mary Medical Center.)

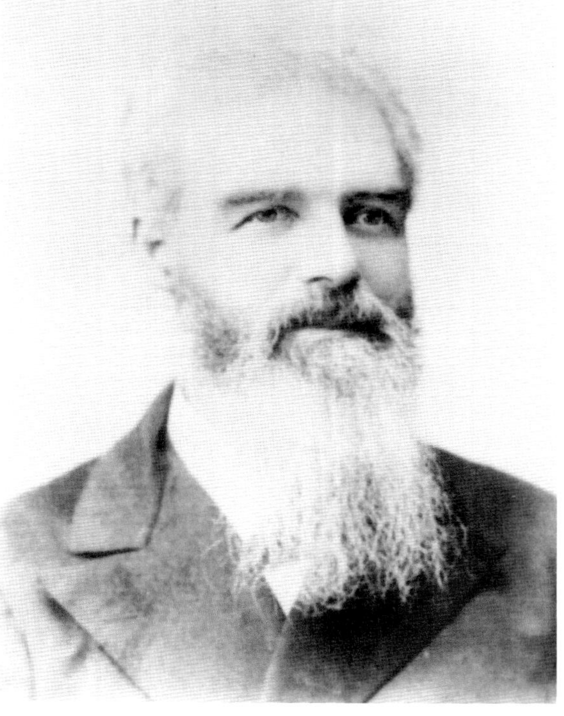

Isaac and Adelia Van Horn, Augusta Moorhouse, Seventh-Day Adventist Pioneers
Augusta Moorhouse and her family came to the valley in 1861. Among of the first Seventh-Day Adventist (SDA) settlers, they made their home south of Walla Walla. Within a decade, more Adventist families had moved to the area and petitioned the General Conference for a minister. In 1874, Isaac (left) and Adelia Van Horn were sent to the valley, where they held a series of evangelistic meetings. One of those converted was Toussaint Chabot, who donated land for the first SDA church in Walla Walla, built in 1875. (Courtesy of Walla Walla University Archives.)

CHAPTER THREE

Growing a City

The maturation of a city is often measured by the establishment of its institutions—government, newspapers, churches, schools, hospitals, colleges, and libraries. Fortunately, Walla Walla grew quickly from a frontier settlement into a city that provided for the needs of its citizens.

Mother Joseph of the Sisters of Providence, who brought Catholic schools and hospitals to the Northwest, established St. Vincent Academy (which operated from 1864 to 1959). In 1880, the order also founded a hospital, which outgrew several buildings and still serves the community as Providence St. Mary Medical Center.

In an effort to survive as an educational institution, Whitman Seminary became Whitman College. Shortly thereafter, newly established Walla Walla College in College Place welcomed Edward Sutherland as its president.

A continuing flow of newcomers to the valley enhanced the rich ethnic diversity of the area. They also introduced Walla Walla sweet onions and some of the first vineyards in the valley.

The growing city needed services. Volunteers became paid professional firefighters. And despite several failed early attempts, the Walla Walla Public Library finally opened for good in 1897 and moved into its expanded Carnegie Library building in 1904.

The opportunity to attract a new territorial penitentiary resulted in an all-out campaign to bring the facility to Walla Walla. It has been a significant local employer since it opened in 1887.

Fort Walla Walla, on the other hand, was living on borrowed time. Despite being the headquarters of the 9th Cavalry (Buffalo Soldiers) from 1902 to 1904, the fort finally closed in 1910. It briefly reopened during World War I, but its days as a military fort were over.

Although Walla Walla continued to grow, by the time that Washington Territory became Washington State on November 11, 1889, Seattle had overtaken the city in size. But with a rich agricultural economy, Walla Walla still looked forward to a prosperous future.

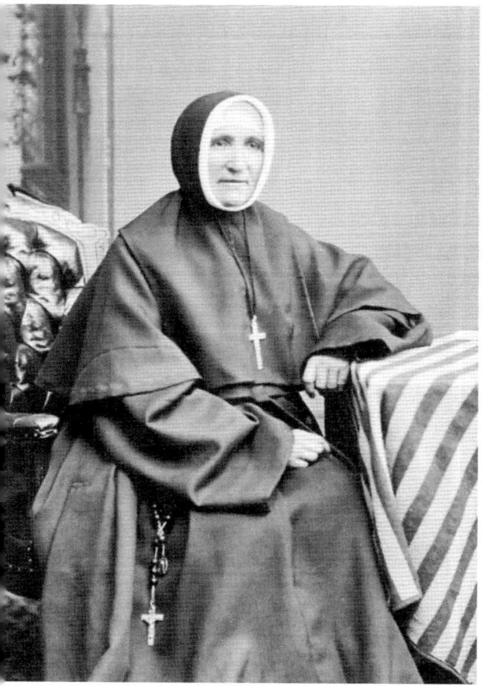

Mother Joseph and the Sisters of Providence, Founders of Providence St. Mary Medical Center, St. Vincent Academy

Mother Joseph (born Esther Pariseau, 1823–1902) designed and/or supervised construction of 29 schools and hospitals in the Pacific Northwest, including a school and hospital in Walla Walla. The first mission of the Catholic Church in the city was St. Vincent Academy, which educated students from 1864 through 1959. As part of the sisters' mission, the academy also cared for the sick until St. Mary Medical Center, the first permanent hospital in the city, was founded in 1880. The new hospital quickly outgrew its home; by 1883, it moved to a larger building, which in turn had to be expanded several times. After a devastating fire in 1915, a five-story building was constructed on the site, including a nursing school (pictured, class of 1929). In 1976, this building was replaced by a modern hospital facility. The present building has been expanded and renovated and now serves the community as Providence St. Mary Medical Center. A statue of Mother Joseph was dedicated in the US Capitol in 1980, noting, "She made monumental contributions to health care, education, and social work throughout the Northwest." (Both, courtesy of Providence St. Mary Medical Center.)

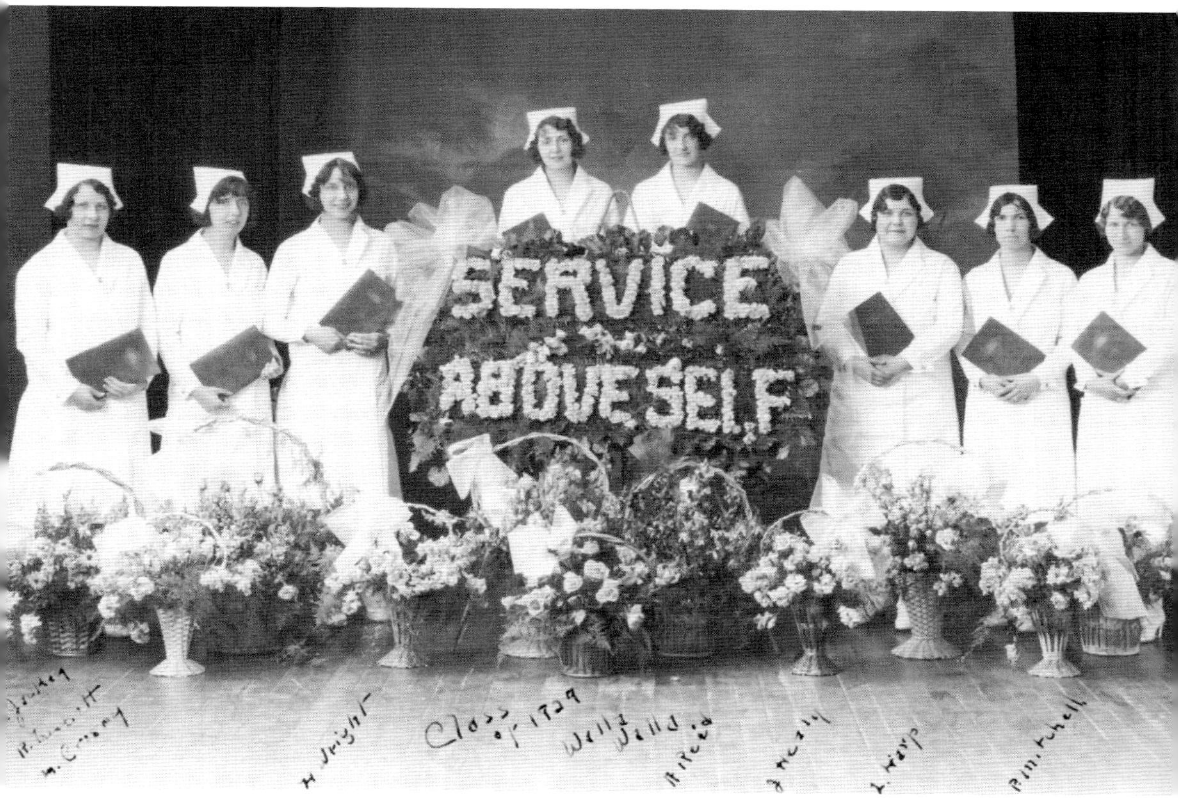

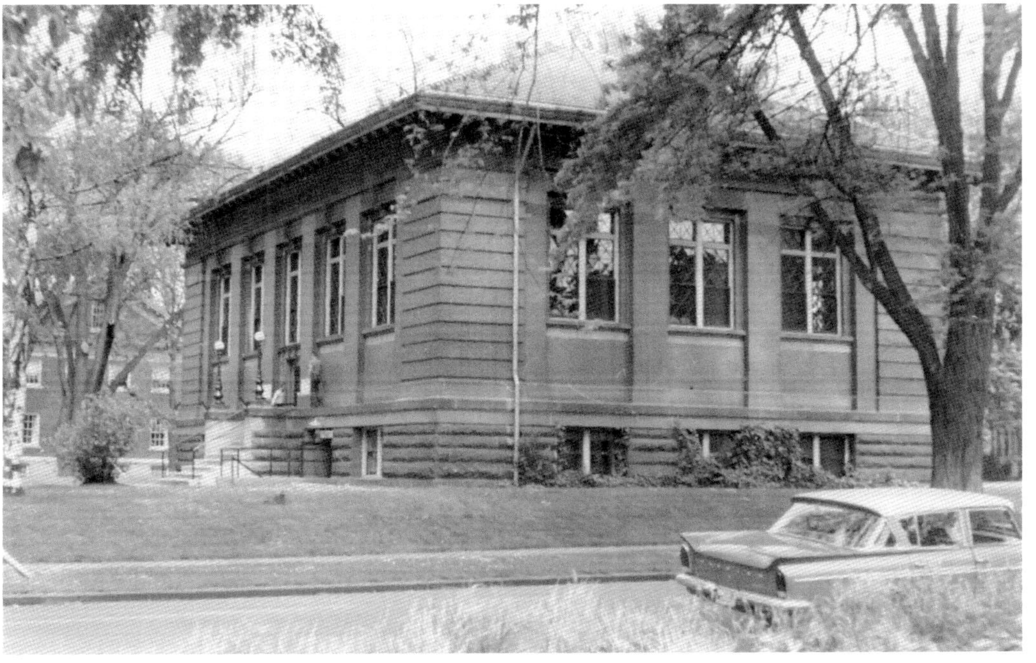

Margaret Welch Center, Walla Walla's First Librarian
The Walla Walla Library Association, founded in 1865, established a small library, but the association soon disbanded. In 1877, a small one-story building was constructed, and Margaret Welch became the first librarian in Walla Walla. The library closed in 1887, and it was not until 1897 that a public library was reestablished. Margaret Welch Center (then married to Solomon Center) was again selected librarian. The Walla Walla Public Library opened its doors to the public in November 1897. In 1904, the new Carnegie Library building, designed by architect Henry Osterman, was dedicated on Palouse Street; it was utilized until the library moved to a new building on Alder Street in 1970. (Courtesy of Whitman College and Northwest Archives.)

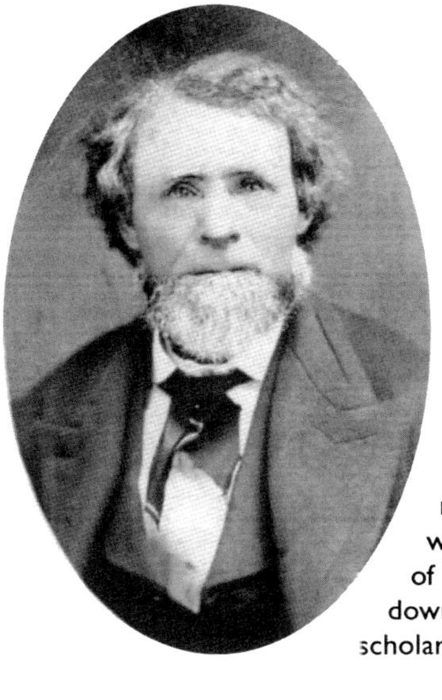

Joseph L. Stubblefield, founder of Stubblefield Home for Orphans
Joseph L. Stubblefield was an early pioneer in Walla Walla County, arriving in 1861. When he died in 1903, he left what was a large trust fund at the time—approximately $130,000—to establish and maintain the Stubblefield Home for orphans and elderly indigent widows. The home, which opened in 1904, was located southeast of Walla Walla near Bryant and Fern Avenues. The building was torn down in 1964, but the J.L. Stubblefield Trust still makes awards and grants scholarships. (Courtesy of Whitman College and Northwest Archives.)

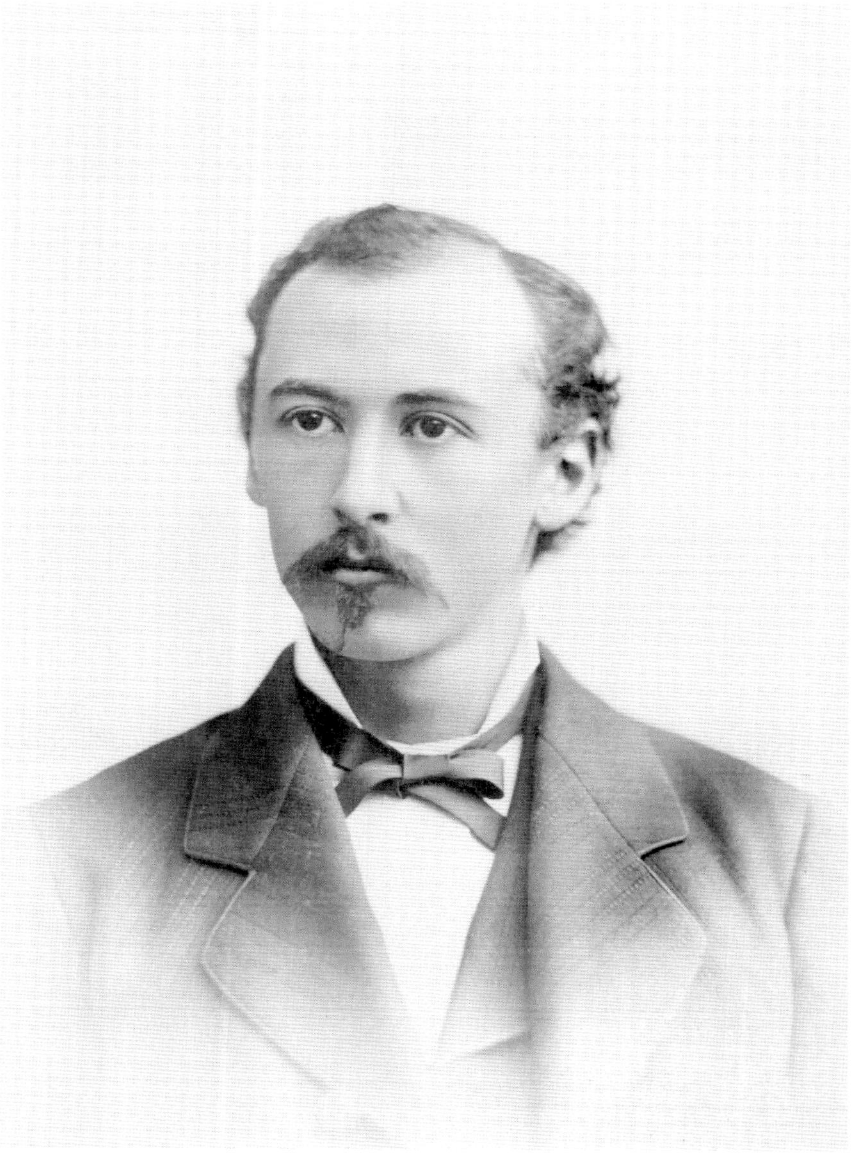

William D. Lyman, Historian and Writer

William Denison Lyman was born in Portland, Oregon, in 1852. Educated at Pacific University, he went on to earn his degree at Williams College in Massachusetts in 1877. After teaching at Pacific University for a decade, he moved to Fresno, California, and later to Santa Fe, New Mexico. But he decided to go back to teaching, coming to Whitman College in 1889. Lyman spent the rest of his teaching career at the college, teaching history and occasionally other subjects and serving as head of the history department. He wrote a number of newspaper and magazine articles. His books included *The Columbia River: Its History, Its Myths, Its Scenery, Its Commerce*; *Lyman's History of Old Walla Walla County*; and *Indian Myths of the Northwest*. Lyman, an avid mountain climber, climbed and wrote descriptions of most of the highest peaks of the Northwest. He was named professor emeritus shortly before his death in June 1920. (Courtesy of Whitman College and Northwest Archives.)

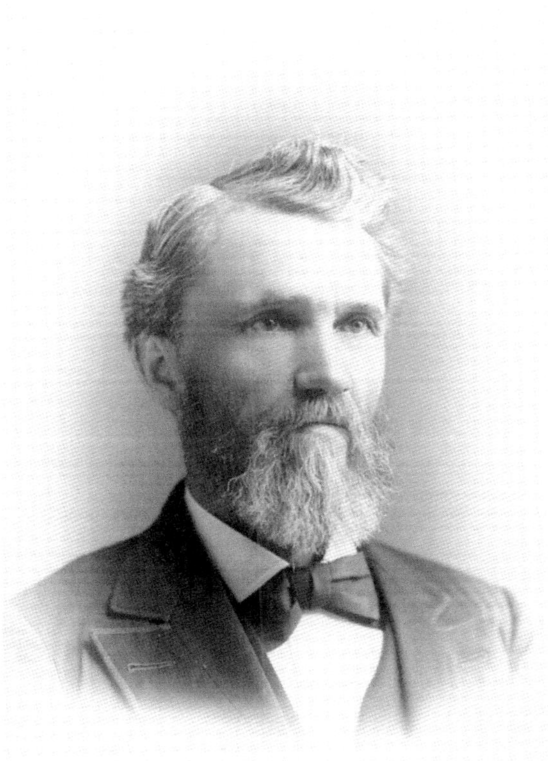

Alexander J. Anderson, First President of Whitman College, 1882–1891
By the 1880s, the Whitman Seminary, founded by Cushing Eells in 1859, was struggling to stay open as a precollege academy. In 1882, the trustees decided that its best chance to survive would be to become a liberal arts college. They called on Alexander Anderson, former president of the University of Washington, to become the first president of the newly formed Whitman College. Anderson developed curricula for the college and affiliated Whitman with the American College and Education Society in Boston, which provided financial assistance to the school. (Courtesy of Whitman College and Northwest Archives.)

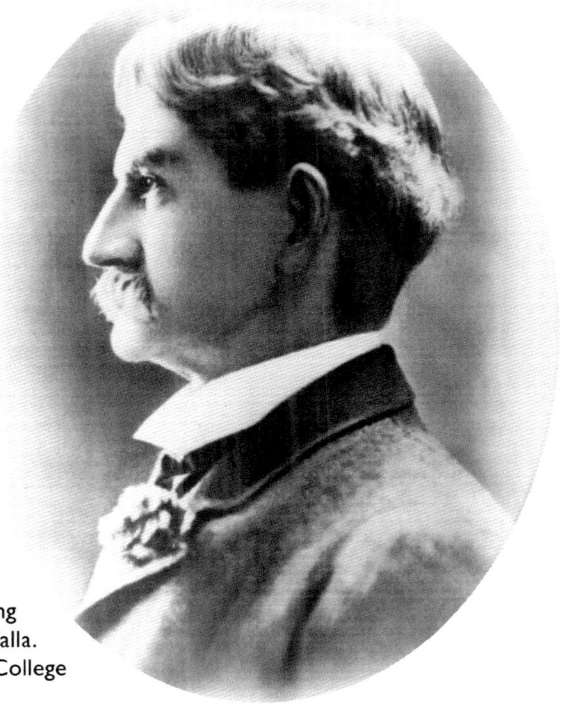

Levi Ankeny, Banker and Politician
Born near St. Joseph, Missouri, Levi Ankeny moved to Portland, Oregon, in 1853 and later ran a general store and bank in Idaho in the 1860s. He served as the first mayor of Lewiston, Idaho, in the early 1870s and shortly thereafter moved to Walla Walla, where he founded the First National Bank in 1902. He was also appointed chairman of the Pan-American Exposition Commission for the 1901 fair. In 1902, he was elected to the US Senate, serving until 1909, when he returned to Walla Walla. Ankeny died in 1921. (Courtesy of Whitman College and Northwest Archives.)

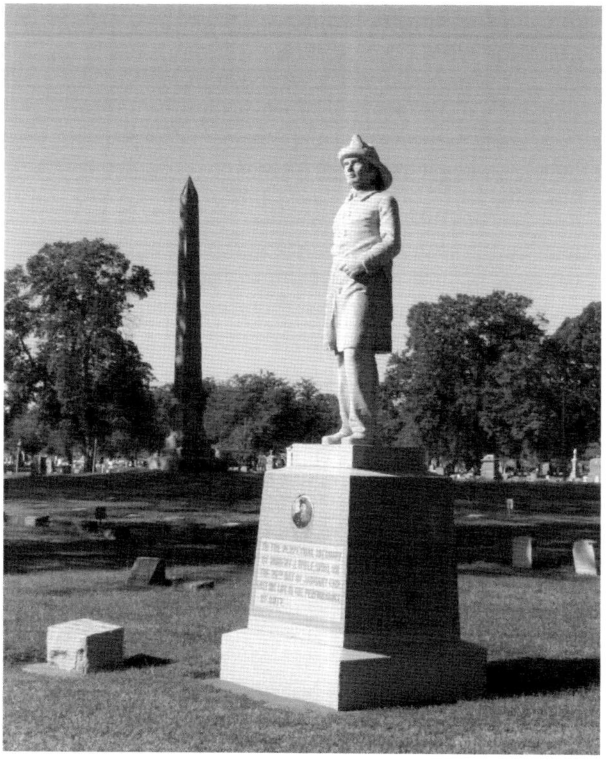

Robert J. Wolf, Firefighter
Robert Wolf was the first professional firefighter in the city of Walla Walla. Prior to that time, volunteer fire companies—with names like Tiger Company, Washington Company, and Our Boys—handled fires competitively. Wolf came to the city in 1883 and was hired as a fire engine driver in 1888. He later became assistant chief. In 1903, the city formed a full-time, paid fire department. Wolf served the city until his death in 1912 in a large downtown fire that consumed the Jones Building at Second Avenue and Alder Street. Two years later, this statue in his honor was erected on the site of the fire, but it was later relocated to his grave at Mountain View Cemetery in Walla Walla. In 1974, a replica of the statue was erected at Crawford Park at Fourth Avenue and Main Street, the site of a blaze that took the lives of two city firefighters. (Both, author photographs.)

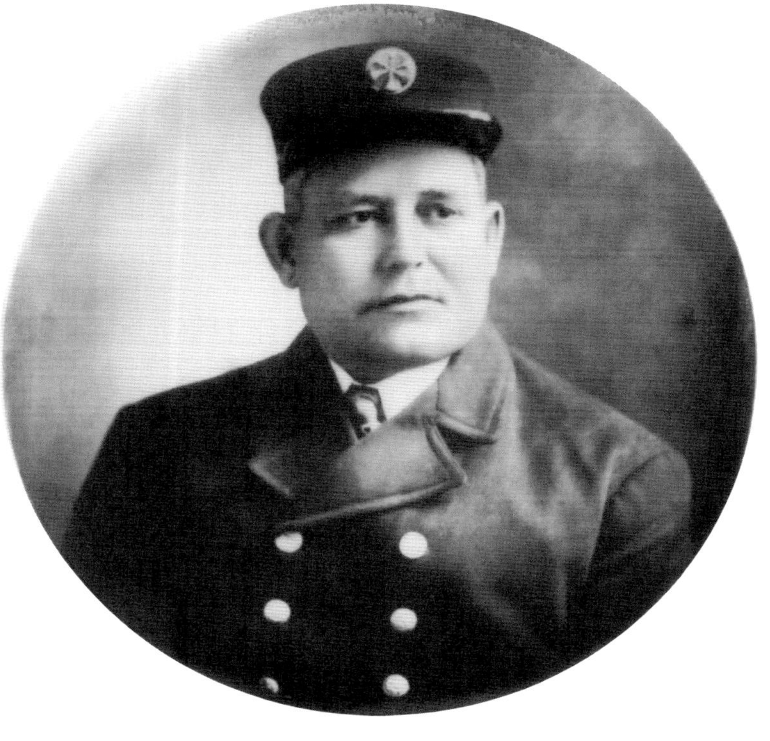

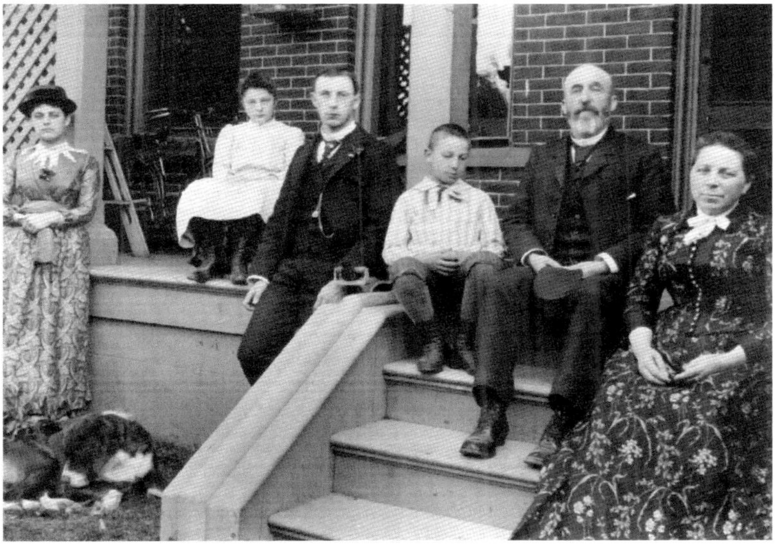

William and Isabelle Kirkman, Ranchers and Pillars of the Community
William Kirkman, a young textile salesman from Bury, England, came to Boston in 1852 and in 1853 settled in San Francisco. It was there he met his wife, Isabelle, a native of Balla Bay, Ireland. The couple married in 1867 and relocated to Idaho City, Idaho. In 1870, the Kirkmans moved to Walla Walla and built a small house on Colville Street. Kirkman partnered with John Dooley in a highly profitable cattle-ranching endeavor, and in 1890, he bought Dooley out. That same year, he founded the Walla Walla Dressed Meat Company and became involved in wheat farming, operating two farms near Dry Creek. When their imposing home at 214 North Colville Street was completed in 1880, William and Isabelle Kirkman moved in with their four surviving children, William Henry, Fanny Ann, Myrtle Bell, and Leslie Gilmore. The family built an addition consisting of a larger dining room and kitchen in 1890. The house is now a museum. The Kirkmans were active in the community, and William served on the city council, school board, and Whitman College Board of Trustees. (Both, courtesy of Kirkman House Museum.)

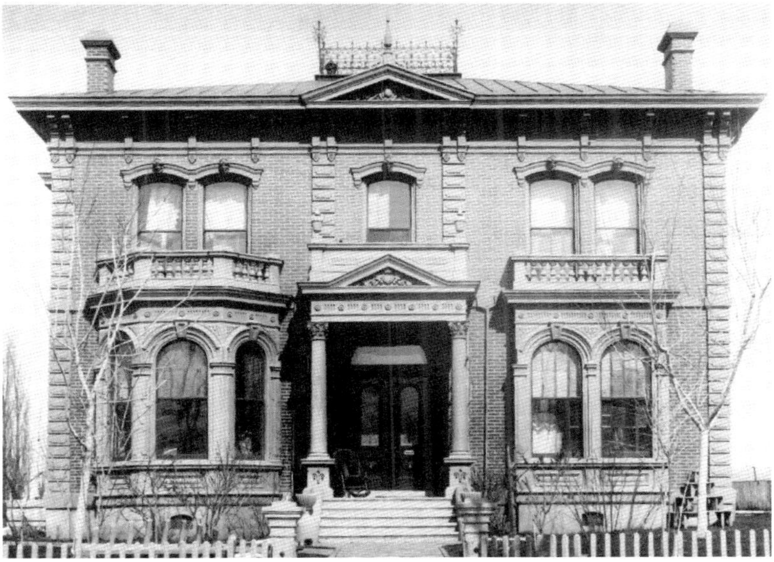

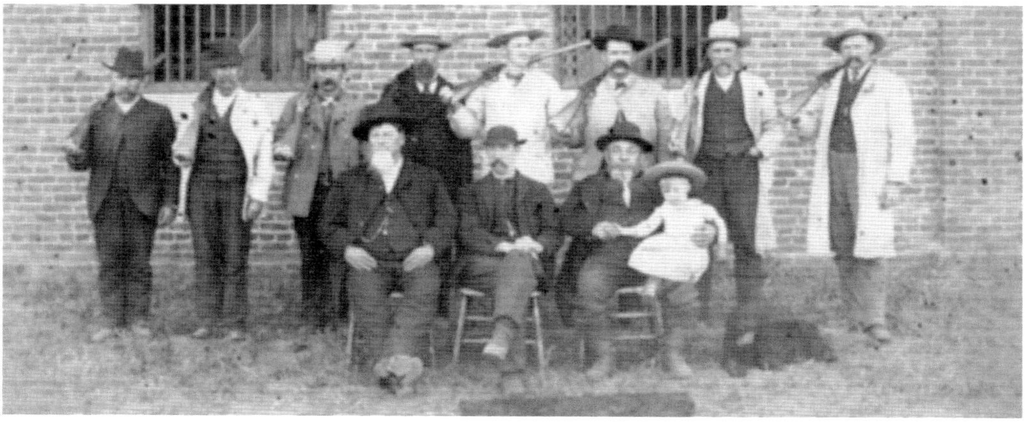

Frank Paine, First Superintendent of Walla Walla Penitentiary

Frank Paine, a Maine native, arrived in Walla Walla in 1862 and found a job with Baker Boyer Mercantile Co. Paine served as mayor, treasurer, and director of schools. When the territorial governor authorized a new penitentiary in 1885, Walla Walla campaigned to be its site. Paine (seated, left) was appointed superintendent, and the first convicts arrived in May 1887. An innovative administrator, Paine put prisoners to work making products for the town, notably bricks and jute. The prison, expanded over the years, is a significant employer in Walla Walla. (Courtesy of Fort Walla Walla Museum.)

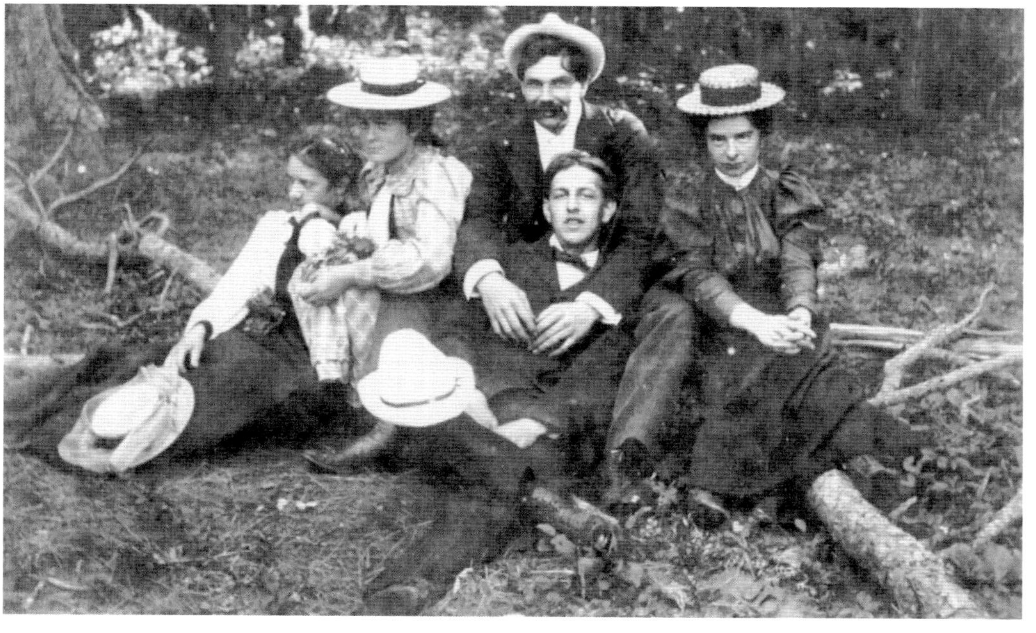

Arminda Fix, First Librarian of Whitman College, Speaker, and Poet

Arminda Fix was born in Walla Walla in 1872. Fix went to Whitman College between 1894 and 1899 and is pictured there (seated, left). She went to library school in New York and served as the first librarian of Whitman College from 1899 to 1916. Fix was active in a number of local organizations, including the Daughters of the American Revolution, historical societies, the YWCA, and the Walla Walla Garden Club. She was well known for her speeches at local club meetings, as well as for her poetry. Fix died in 1965. (Courtesy of Whitman College and Northwest Archives.)

Buffalo Soldiers, Fort Walla Walla

From October 1902 to October 1904, Fort Walla Walla was home to the famed Buffalo Soldiers, the elite African American troop of the 9th Cavalry. The 9th and 10th Cavalry were established in 1866 as regiments of African American soldiers by Maj. Gen. Philip H. Sheridan, and the group was nicknamed the "Buffalo Soldiers" by the Indian tribes they fought. The Buffalo Soldiers served in the Indian Wars and in the Spanish-American War, where they served alongside Theodore Roosevelt's Rough Riders at the battles of Kettle Hill and San Juan Hill. In 1902, fresh from duty in the Philippines, four troops of the 9th Cavalry were assigned to Fort Walla Walla. The troops consisted of 16 white officers and 375 African American troopers. The Buffalo Soldiers provided extraordinary service, including opening the West to settlement. The 9th Cavalry disbanded in 1905, and the 14th Cavalry replaced it and served at Fort Walla Walla until 1908, with its main responsibility being maintenance of law and order. (Courtesy of Library of Congress.)

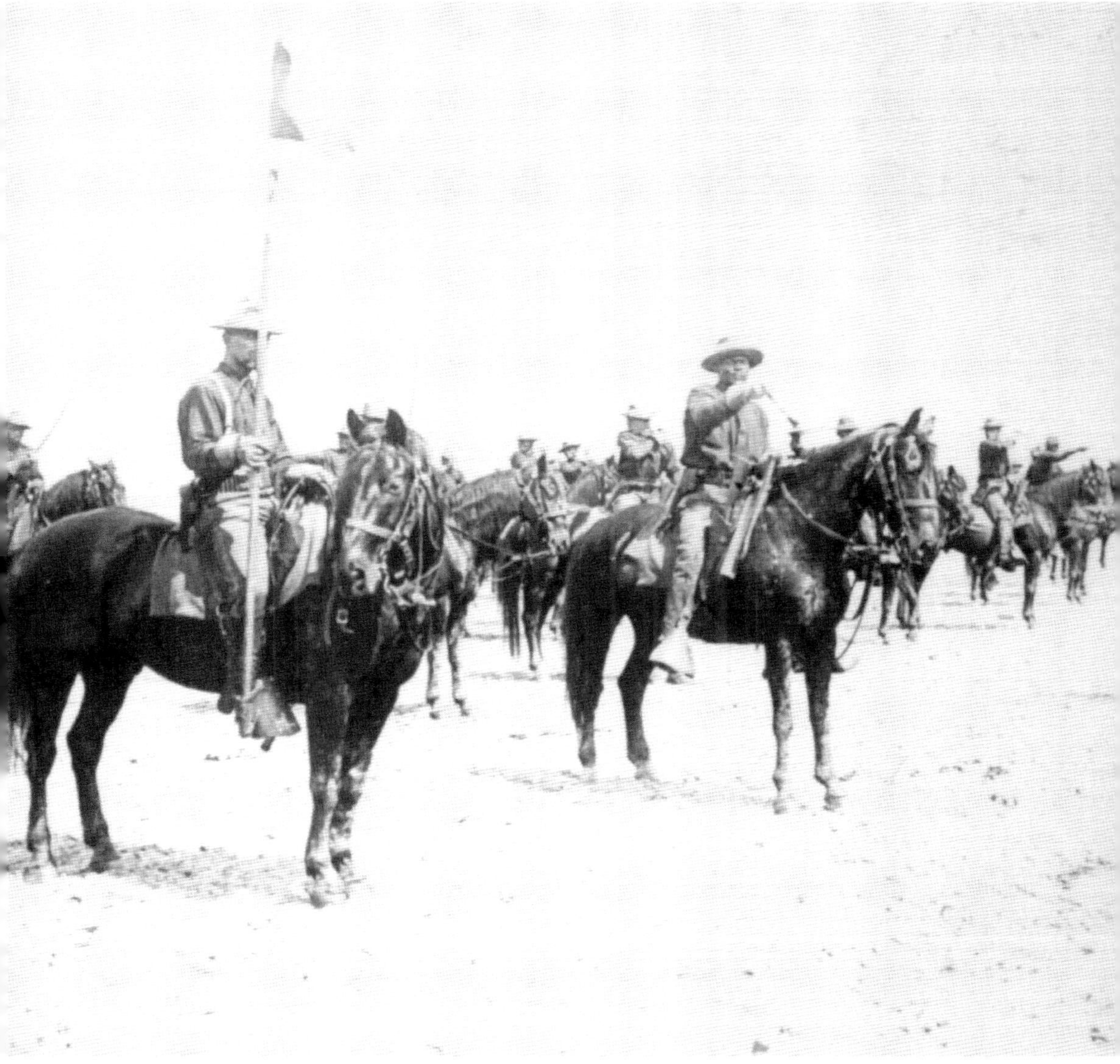

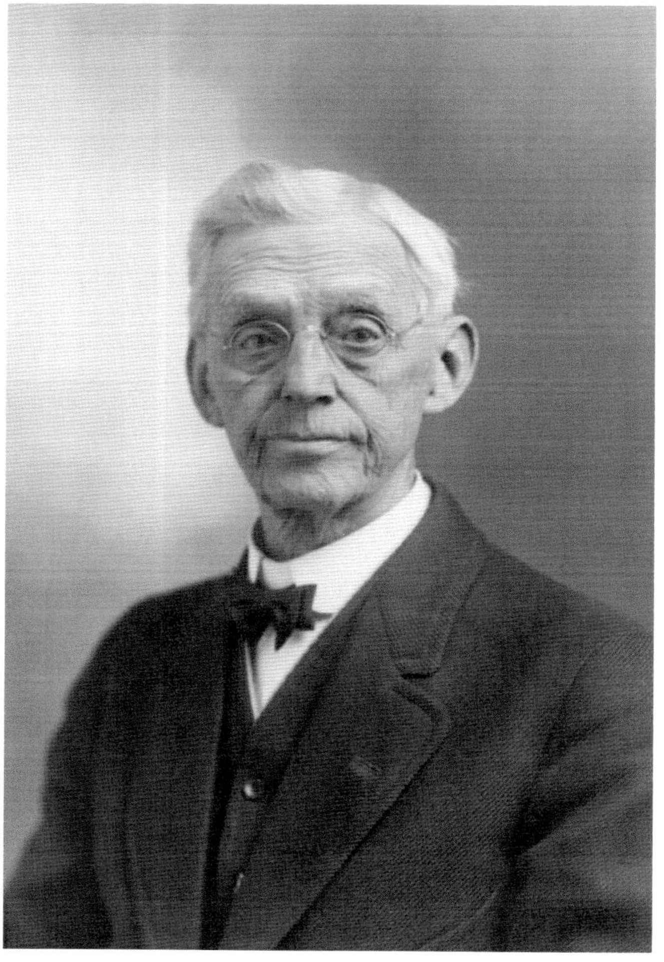

Dr. Nelson Blalock, Physician, Pioneer Orchardist

Dr. Nelson G. Blalock, a graduate of Jefferson Medical College, served as a regimental surgeon in the Civil War with the 115th Illinois Volunteers. After practicing medicine in Mount Zion, Illinois, from 1863 to 1872, Blalock left to scout a trail to Washington Territory, looking for a healthier climate. He was so impressed with Walla Walla that in 1873 he moved his family to the valley. Although he continued to practice medicine, he initially made most of his living freighting goods from Wallula to Walla Walla. He also set up a mill and flume to produce lumber. In 1876, Blalock bought 160 acres west of town and began planting apple and pear trees. By 1893, Blalock Orchards was able to ship two carloads of fruit to the World's Columbian Exposition in Chicago. Blalock expanded his orchards, irrigating 1,600 acres with 20 miles of pipelines that ran from eight artesian wells. He also diversified into wheat, cultivating 1,000 acres south of town. Blalock was also involved in civic endeavors. He was a member of the constitutional convention, which framed the state constitution in 1889, and served as president of the Columbian Exposition for the state of Washington. Locally, he served two terms as mayor of Walla Walla and was a member of the school board for eight years. He was a member of the board of trustees of Whitman College for 30 years and served as president of the board for 12 years. Blalock gave land to Whitman College and also donated 40 acres to Walla Walla College (now Walla Walla University). Blalock died in 1913 and is buried in Mountain View Cemetery with a Civil War marker simply showing his name and his regiment. (Courtesy of Whitman College and Northwest Archives.)

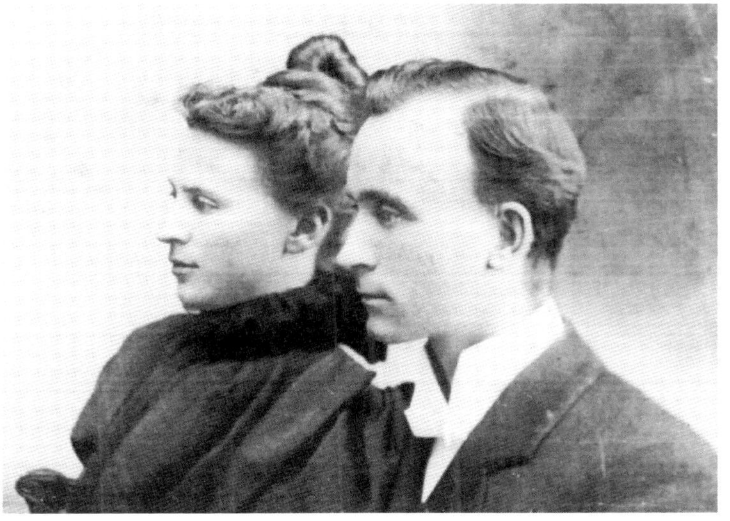

Edward Sutherland, President of Walla Walla College

Edward A. Sutherland was associated with the Seventh-Day Adventist–affiliated Walla Walla College from its opening in 1892. He acted as the school's administrator until 1894, when he became the college's president. Under Sutherland's tenure, the school instituted Bible studies and emphasized practical courses that could be completed within a short period of time—food production and preparation, printing, farming, dressmaking, and basket weaving. The college also trained ministers, missionaries, and church school teachers. Today's curriculum includes liberal arts, professional, and technical programs. The college added master's degree programs as early as 1948 and became Walla Walla University in 2007. (Both, courtesy of Walla Walla University Archives.)

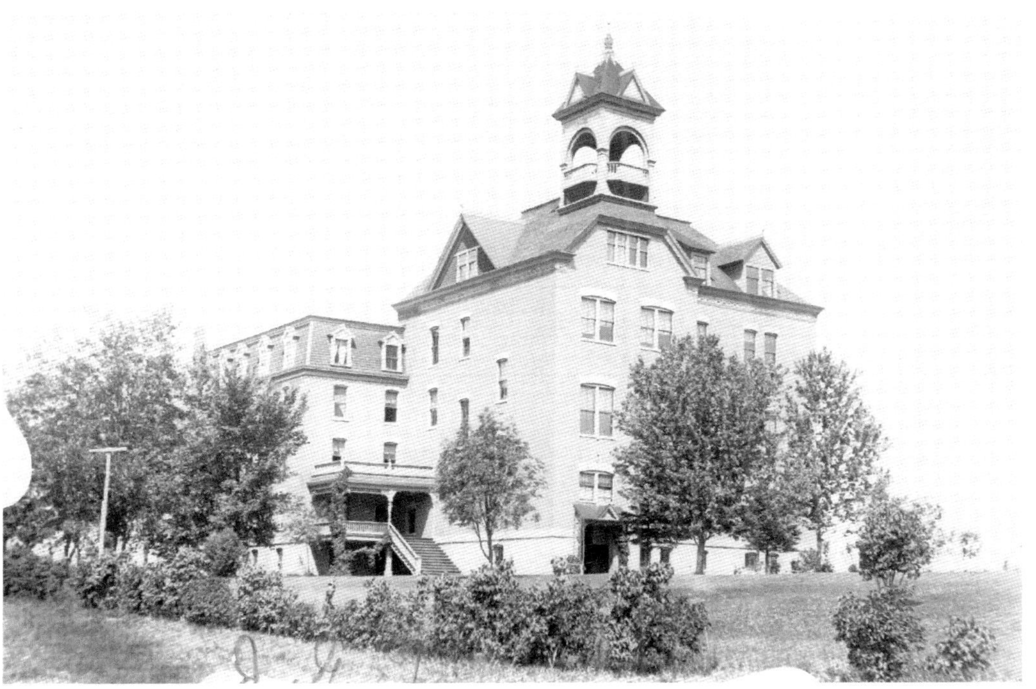

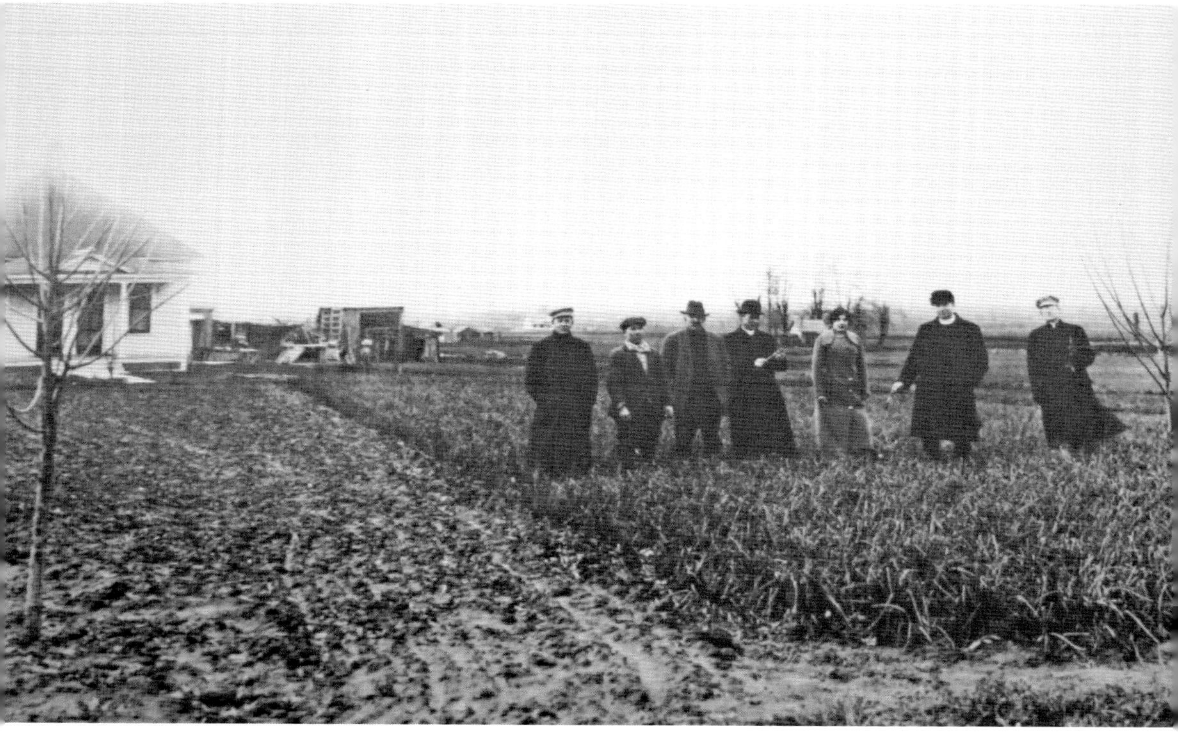

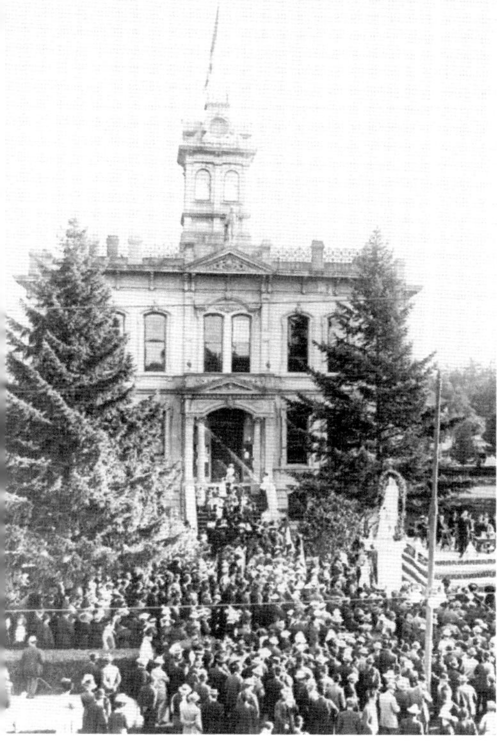

Italian Pioneers

Locati, Venneri, Saturno, Orselli, Tachi, Rizzuti, Leonetti, Castaldi, Deccio—names that roll off the tongue—draw to mind the deep roots of the Italian community in the Walla Walla Valley. Since Frank Orselli arrived in 1857, Italians have brought richness to the valley's agriculture, culture, cuisine, and wine. Although Walla Walla sweet onions may have been brought to the valley by a French soldier, Italian families have long been associated with this seasonal favorite. The Italians were also among the earliest to cultivate grapes in the valley. It may have been Frank Orselli who planted one of the first vineyards. Pasquale Saturno, known for his Walla Walla sweet onions, also made wine and sold it to Fort Walla Walla. Doug Saturno, whose family farm (above) is pictured around 1876, portrays his great-grandfather Pasquale in the Living History Company at Fort Walla Walla Museum. The institutions Italian immigrants formed—St. Francis of Assisi Church, the Knights of Columbus, and the Italian Heritage Association—left a strong imprint on the area and help preserve Italian culture for future generations. The photograph at left shows the dedication of the Christopher Columbus statue in front of the Walla Walla County Courthouse on October 12, 1911. The statue is still the centerpiece of an annual celebration of Italian culture. (Above, courtesy of Doug Saturno; left, courtesy of Fort Walla Walla Museum.)

CHAPTER FOUR

A Golden Age

By the turn of the 20th century, Walla Walla was in full bloom. It had transitioned from a wide-open frontier town, geared to supplying miners and hosting an assortment of rough-and-tumble characters, to a more genteel city and agricultural center.

Downtown saw the erection of impressive buildings more fitting for a city that had become the commercial and agricultural center of southeastern Washington. Walla Walla had discovered wheat was the best kind of gold to ensure prosperity for the city.

The new century brought more institutions associated with a prosperous regional center, including Walla Walla General Hospital, the YMCA, the YWCA, and even the Walla Walla Symphony (now the oldest continuously operating symphony west of the Mississippi River). The city began laying out parks, and Pioneer Park was established in 1902, inspired by a plan suggested by the renowned Olmsted Brothers.

Area colleges continued to offer high-quality education to incoming students and valley residents. Luminaries like Supreme Court justice William O. Douglas and Nobel Prize winner Walter Brattain, both graduates of Whitman College, enjoyed lifelong associations with their alma mater. Legendary coach Raymond Borleske earned acclaim at Whitman and was the first inductee into the State of Washington Sports Hall of Fame.

An architectural renaissance provided Walla Walla with many of its landmark buildings, including the Marcus Whitman Hotel, the Walla Walla County Courthouse, the Carnegie Library, and many schools. Streets were lined with elegant residences befitting the prosperity of the city. Palouse Street is still graced with many of these symbols of the flourishing community. A new pavilion at the Walla Walla Fairgrounds established a backdrop for the Walla Walla Fair & Frontier Days. In 1913, the first Walla Walla Stampede Rodeo was held at the fairgrounds.

Business and manufacturing was bustling. Hotels, breweries, and shops were in demand. Factories, canneries, and food-processing enterprises were spurred on by promoters like John Grant Kelly, owner of the Walla Walla *Union-Bulletin* newspaper. Life was good in up-and-coming Walla Walla.

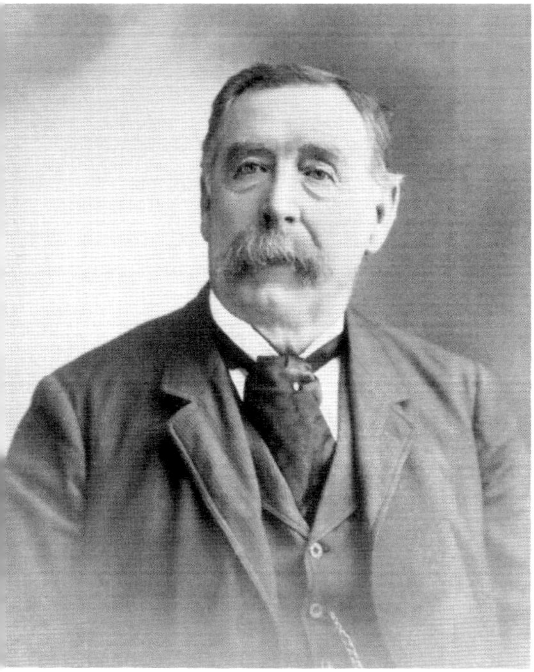

George Dacres, Hotelier

George Dacres was born in Ireland around 1828. He came to America in 1849 and worked as a store clerk in California before coming to the Northwest. Dacres worked on a survey between Washington and British Columbia. After leaving the survey team in 1860, Dacres operated pack trains (he owned more than 40 mules) during the Idaho and Kootenay, Canada, gold-mining boom. By 1875, Dacres had shifted his interests to farming in the Walla Walla Valley, gradually acquiring 1,000 acres. He also became active civically, serving on the Walla Walla City Council for two years. After an 1892 fire destroyed Fred Stine's 1870s hotel, Dacres bought the ruins. His new hotel, completed in 1899, featured a cast-iron frieze. Dacres died in 1902. In 1907, Portland architects Bennes, Hendricks & Tobey added an additional story and remodeled much of the interior. Over the years, the hotel welcomed luminaries including Louis May Alcott, John Philip Sousa, and Al Jolson. The hotel closed in 1963. The restored building, on the corner at Main Street and Fourth Avenue, is listed in the National Register of Historic Places and retains its architectural integrity. (Both, courtesy of Joe Drazan.)

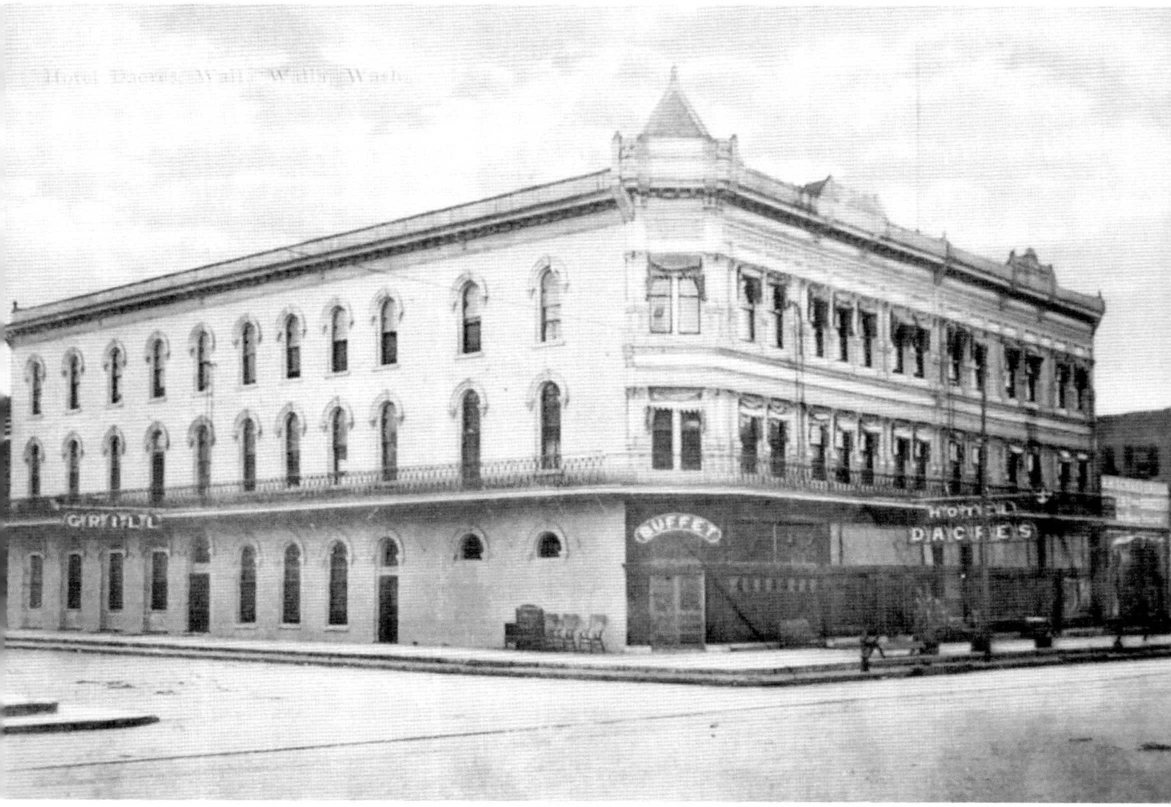

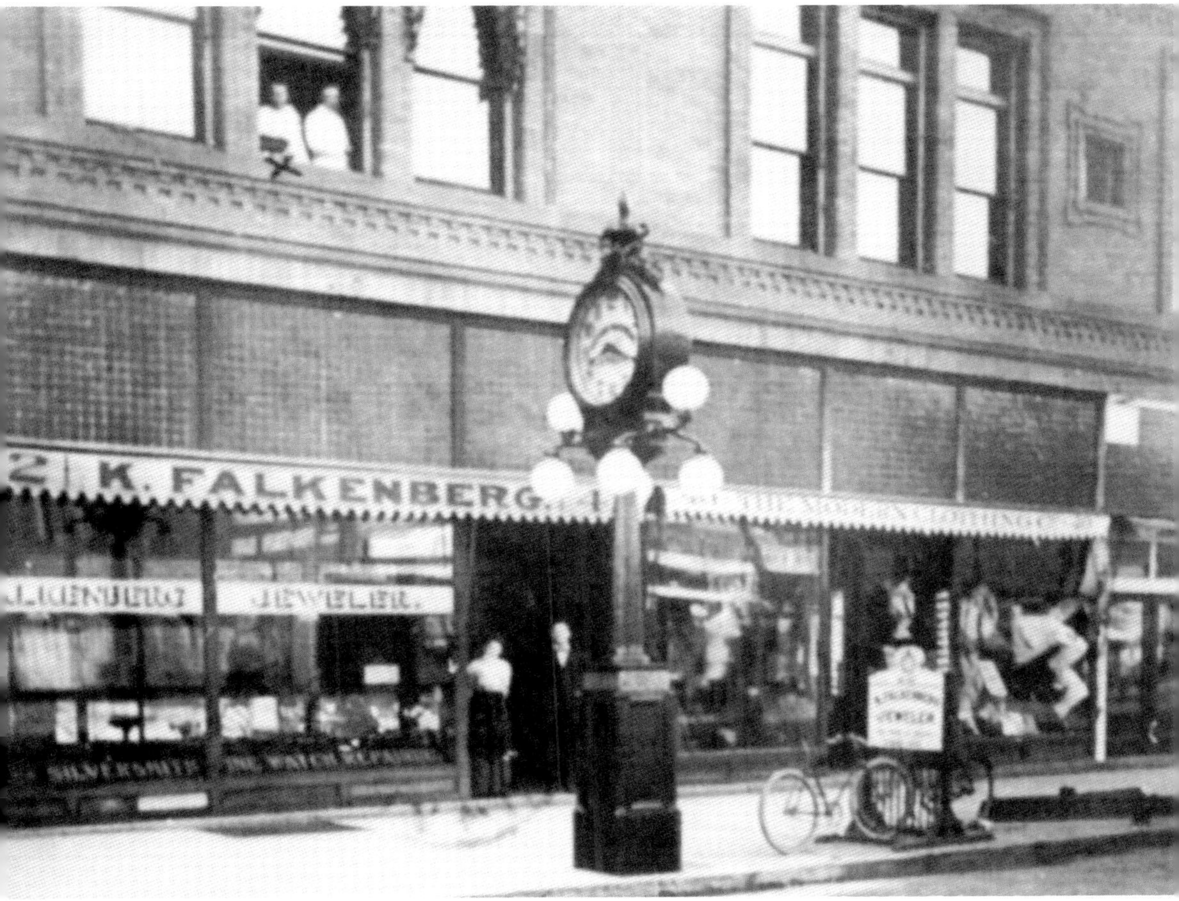

Kristian Falkenberg, Jeweler
Kristian Falkenberg was born in Norway in 1872 and came to the United States in 1893. By 1905, he was looking for a place to start his business in the West. When he came to Walla Walla, he was impressed with "tree-lined streets on which were located rows of substantial and pleasant looking homes." In November 1905, he opened his first store at Fourth Avenue and Main Street. In less than a year, he was so successful that he moved to 42 East Main Street, pictured above (Falkenberg stands proudly in the doorway). In 1911, Falkenberg installed a Howard street clock in front of his store. In the summer of 1916, an incoming Whitman freshman came to Walla Walla to look for a job to help pay his way through college. On the recommendation of assistant Philo Rounds and young clerk Jerry "Spud" Cundiff, Falkenberg hired a future US Supreme Court justice, William O. Douglas, to work in the store. Kristian Falkenberg died in 1962. In 1932, watchmaker Knute Glimme and Jerry Cundiff bought the store. Today, Jerry's grandson Skip Cundiff runs the business, which moved to 6 East Main Street in 1974. The clock moved as well and still graces the sidewalk in front of Falkenberg's. (Courtesy of Joe Drazan.)

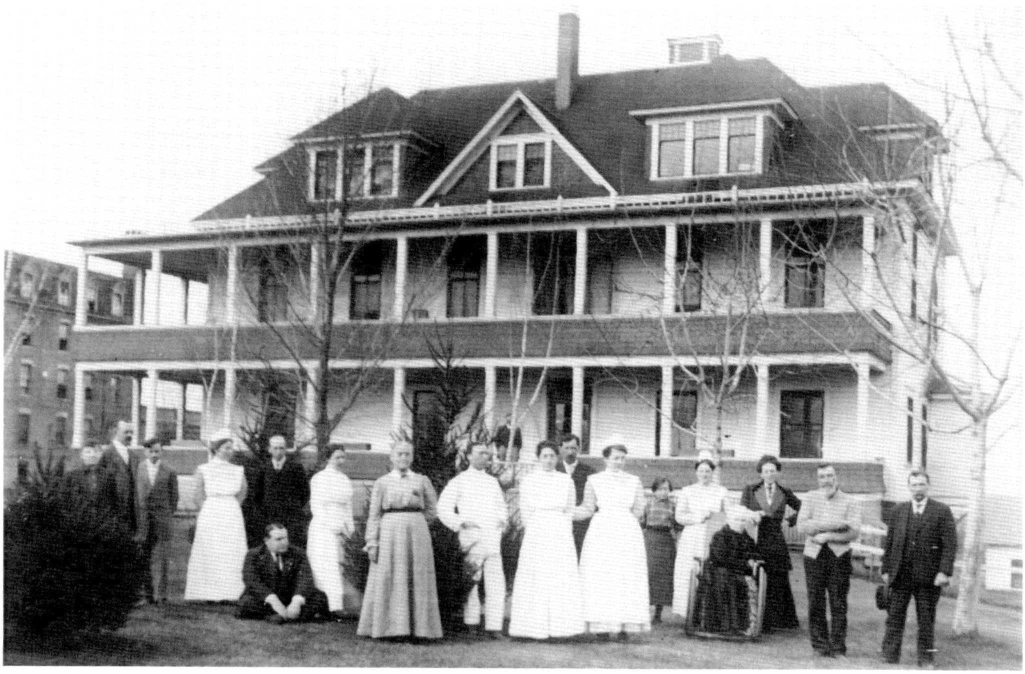

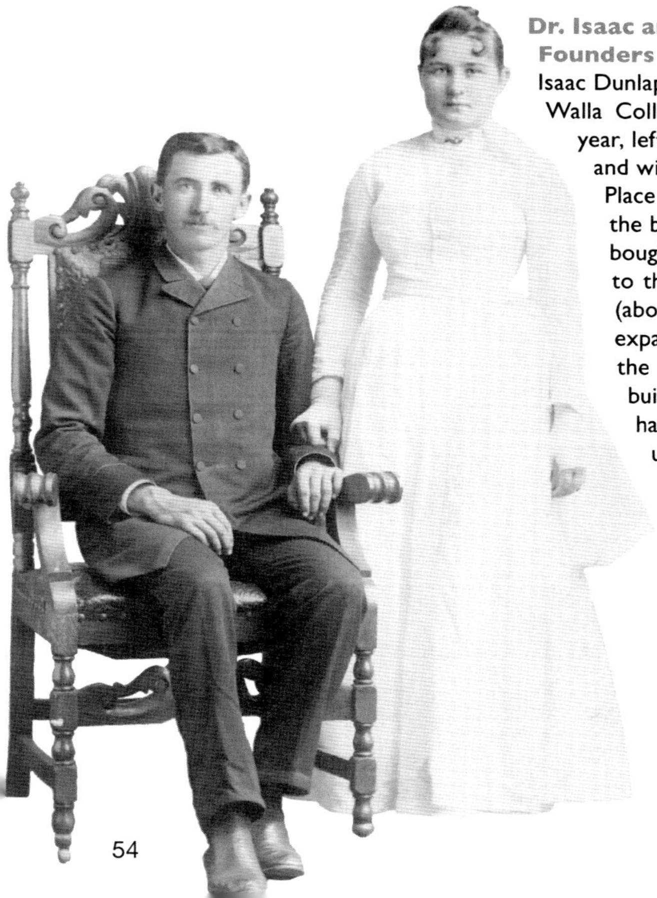

Dr. Isaac and Maggie Dunlap, Founders of Walla Walla General Hospital

Isaac Dunlap, who served as the business manager of Walla Walla College (WWC) in College Place during its first year, left the school for his medical training. In 1898, he and wife Maggie, a trained nurse, returned to College Place and opened sanitarium treatment rooms in the basement of the college. In 1906, the sanitarium bought the old public school, which they moved to the WWC campus. They jacked up the building (above) and added a first floor. The sanitarium expanded several times before finally moving off the Walla Walla College campus into a hospital building the city had built on Bonsella Street but had never opened. The hospital remained there until a modern facility was built in 1977. Now part of the Adventist Health Medical Group, the hospital was extensively remodeled and expanded in 2013. (Both, courtesy of Walla Walla University Archives.)

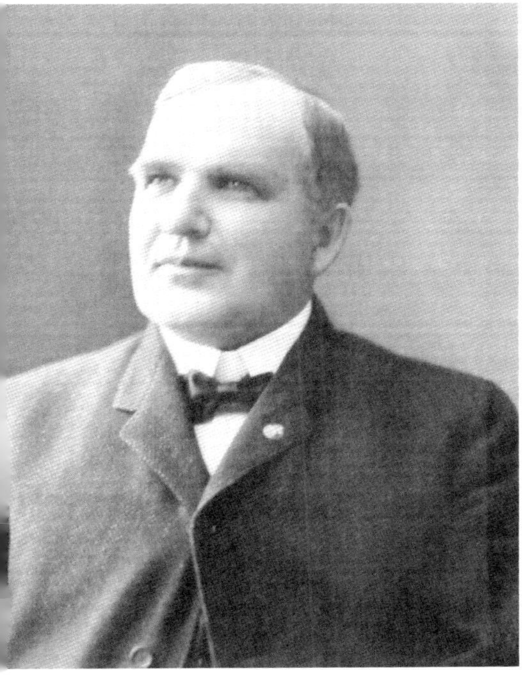

Gilbert Hunt, Threshing Machine Inventor and Manufacturer

Gilbert Hunt came to town in 1883 with $10 in his pocket. After working in Byron Jackson's mill making feeders for stationary threshing machines, he bought the business. Gilbert Hunt Company was the only manufacturer of threshers and threshing-machine engines west of the Missouri River. One of the largest producers of farm machinery in the region, Hunt invented the Pride of Washington steam thresher. He served as mayor and was on the school board. He was a strong proponent for paving the downtown business district, extending the water system, and establishing public parks. (Courtesy of Joe Drazan.)

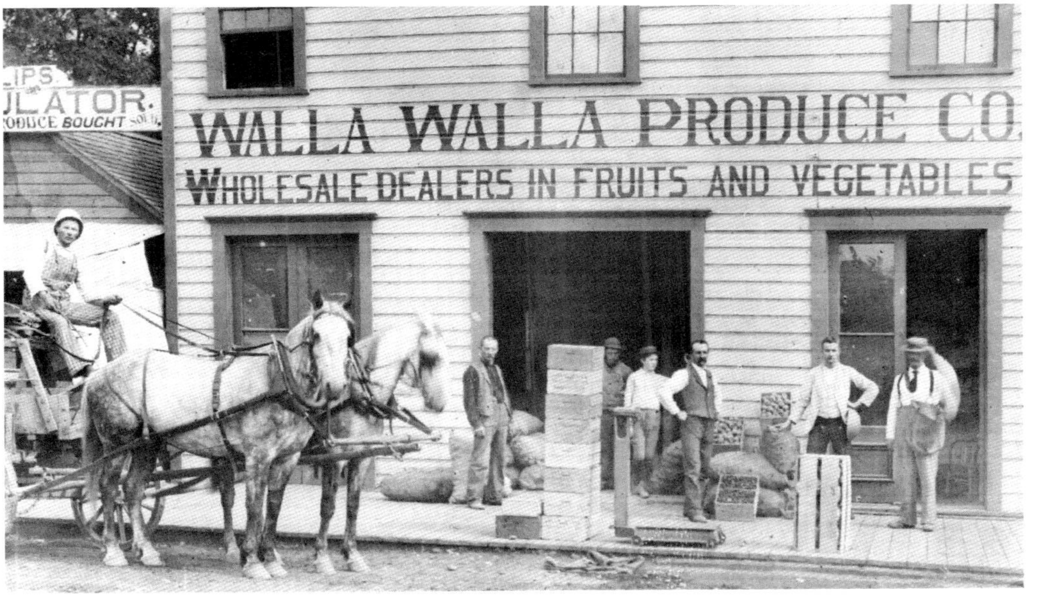

Frederick E. Mojonnier, Pioneer in Hothouse Vegetable Business

Born in Illinois in 1874, Frederick Mojonnier came to town in 1895 to work for the Walla Walla Produce Company. By 1900, he was a stockholder and was running the business. After buying out John Thonney, Mojonnier ran the company until 1914, when he sold it to devote himself to his Walla Walla Hothouse Vegetable Company (founded in 1909). At Mojonnier Station, west of Walla Walla, he had three acres under glass. His company was known as one of the leading hothouse vegetable growers in the Northwest, shipping cucumbers, lettuce, and tomatoes all over the West. (Courtesy of Fort Walla Walla Museum.)

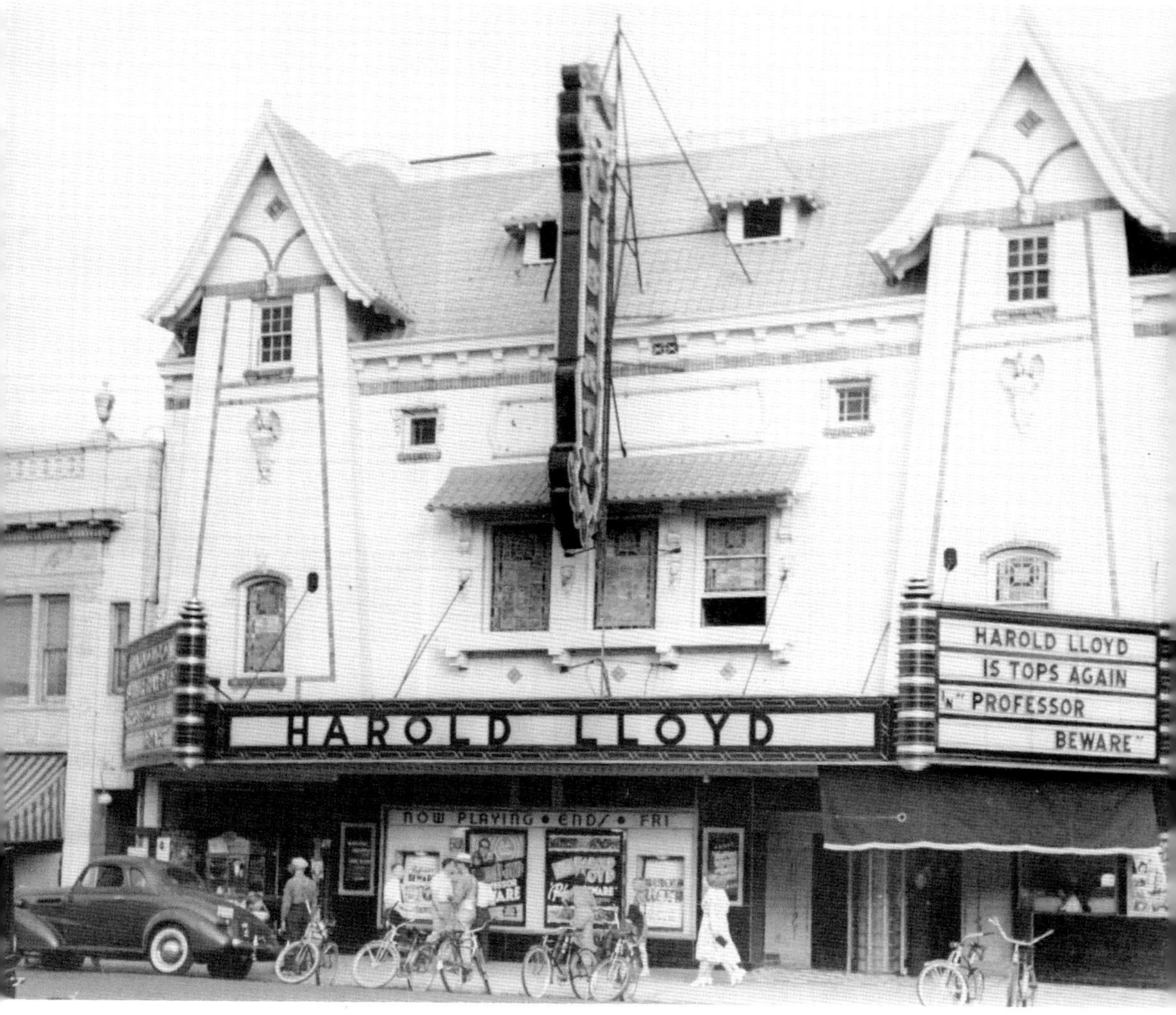

Henry Osterman, Architect

If any one architect put his stamp on Walla Walla, it was Henry Osterman. Osterman, born in 1862, came to the United States from Essen, Germany, in 1889 with brothers William, Frank, and August. The siblings settled in Walla Walla and found work as carpenters, but by about 1896, all but Henry had returned to Germany. Within a few years, Osterman was advertising himself as an architect, although it is not known if he had any formal training. There are some references to him having been trained in Dusseldorf before he came to the United States. Osterman designed a number of the most significant buildings in the Walla Walla Valley, including the county courthouse, city hall, Green Park School, Central Christian Church, Dixie School, and numerous residences. Six Osterman-designed buildings are listed in the National Register of Historic Places, including the Liberty Theatre (above), the Carnegie Library, the pavilion at the Walla Walla Fairgrounds, and Osterman's home at 508 Lincoln Street. (Courtesy of Fort Walla Walla Museum.)

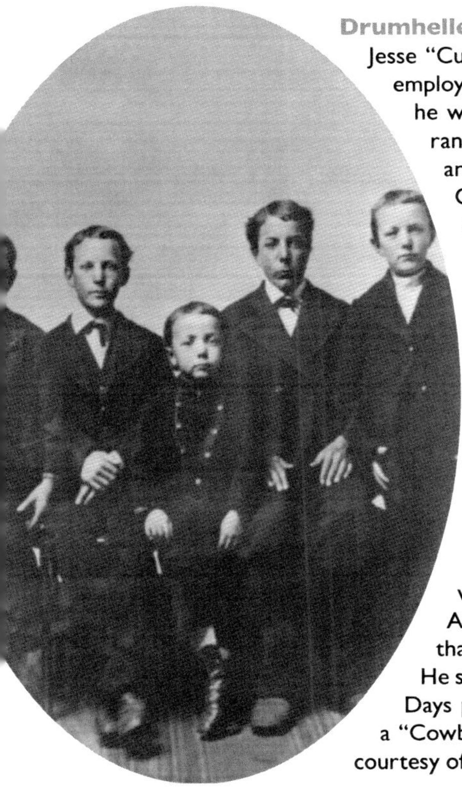

Drumheller Family, Hardware, Horse Racing, and Rodeos

Jesse "Curley" Drumheller came to Walla Walla in 1855 as a civilian employee of the Army, buying and caring for their horses. By 1856, he was raising cattle in the valley. His family went on to build a ranching empire. Drumheller married Martha Maxson in 1863, and the couple had five sons (at left, from left to right, George, Oscar, Thomas, Samuel, and Albert). In 1900, Jesse founded a hardware and agricultural supply store, one of the largest establishments of its time in Walla Walla, with his sons Thomas and Oscar. Samuel founded a town in Alberta, Canada, that bears the Drumheller name. Albert died at age 28 of a ruptured appendix. George farmed his 5,000 acres of wheat with 500 mules—he was one of the last wheat farmers to use the animals. George is also considered the father of Thoroughbred racing in Washington State, and he was a successful horse breeder as well. In 1913, George and his wife, Anna Bush Drumheller, staged the first Walla Walla Stampede Rodeo, a tradition that still continues at the Walla Walla Fair & Frontier Days. George and Anna's son Allen was a cowboy and renowned horse trainer. Allen and his father were both inducted into the Washington Racing Hall of Fame. Allen's brother Dewey (below) enjoyed an active rodeo career that including calf roping, steer wrestling, and wild-cow milking. He served as the marshal for the 1968 Walla Walla Fair & Frontier Days parade. Dewey passed away in 1971. In 2013, he was named a "Cowboy Legend" by the Walla Walla Fair & Frontier Days. (Left, courtesy of Drumheller family; below, courtesy of Judy Frazier.)

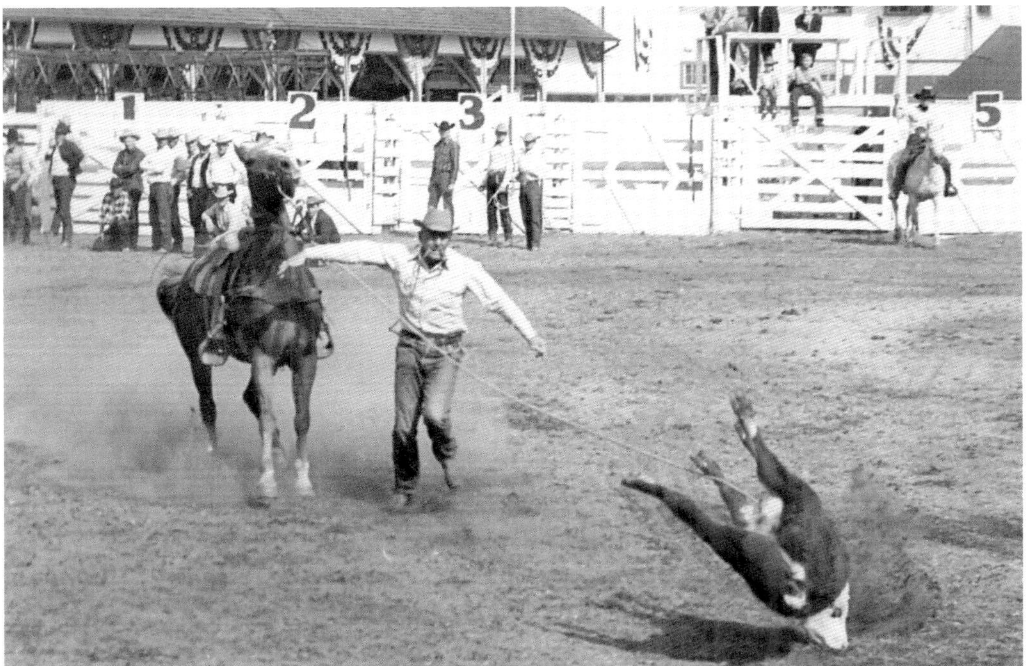

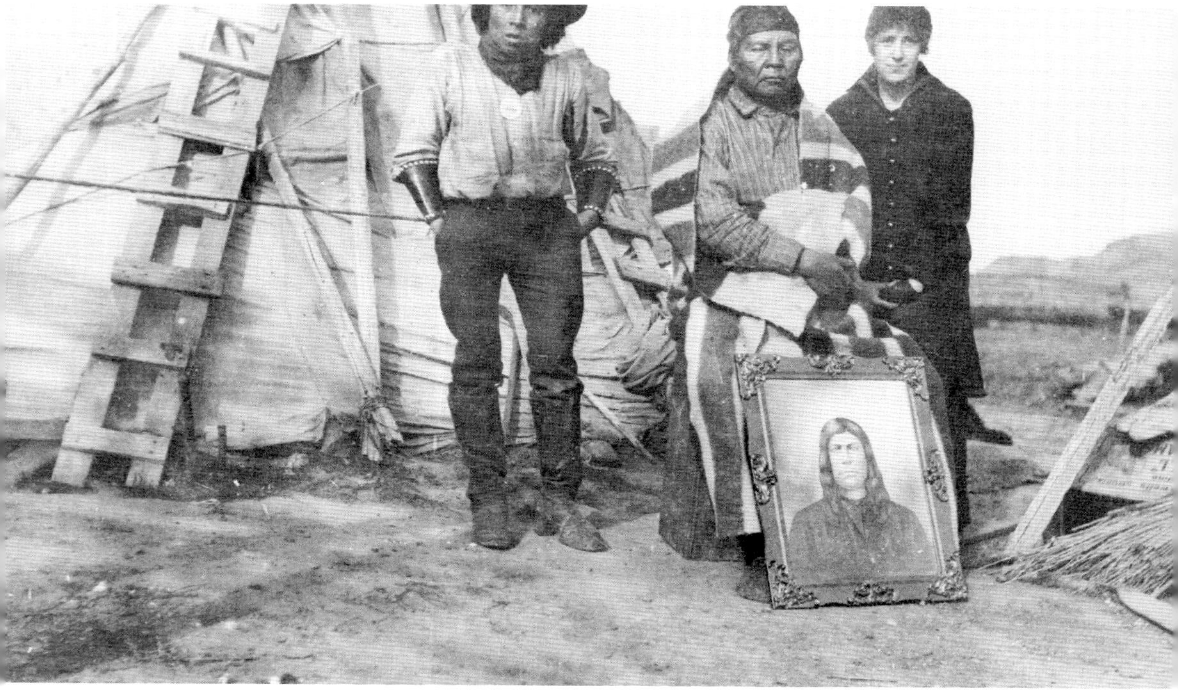

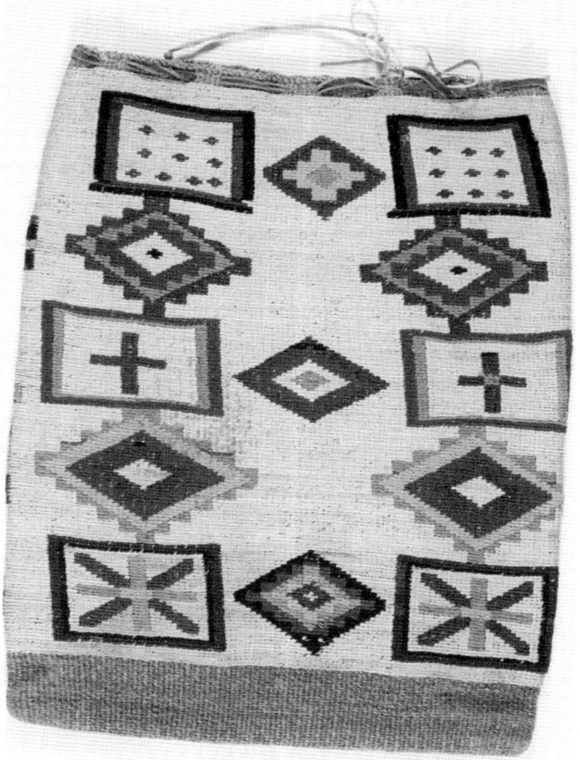

Old Bones, Palouse Indian Leader
Born into a band of Cayuse, Old Bones (earlier known as Waughaski) became the leader of a band of Palouse people who lived at the mouth of the Palouse River. Old Bones's father, Umtippe, is said to have been the young man who recovered Marcus and Narcissa Whitman's daughter Clarissa after she drowned in a stream near the mission. A charcoal portrait of Old Bones, now in the collection of Fort Walla Walla Museum, depicts him wearing a shirt believed to have been given to his father, Umtippe, by the Whitmans—a shirt that Old Bones is said to have been buried in when he died in 1916. Above are Peter (left) and Susie Bones (center) with the portrait. Old Bones became a great friend of pioneer Albert Lloyd and his family, who settled near Waitsburg in 1859. The Lloyds' relationship with Old Bones's family led to Albert and Lois Lloyd and their descendents preserving important artifacts like the twined bag at left, many of which are on display at the museum. (Both, courtesy of Fort Walla Walla Museum.)

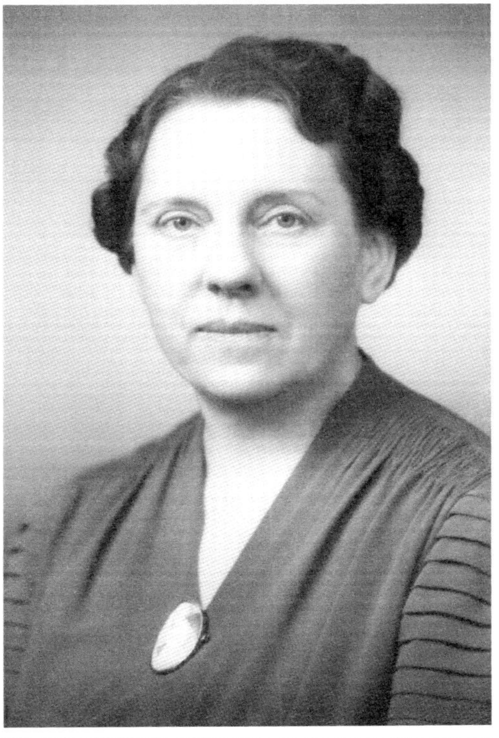

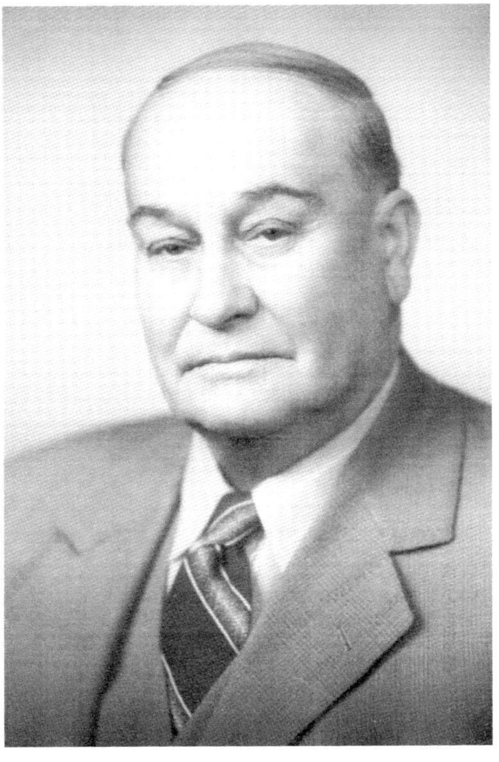

Wesley and Ina Lloyd, Friends of Indian People

Pioneer Albert Lloyd came to the Northwest as a child, traveling in a wagon train from Missouri to Oregon in 1845. Stopping at the Whitman Mission on their way, the family settled in the Willamette Valley. In November 1855, Lloyd returned to the Walla Walla Valley with the Oregon Volunteer Militia and participated in the Battle of Walla Walla against Indian tribes. Following his militia service, he and wife Lois (Jasper) settled in Walla Walla County. Their farm was near the Nez Perce Trail, and the Lloyds fed many Indian warriors, soldiers, and prospectors that traveled through. In 1909, their son Wesley and his wife, Ina (both at left), took over the farm. Wesley became known as a friend of the Indians in the area. Gift exchanges between Plateau Indian people are a way of showing mutual respect. In that tradition, the Lloyds commonly exchanged gifts with their Indian friends, often offering food (particularly meat and produce). In return, the Indians gave them a number of artifacts and regalia, which the Lloyds carefully preserved. When the Indian families were camped nearby, their children played with young Milton and Tony Lloyd. During the 1910s and 1920s the Indians gave the children moccasins, gauntlets, and a teepee. The special relationship between the families spanned generations into the 1940s, and many of the artifacts in the family's collection were given to them by Old Bones's family. The Lloyd collection was donated to Fort Walla Walla Museum by the estate of Bertha Lloyd, Milton's widow. The artifacts are used to tell the story of the Plateau Indians and their positive interactions with a local pioneer family. (Both, courtesy of Fort Walla Walla Museum.)

Almina "Grandma" Klicker, Klicker Strawberries

The story of the Klicker family in the Walla Walla Valley begins with Almina Ross Garland, born in Brodhead, Kentucky, in 1863. After the death of her husband, Charles Garland, Almina and her children, Virginia and Marion Garland, came west. The widow staked her homestead claim in 1889 on a logged-off mountain slope 13 miles outside Walla Walla on Klicker Mountain. Almina soon caught the eye of her neighbor Jake Klicker, and the couple was married in 1893. In 1895, they opened a hotel on the mountain, and Almina soon proved herself to be a savvy proprietress. The couple had three children: Jake, Kitty, and Delbert. When Jake and Delbert were in their teens, they worked for Joe Thomas on his ranch just west of Walla Walla. Thomas was planting strawberries, but at the end of the day, the extra plants were tossed. Jake and Delbert asked Thomas for the leftovers and then rushed home to start their own berry patch—the beginning of Klicker Strawberries. The enterprise soon proved more lucrative than the hotel. To ensure a long season, Klicker has strawberry fields at a range of elevations, from 1,100 to 4,200 feet. The family is also proud of their role in providing seasonal jobs for thousands of young people in the valley, jobs that came with a dose of work ethic and responsibility. Over the years, the Klicker family and their descendants have made their mark in Walla Walla in cattle ranching, farming, and providing Christmas trees. But when asked what they associate with the name "Klicker," locals are likely to respond, "strawberries!" (Courtesy of Klicker family.)

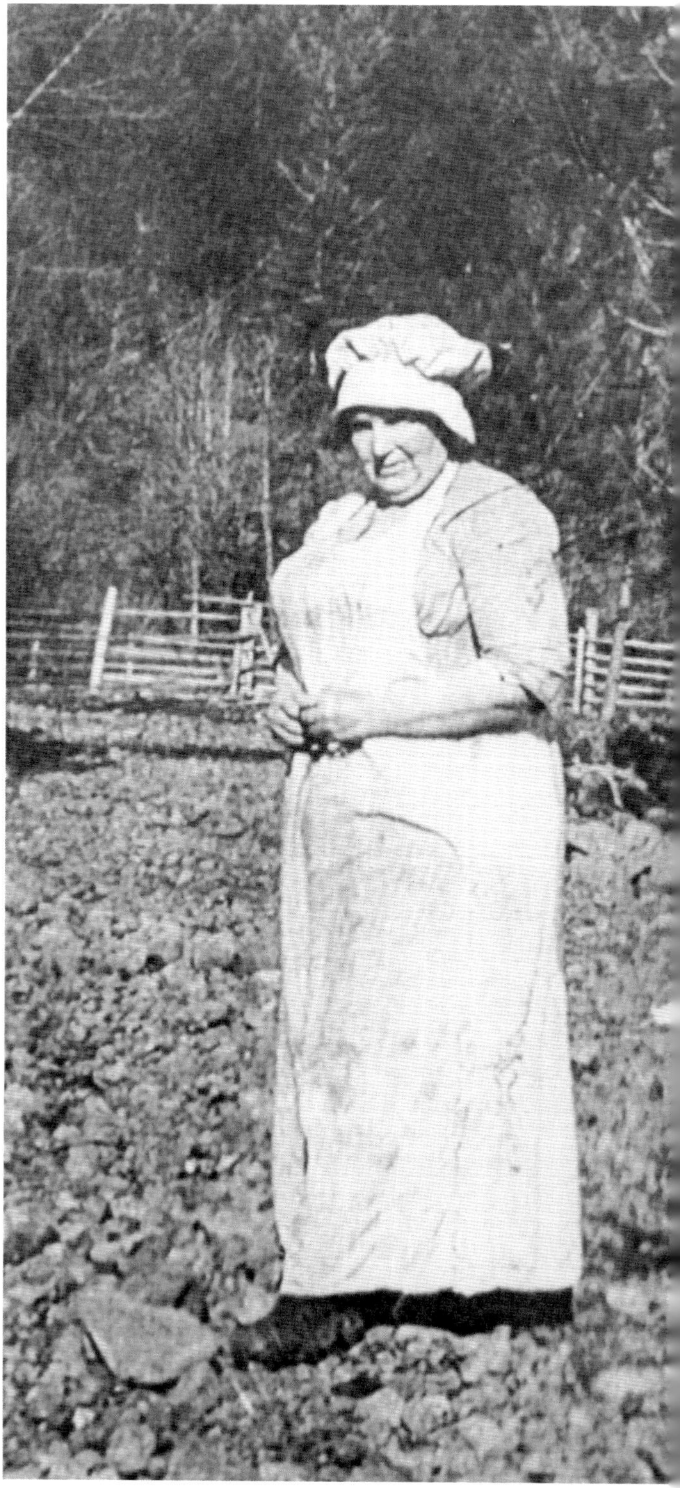

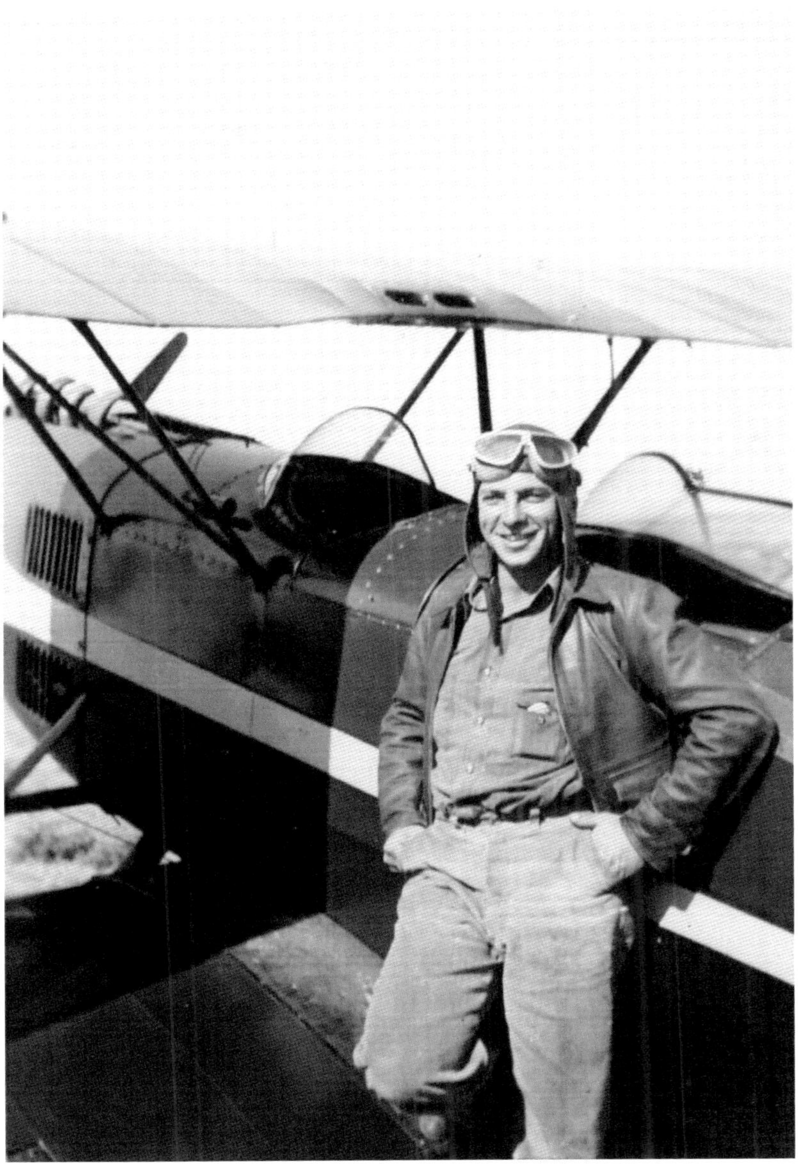

Uriah Franklin Corkrum, Farmer, Decorated Veteran, and Entrepreneur
Uriah Franklin "Bill" Corkrum was born in 1917 in nearby Dixie, Washington, to a pioneer Walla Walla County family with roots going back to the 1850s. After graduating from Dixie High School and spending several years at Washington State College, Corkrum joined the US Army Air Corps in 1941. He served as a pilot in the Pacific theater, earning four Distinguished Flying Crosses and three Air Medals. After his discharge as a lieutenant colonel in 1947, he and wife Annie returned to Dixie, where he owned and operated one of the largest wheat and green pea operations in Walla Walla County. Corkrum always loved flying, airplanes, and aviation history. He built and collected model airplanes. He was an early technology innovator, founding Ag-Data, Inc., in 1966 to provide computerized accounting services to the agricultural community. The company is still going strong today. Corkrum died in 2007. (Courtesy of Barlow Corkrum.)

Mary Shipman Penrose, National Leader of YWCA

Mary Deming Shipman was born in Hartford, Connecticut, in 1868. In 1897, she married Stephen Penrose, who served as president of Whitman College from 1894 until 1934. Mary served ably as the president's wife, not only acting as hostess but also teaching classes and, in the 1920s, leading fundraising efforts on behalf of the school in the northeastern United States. Mary Shipman Penrose served as national president of the YWCA from 1913 to 1915 and as a member of its board for many years. She was instrumental in founding the YWCA in Walla Walla in 1916. (Courtesy of Whitman College and Northwest Archives.)

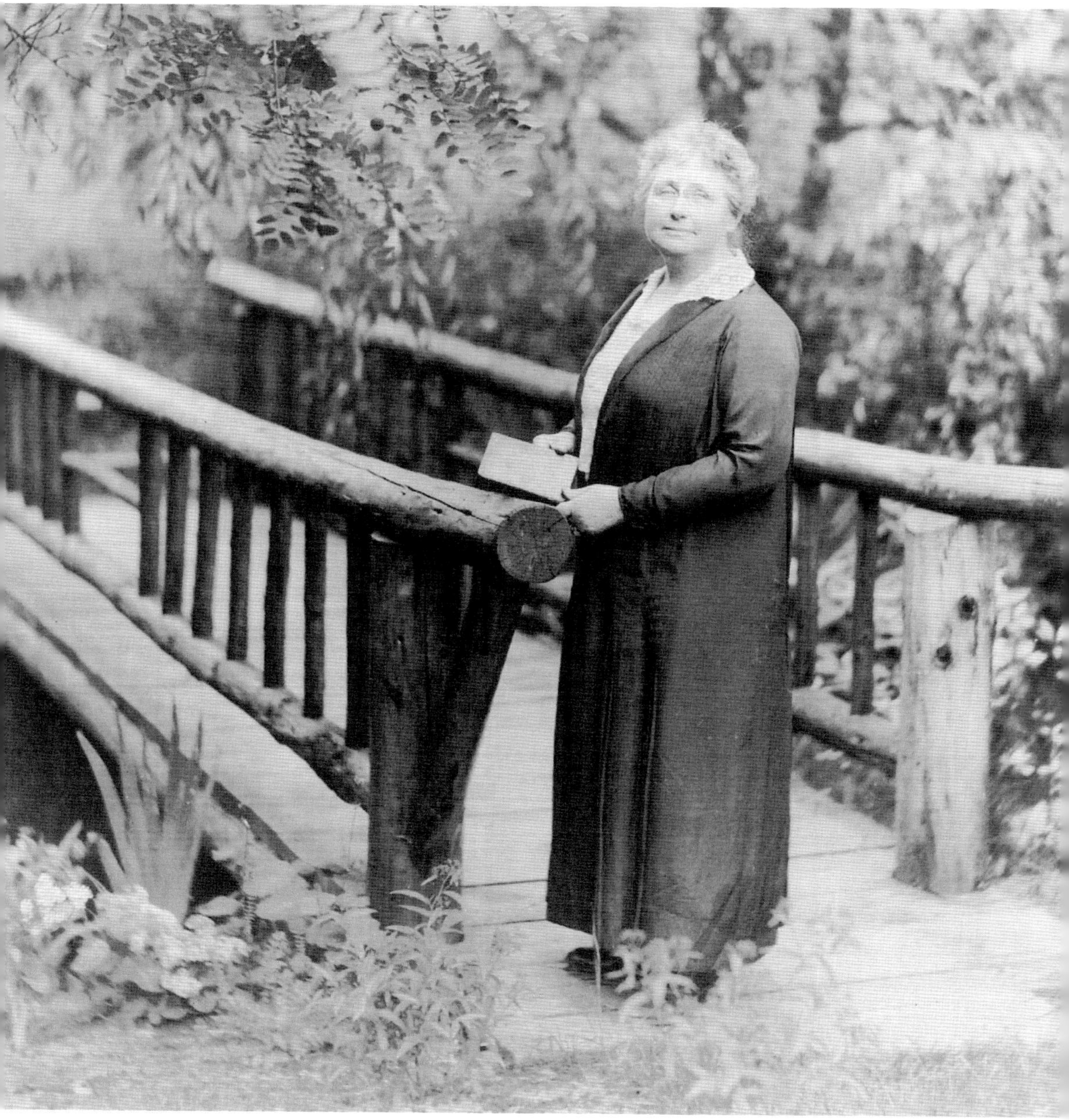

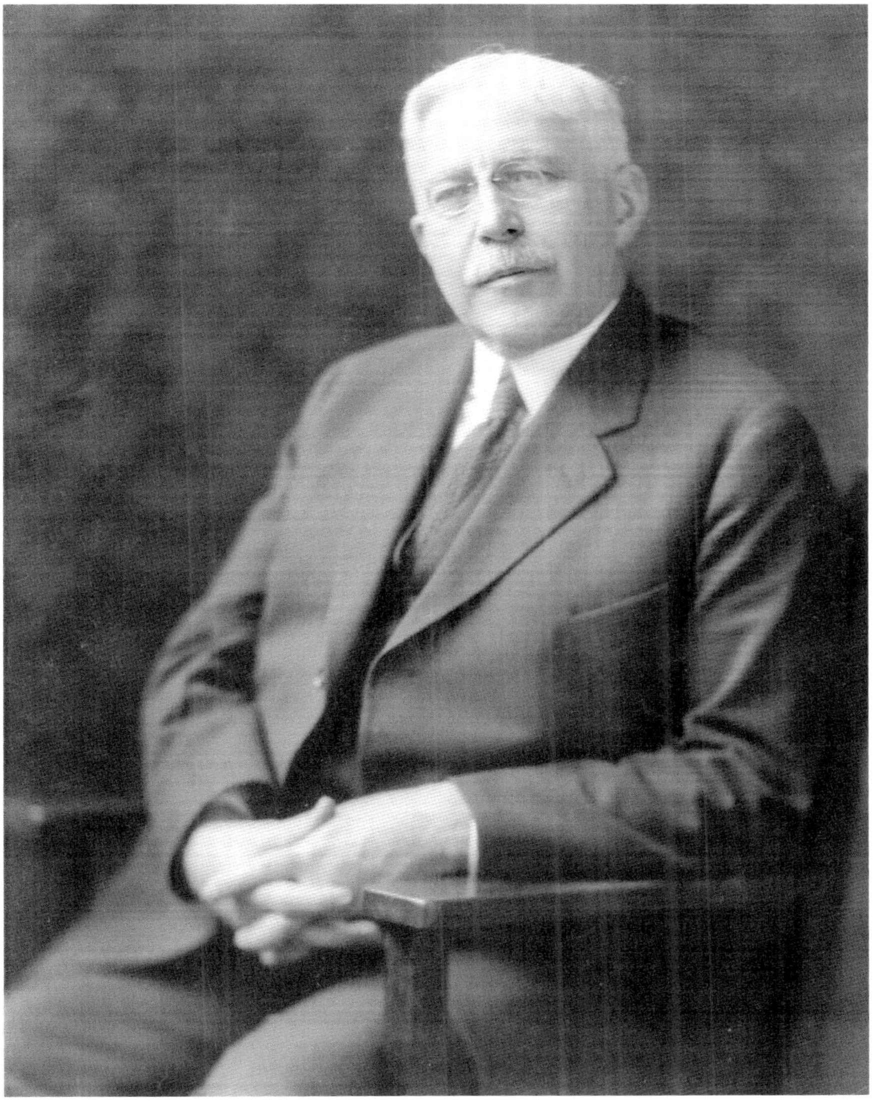

Stephen B.L. Penrose, President of Whitman College
Stephen Beasley Linnard Penrose was born to a prominent Philadelphia family and educated at Williams College, Princeton Theological Seminary, and Yale Divinity School (1890). He came to the Northwest right after graduation to become the minister of the Congregational church in Dayton, Washington. In 1892, he was named to the board of trustees of Whitman College, and in October 1894, he was called to be president of the college. At 29, Penrose was the youngest college president in the United States. Knowing the college's precarious finances, he began his presidency with a massive fundraising effort. He was able to establish a substantial endowment, and he oversaw the construction of the first masonry buildings on the campus, including the Whitman Memorial Building. Penrose's accomplishments over his 40-year tenure at Whitman included gaining a national reputation for the college and positioning Whitman as a premier liberal arts college. In 1934, Penrose, who had lost his eyesight, resigned as president. When he died in 1947, the *New York Times* noted that his devotion to Whitman College had "few parallels in the field of American education." (Courtesy of Whitman College and Northwest Archives.)

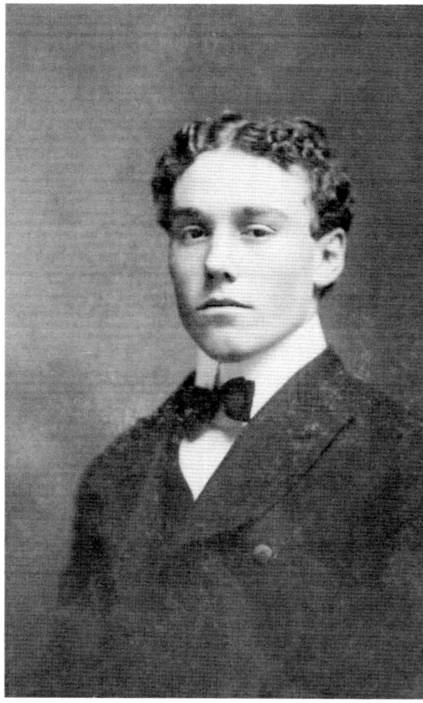

Frederick D. Applegate, Physical Director and Secretary of the YMCA, 1906–1950

The Young Men's Christian Association (YMCA) was founded in Walla Walla in 1886 and featured a reading room and assembly hall in the Paine Building. The town felt that there needed to be a place for indoor sports. Lettice Reynolds donated the funds, and the new building was completed in 1907 (below). It featured a gymnasium, swimming pool, and a tennis court as well as reading and game rooms. It was a remarkable facility for a town the size of Walla Walla. At the helm was Frederick "F.D." Applegate, an Iowa native who had been working at the YMCA in Portland, Oregon. He was appointed as physical director of "the Y" in 1906. A decade later, he was named secretary, a position he held until 1950—a distinguished 44-year career. Applegate also coached the newly formed Whitman College baseball team in 1908. He died in 1962 and is buried in Mountain View Cemetery. (Right, courtesy of Whitman College and Northwest Archives; below, courtesy of YMCA.)

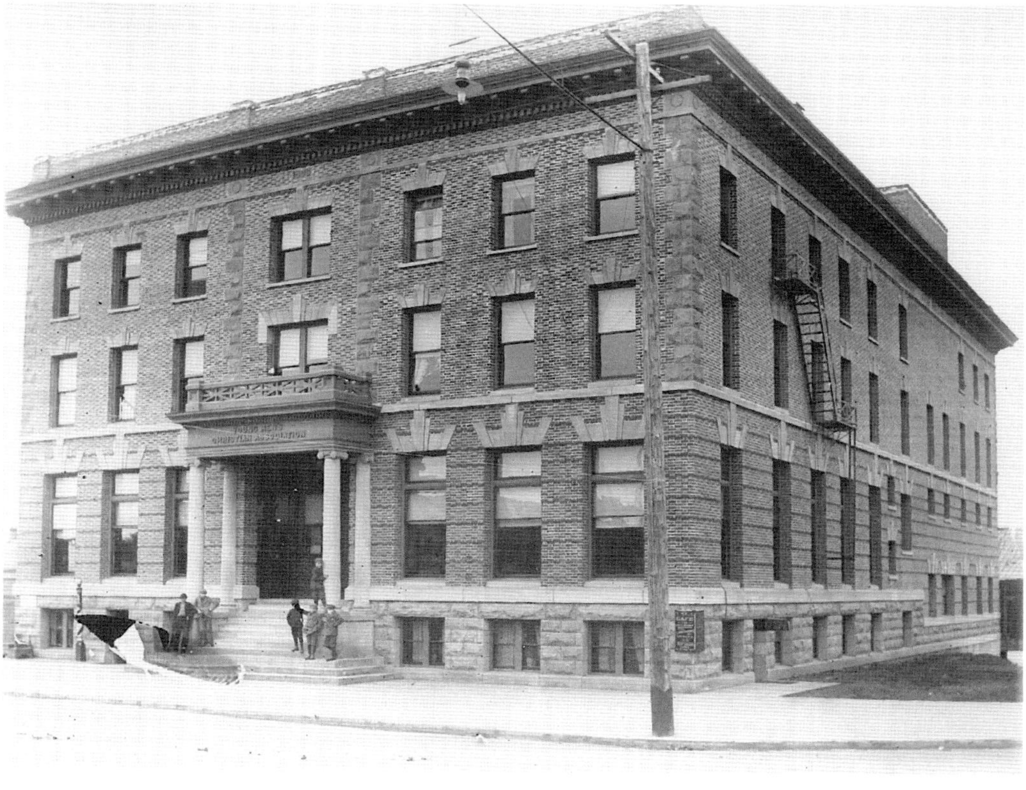

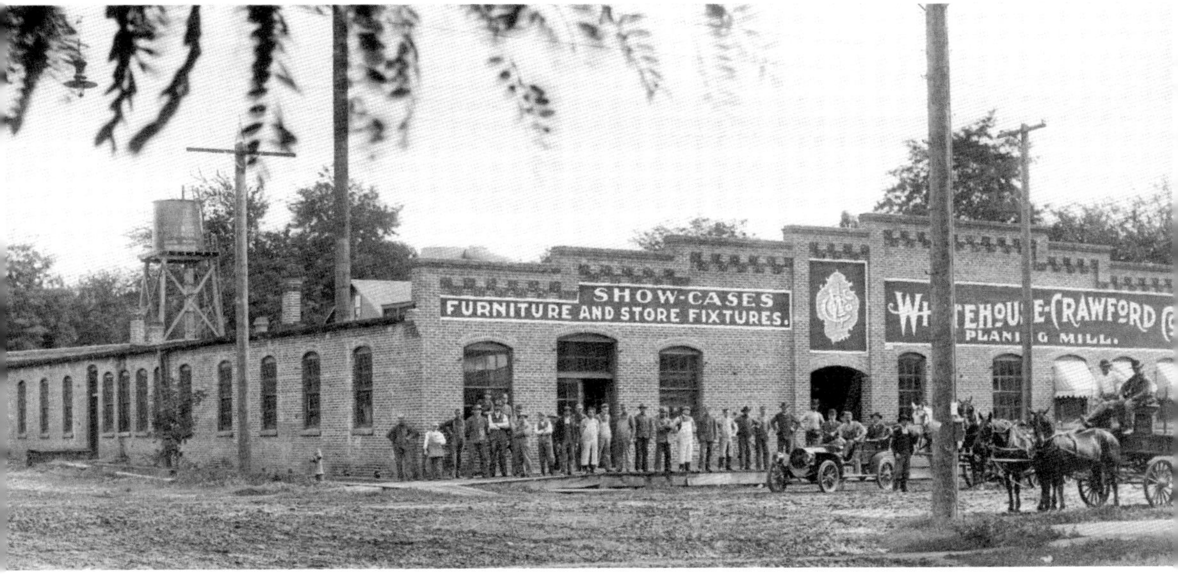

J.M. Crawford, Whitehouse-Crawford Planing Mill

J.M. Crawford came to Walla Walla in 1904, buying into the Whitehouse-Crimmins Lumber Company. Buying out the other investors, he began an expansion that included the Tum-a-Lum Lumber Company in Touchet. By 1921, Crawford had more than 50 lumberyards in the Northwest. The 1904 Whitehouse-Crawford planing mill operated until 1988, when it was sold to the City of Walla Walla, which intended to raze the building. Carl and Sonia Schmitt stepped in, restored the building in 2000, and turned it into an upscale restaurant. The building is listed in the National Register of Historic Places. (Courtesy of Whitehouse-Crawford Restaurant.)

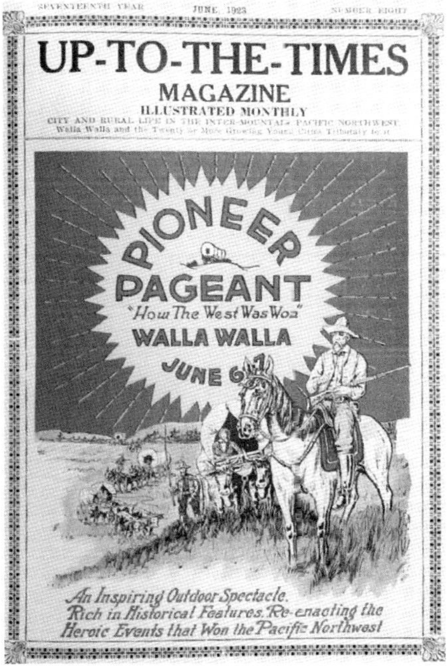

Robert C. MacLeod, Editor and Publisher of *Up-to-the-Times* Magazine

The historical record of Robert C. MacLeod's (1871–1931) monthly magazine, *Up-to-the-Times*, left a vibrant and important narrative of Walla Walla history. MacLeod, an unabashed promoter of Walla Walla, felt the city would eventually become a major hub in eastern Washington. Published from 1906 into the 1920s, the magazine was touted as "an illustrated magazine full of interesting local topics and devoted to the interest of progressive residents of the great Walla Walla Valley and the Inland Empire." The magazine folded in 1930, and MacLeod died in 1931. (Courtesy of Joe Drazan.)

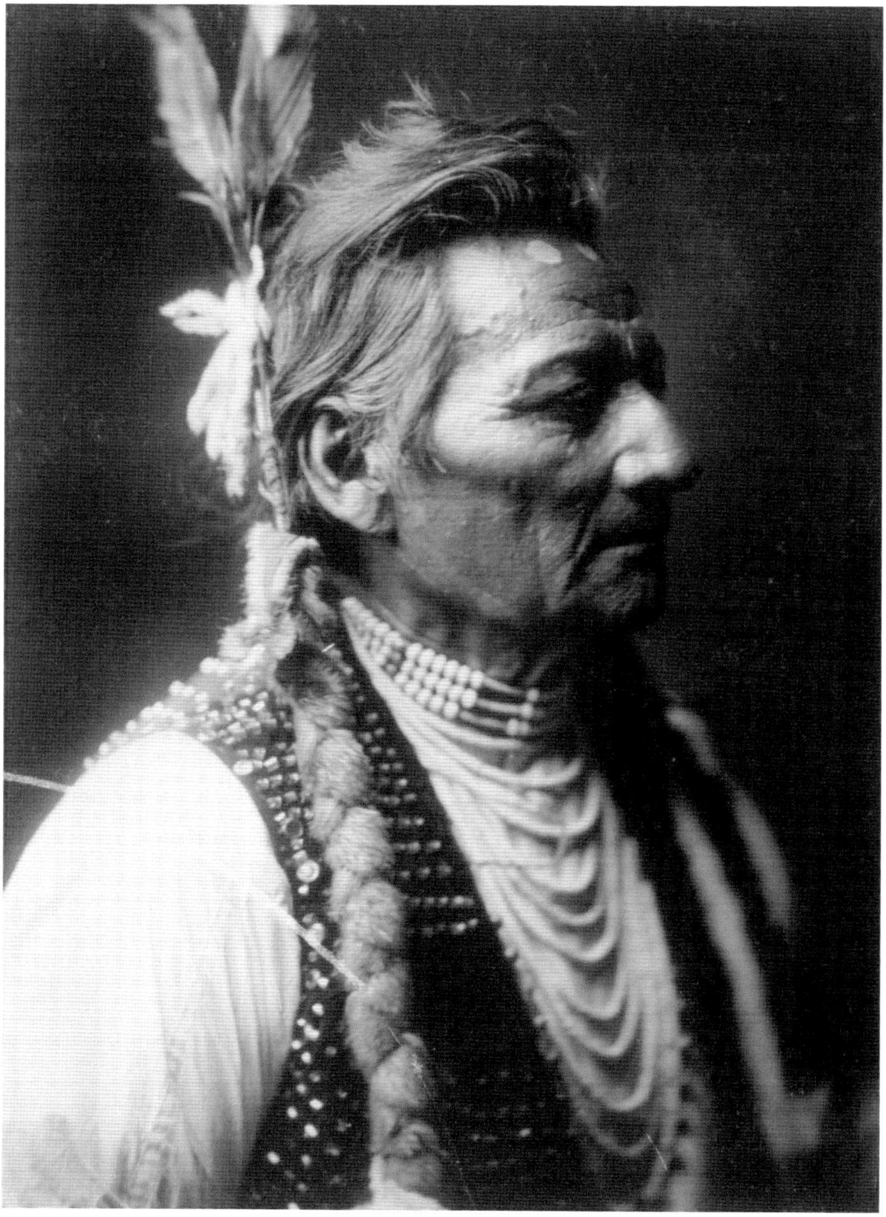

PioPio-Maksmaks, Walla Walla Indian, son of Peo-Peo-Mox-Mox
By the time PioPio-Maksmaks was photographed by Edward Curtis in 1905 for his North American Indians series, the Walla Walla Indians had been living on the reservation with the Umatilla and Cayuse Indians for decades. The photograph depicts him in a romantic way, recalling the earlier days when his people were powerful. Still, Curtis remarked, "PioPio-Maksmaks possesses as unusually strong face, and his remarkably piercing eye betokens a man possessing the courage characteristic of his family and tribe." Curtis struggled to get his ambitious series of large-format books on North American Indians published. He was fortunate to gain the support of Alden J. Blethen, publisher of the *Seattle Times*, who published Curtis's photographs along with tales of his adventures. (Library of Congress.)

Edgar Fischer, First Conductor of the Walla Walla Symphony, Collected Tribal Songs of Northwest Indians

Edgar Simpson Fischer, born in Philadelphia, graduated from the Philadelphia Music Academy and studied overseas. Upon his return from Europe in 1899, he accepted a position as head of the violin department at Whitman College, a role he filled until he and wife Alice opened the private Fischer School of Music in 1906. An interesting sidelight of Fischer's musical career was the work he did with noted photographer Edward S. Curtis, who published a 20-volume series, North American Indians. In Volume 3 of the series, *The Teton Sioux* (1908), Curtis notes, "Edgar Fischer has transcribed the music from his personal field notes and from phonographic records made by other members of my party." Fischer was the first conductor of the fledgling Walla Walla Symphony, organized in 1907. He continued as its conductor until his untimely death in 1922. Today, the symphony is the oldest continuously operating symphony west of the Mississippi; it celebrated its 100th anniversary in 2007. (Courtesy of Whitman College and Northwest Archives.)

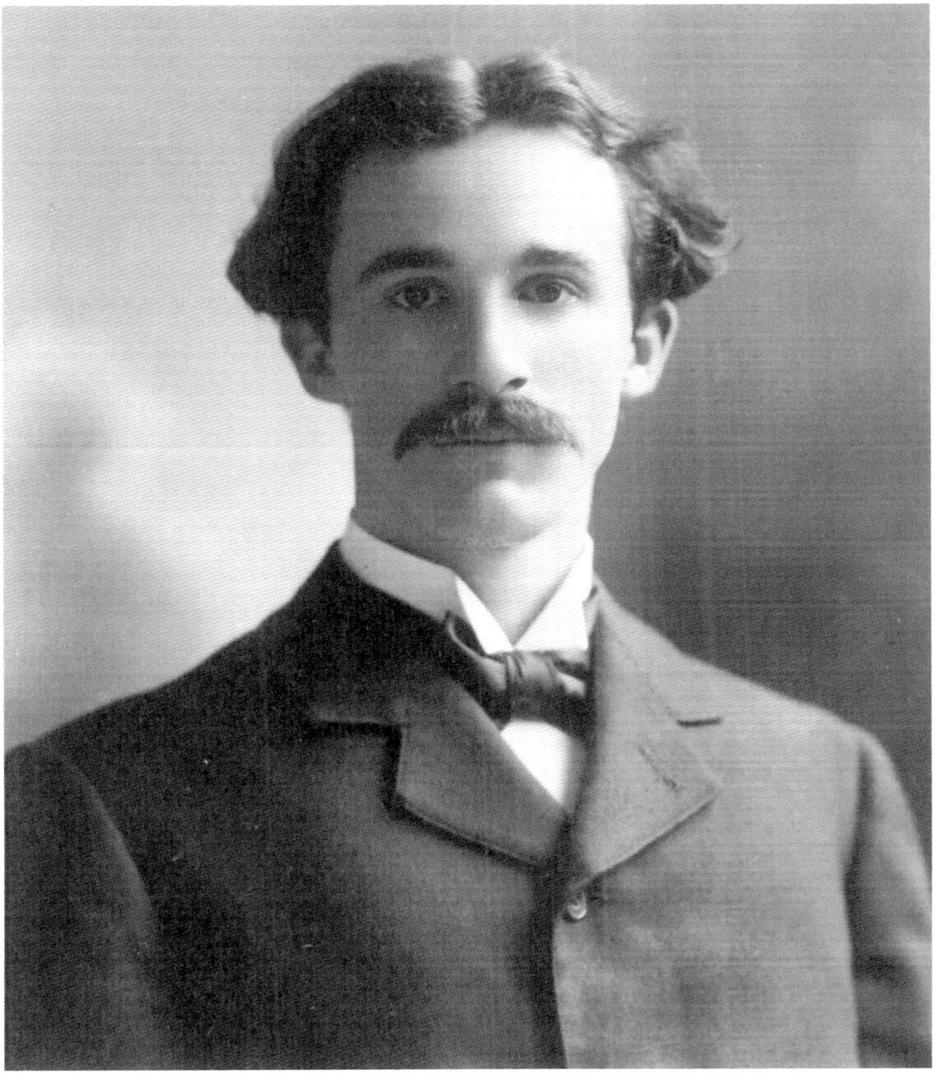

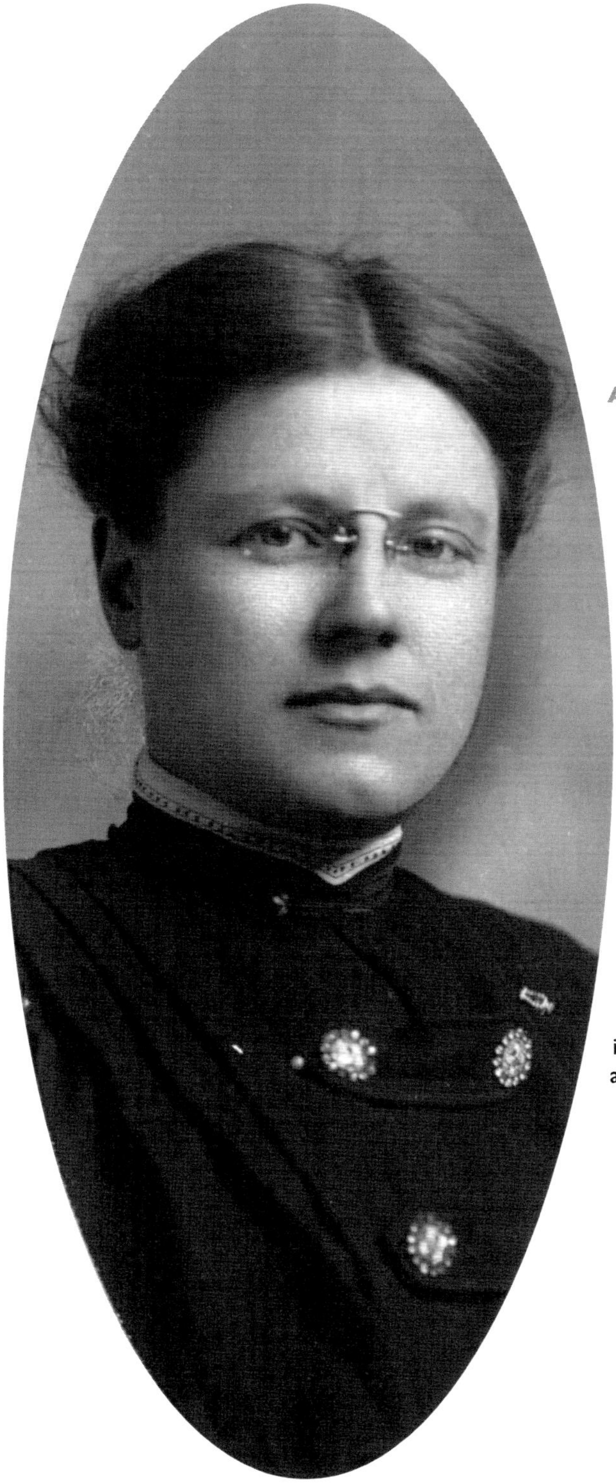

Alice Reynolds Fischer, Walla Walla Symphony Conductor and Music Teacher
Alice Reynolds, born in 1878, graduated from the University of Michigan School of Music with degrees in piano and voice in 1901. A talented pianist and singer, she took a position as a piano teacher at the Whitman Conservatory of Music. It was there that she met and married Edgar Fischer. In 1906, she and her husband founded the Fischer School of Music, which gained a reputation as one of the best music schools in the Northwest. After Edgar Fischer's sudden death in 1922, the Walla Walla Symphony had several interim leaders. In 1924, Alice was named as the orchestra's leader. At that time, women conductors were rare. Alice proved to be an effective and inspiring leader and led the orchestra as it celebrated its 25th anniversary in 1932. She stepped down in 1934 and died in 1945. (Courtesy of Whitman College and Northwest Archives.)

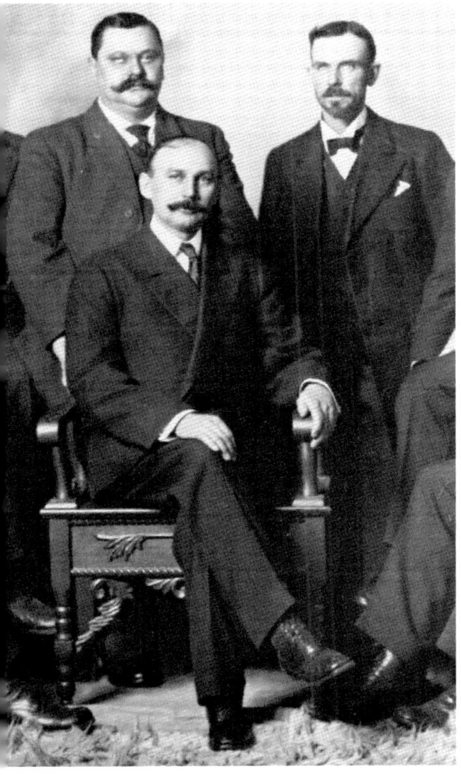

Eugene Tausick, Businessman and Mayor
Eugene Tausick was a self-made man. Born in 1868 in Massachusetts, he was only nine years old when he was out on his own. He put himself through night school working odd jobs. At age 20, he was offered an opportunity to buy into a steam laundry in Walla Walla. He was able to buy out his partner in a few short years; by 1908, his Walla Walla Steam Laundry was one of the largest employers in the valley. Known for his honesty and integrity, Tausick (seated at center) also served as mayor. (Courtesy of Whitman College and Northwest Archives.)

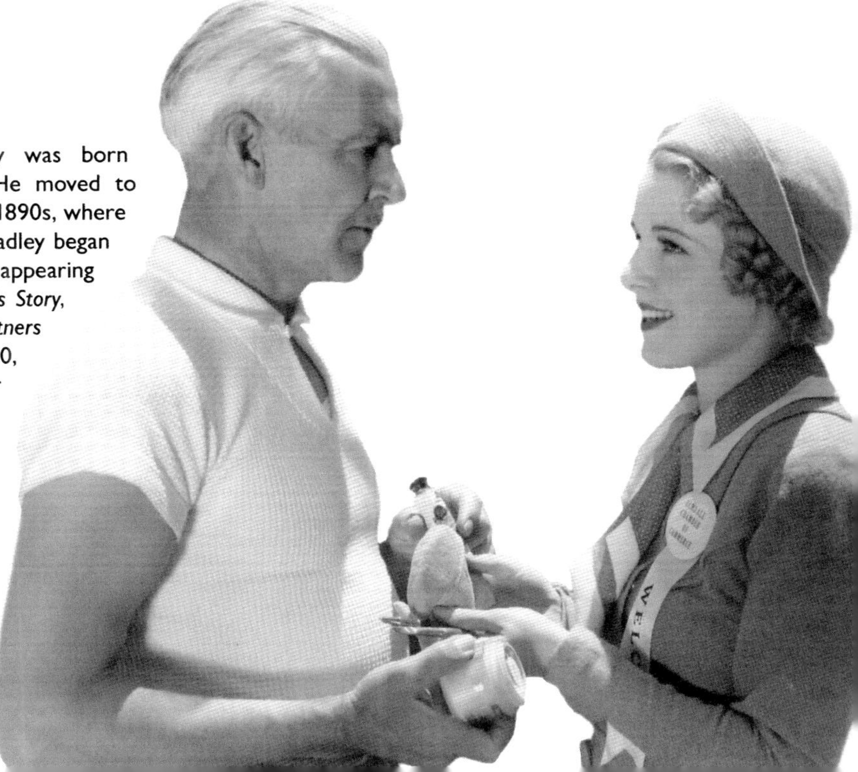

Bert Hadley, Actor and Makeup Artist
Robert C. "Bert" Hadley was born in Walla Walla in 1882. He moved to Lewiston, Idaho, in the late 1890s, where he made his stage debut. Hadley began acting in silent films in 1912, appearing in *A Forlorn Hope*, *A Convict's Story*, *The Scarlet Pimpernel*, and *Partners of the Tide*. As he neared 40, Hadley shifted his career away from acting, working for a time as a film editor and eventually becoming a studio makeup artist. By the late 1930s, he was head of the makeup department of Paramount Studios. He is shown here with actress Rosina Lawrence. (Author's collection.)

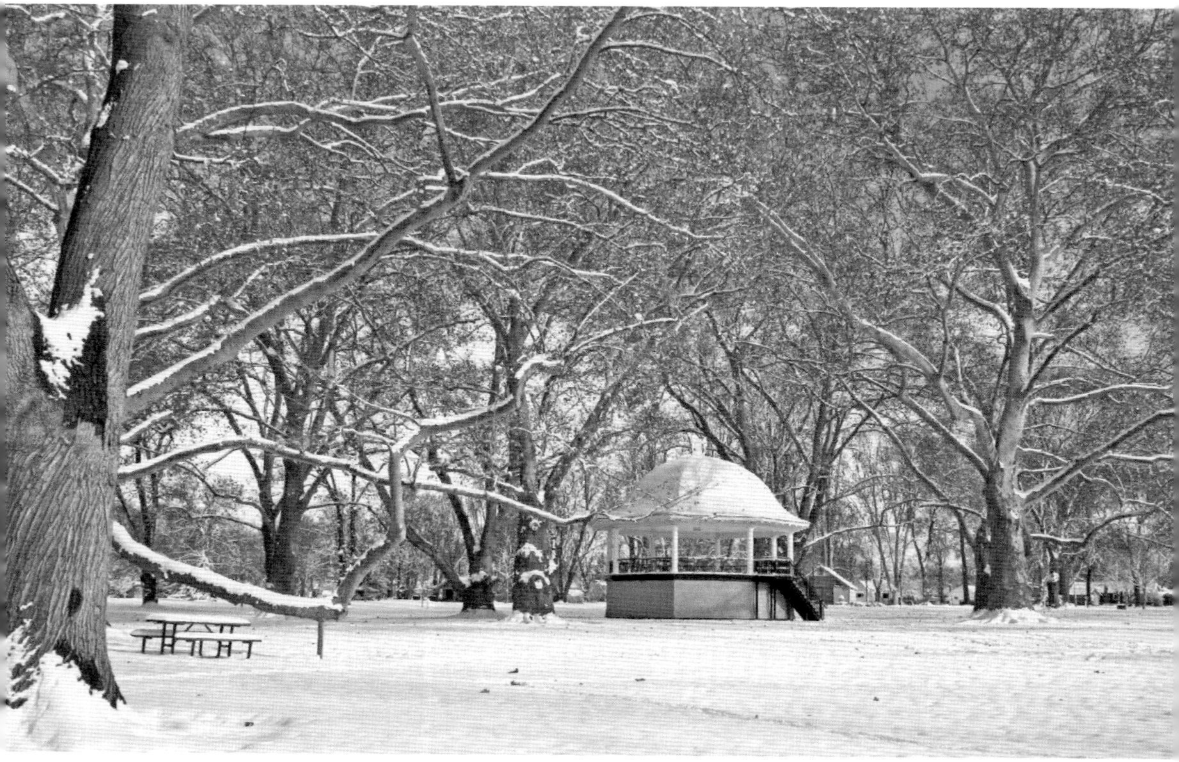

John Warren Langdon, Park Advocate

John W. Langdon came to Walla Walla in 1889 and made a name for himself as a successful businessman with his Green Investment Company and as co-owner of the Baker-Langdon Orchard Company. Active in a number of civic organizations, he was also a member and president of the city's park board. Inspired by the 1906 visit of John Olmsted of the Olmsted Brothers landscape architecture firm, Langdon envisioned Pioneer Park as a cool oasis with both formal and naturalistic elements. The centerpiece was a large concert ground and bandstand (above) in the middle of the park, accessed by a formal, tree-lined drive. The park also featured leafy walks, meandering streams, low waterfalls, rustic bridges, duck ponds, and sweeping lawns. Langdon took the Olmsted Brothers' recommendations, and his resulting plan is considered by many to be a Langdon-Olmsted collaboration. More than 6,000 trees and shrubs transformed the bare ground into a fledgling arboretum. Nearly a century later, a number of these trees are the largest of their kind in the state. Langdon was also a photographer of some note, taking pictures of a number of Yakama and Nez Perce Indians. Langdon died of a self-inflicted gunshot wound in 1930. (Author photograph.)

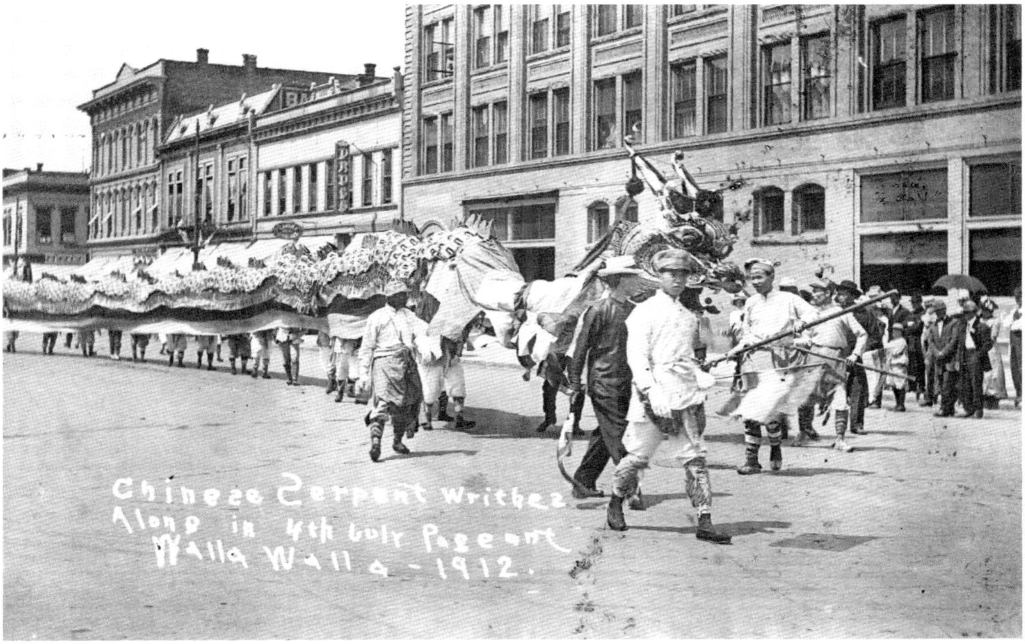

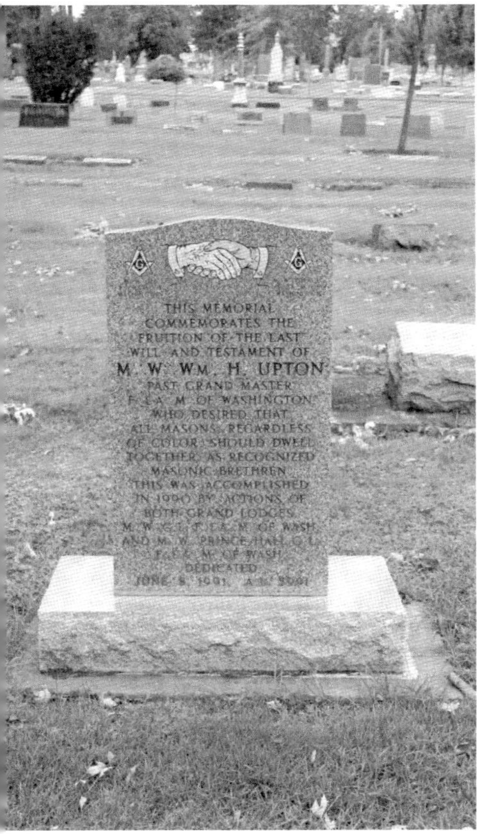

Charles Tung, Chinese American Merchant and Interpreter

Charles Tung was born in California around 1868 to Chinese immigrants and came to Walla Walla around 1880. By then, the city had 600 Chinese residents, and Tung's services as an interpreter were in demand. (Above, Chinese dragon in the Fourth of July parade, 1912.) Tung's Kwong Chung Sing Company imported Chinese silk, porcelain, and tea to Walla Walla. Tung also served as secretary-treasurer of Pacific Enterprise Corporation, which built a two-story building downtown in 1911. In 1930, Tung left for China, but he returned in 1939. (Courtesy of Whitman College and Northwest Archives.)

William Upton, Promoter of Equality

William Upton—attorney, judge, and legislator—served as grand master in the Grand Lodge of Washington State Mainstream Masonry. He was the first to recognize an African American Masonic lodge—the Prince Hall Masons—in 1898. To his dismay, the Prince Hall Masons were later forced to rescind their recognition. When Upton died in 1906, his will specified that there should be no marker on his grave until such time as African American and white Masonry recognized each other in Washington State. That recognition finally came about in 1990, and in 1991, both lodges dedicated this monument in his honor. (Author photograph.)

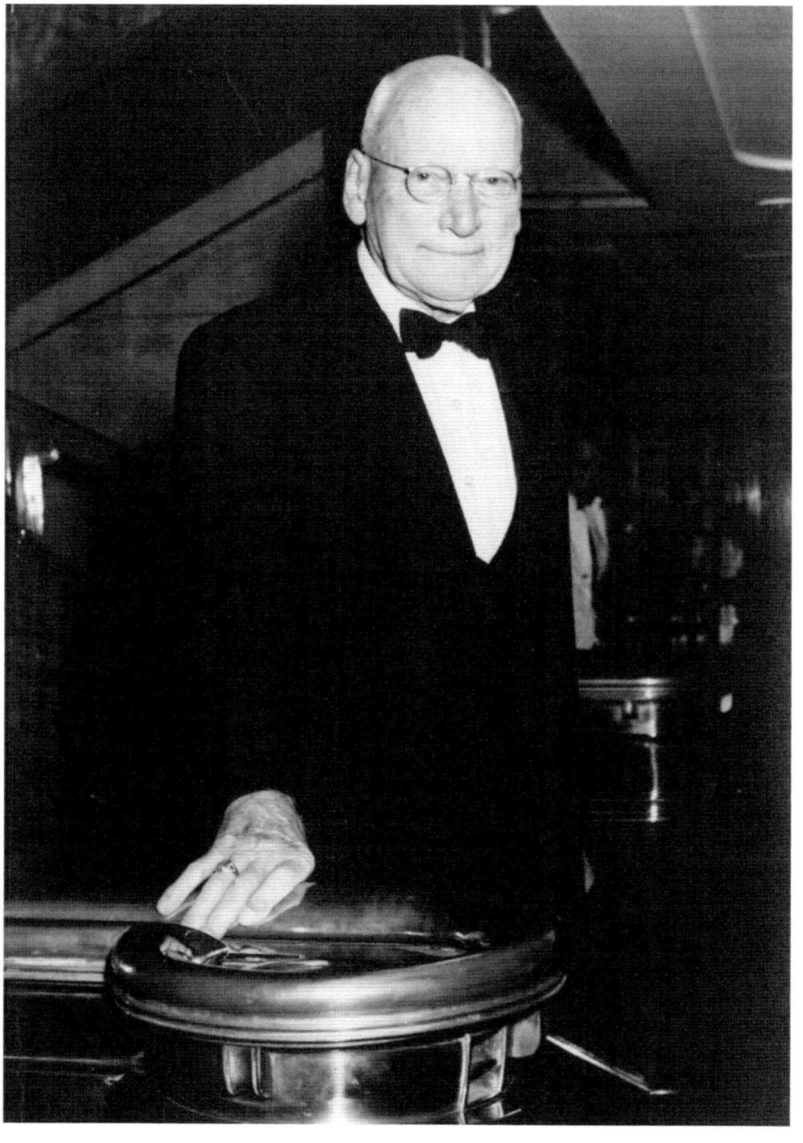

John Grant Kelly, Newspaperman, Business Promoter, and Entrepreneur
Illinois native John Kelly and his wife, Martha, came to Walla Walla in 1912 when Kelly bought the Walla Walla *Union-Bulletin* newspaper. He quickly became an advocate for business development in the valley with a keen interest in attracting a cannery and food-processing facilities. He invested in the Church Grape Juice Company and served as an officer. He and his son-in-law Donald Sherwood successfully convinced Continental Can Company to build a plant in Walla Walla. Recognizing the need for improved transportation to Walla Walla and southeast Washington, Kelly was involved in the Northwest Toll Bridge Company and the development of bridges on the Columbia and Snake Rivers. John and Martha Kelly had a long association with Whitman College, and John served on the school's board of overseers. Kelly received numerous accolades for his efforts in promoting the valley, including the Walla Walla Chamber of Commerce Award of Merit in 1940. Kelly's illustrious career is chronicled in *John G. Kelly, His Life and Legacy*, by Alfred McVay. (Courtesy of Whitman College and Northwest Archives.)

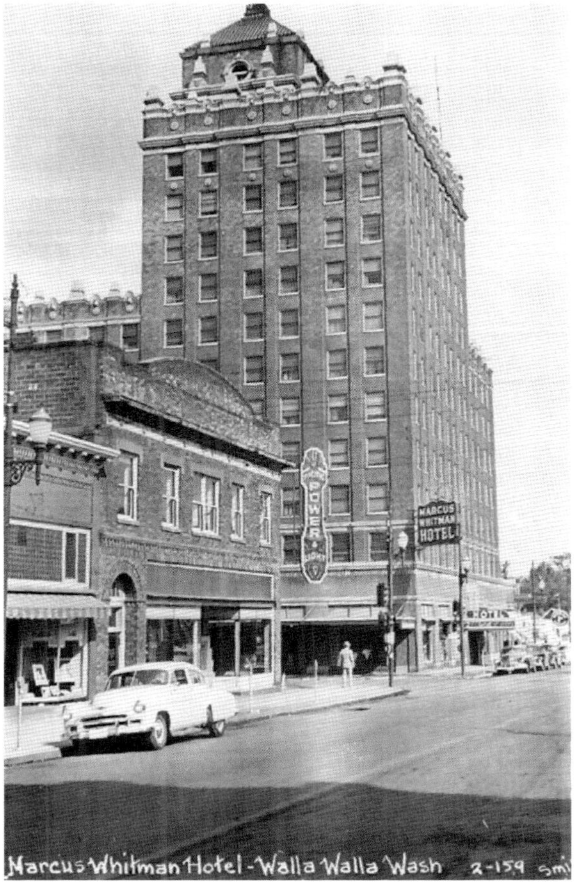

William W. Baker, Marcus Whitman Hotel

By the 1920s, it was clear that Walla Walla needed a luxury hotel to attract visitors and conventions. In 1927, William Baker, president of Baker Boyer Bank, brought the community together to spearhead the construction of one. Seattle Real Estate Company offered to put up $300,000 if the community could raise an additional $150,000, which it did in 90 days. The landmark was completed in 1928, and the Marcus Whitman Hotel has welcomed notables including Louis Armstrong, Shirley Temple, and Pres. Dwight D. Eisenhower. Additionally, all the big bands played at the hotel. (Author's collection.)

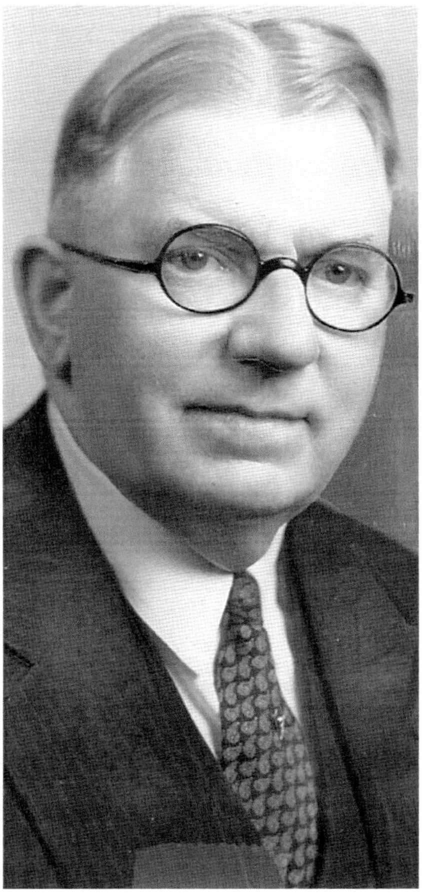

Brig. Gen. Paul Weyrauch, Washington National Guard

Paul Weyrauch, born in Germany in 1873, came to the United States in 1889. He joined the US Army in 1895 and served as a second lieutenant at Fort Walla Walla in 1904. In 1908, he returned to Walla Walla as a civilian. During World War I, he served as a captain in the National Guard, training two batteries of the 146th Field Artillery at Fort Walla Walla to serve in France. Weyrauch retired from the National Guard in 1933 as a brigadier general commanding the 81st Infantry Brigade, Washington and Montana National Guards. (Author's collection.)

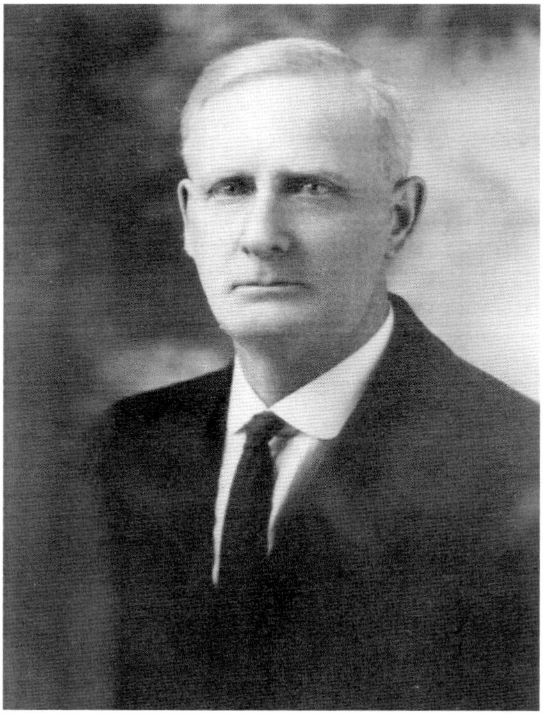

Benjamin Brown, Inspiring Professor
Benjamin Brown taught at Whitman College from 1895 to 1926. Head of the physics department, he was known as an inspiring teacher. Brown used innovative ways to teach his students—for instance, building a scale to weigh the Earth as a teaching tool when introducing the subject of physics. Justice William O. Douglas, a Whitman graduate, cited Brown as one of his most influential professors in his 1974 autobiography, *Go East, Young Man.* Walter Brattain, winner of the 1956 Nobel Prize in Physics, credited Brown with inspiring him to continue his physics studies. (Courtesy of Whitman College and Northwest Archives.)

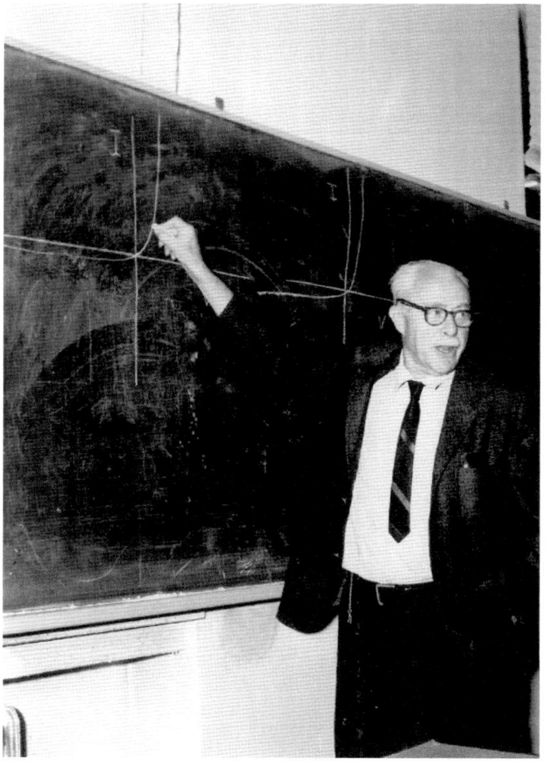

Walter Brattain, Nobel Prize Winner in Physics
Benjamin Brown's distinguished student Walter Brattain earned his bachelor of science degree from Whitman College in 1924, a master's degree from the University of Oregon in 1926, and a doctorate from the University of Minnesota in 1929. Brattain won the Nobel Prize in Physics in 1956 with Dr. John Bardeen and Dr. William B. Shockley "for research on semiconductors and the discovery of the transistor effect" at Bell Laboratories. Brattain was a visiting lecturer at Whitman College from 1962 to 1963, a visiting professor from 1963 to 1972, and an adjunct professor from 1972 to 1976. (Courtesy of Whitman College and Northwest Archives.)

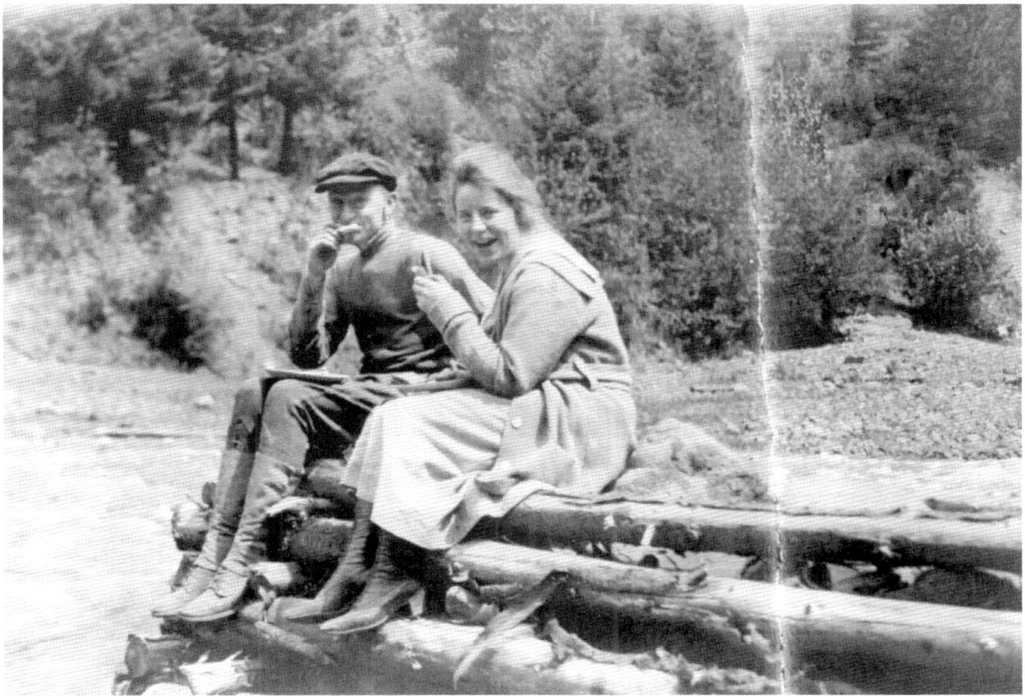

William O. Douglas, US Supreme Court Justice

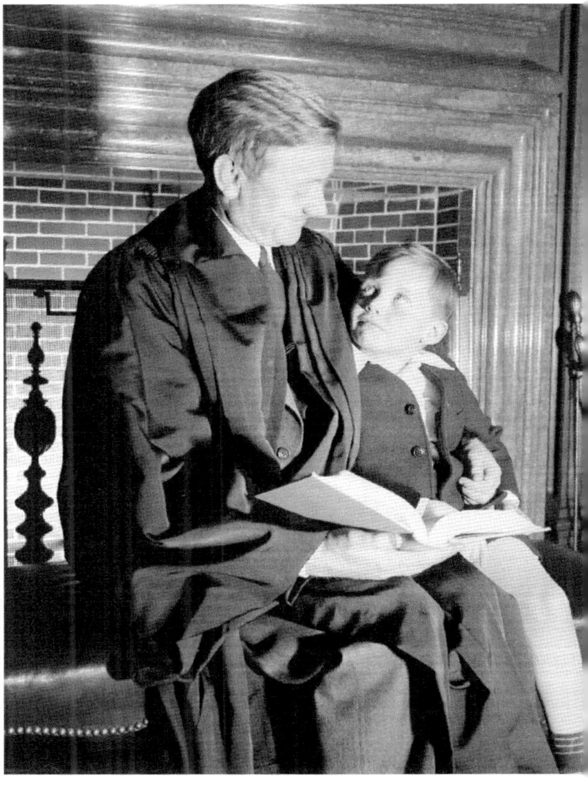

William Orville Douglas was born in Minnesota but spent his childhood in Yakima, Washington. He overcame childhood illness, his father's death when he was six, and his family's financial hardships. Fortunately, he received a scholarship to Whitman College and graduated in 1920. Douglas, who majored in English and economics, was a member of the debate team and class president in his senior year. He is pictured above at Whitman College with Frances Penrose. After teaching for several years, he went to Columbia University Law School. He served on the Securities and Exchange Commission under Franklin Delano Roosevelt, and in 1939, Roosevelt appointed him as one of the youngest Supreme Court justices in history. The image at right shows Douglas with his son on the day he was sworn in as a justice. Douglas was known for championing individual rights and for his advocacy of the preservation of the natural environment. He wrote a number of books, including *My Wilderness: The Pacific West* and his memoir, *Go East, Young Man*. Douglas Hall at Whitman College is named in his honor. (Above, courtesy of Whitman College and Northwest Archives; right, courtesy of Library of Congress.)

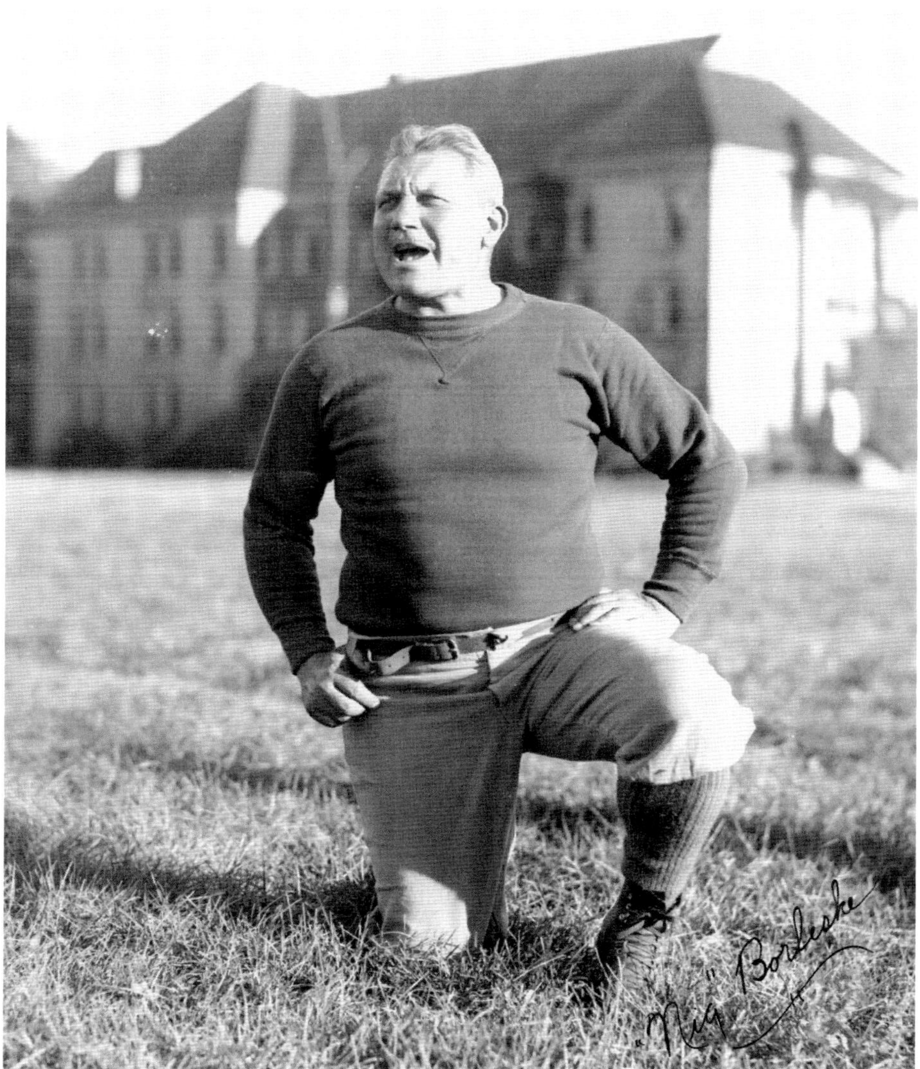

Raymond V. Borleske, Athlete, Legendary Coach

Raymond Borleske came to Whitman College from Spokane in 1906 and quickly established himself as a star athlete—perhaps the best in the college's history. He excelled in football and served as team captain in his final two seasons. In his junior and senior years, Borleske also captained the college's baseball team, leading it to successful seasons. After Borleske received his law degree from the University of Oregon in 1915, the president of Whitman College, Stephen Penrose, asked him to return to the college to coach its football, baseball, and basketball teams. Under his tutelage, Whitman enjoyed enormous success in football, winning conference titles in 1921, 1928, 1930, and 1931. The baseball team won 10 conference championships, and the basketball program won seven conference titles in a 12-year span. Borleske retired from coaching in 1947. He was inducted in the National Association of Intercollegiate Athletics Hall of Fame and was the first inductee into the Washington Sports Hall of Fame. Borleske Stadium, home to Whitman College teams and the Walla Walla Sweets baseball team, is named in his honor. (Courtesy of Whitman College and Northwest Archives.)

CHAPTER FIVE

Changing Times

The 1940s brought more changes to Walla Walla and, in a sense, delivered the world to its doorstep. The airport became the Walla Walla Army Air Base and was used for training the USAAF's 91st Bombardment Group, which flew B-17s in the European theater of World War II.

The war also brought about a dark chapter in American history with the restriction and internment of Japanese Americans. Although Japanese families in Walla Walla were not sent to internment camps, they were put under a restrictive curfew—one that forced many of them to give up their businesses. After the war, some Japanese families that had been in internment camps came to Walla Walla, encouraged by opportunities in the region.

The same opportunities brought many Latino families to the valley in the 1940s looking for a better life. Although many initially worked primarily in agriculture and the canning industry, Latinos became integral to the fabric of the area as business people, teachers, firemen, and elected officials.

Walla Walla's military tradition continued after the war when the US Army Corps of Engineers established its new Walla Walla District in 1948. The district also created new recreation areas, including Rooks Park and Bennington Lake. Construction of Ice Harbor Lock and Dam in the western part of Walla Walla County brought Vice Pres. Lyndon B. Johnson for its dedication in 1962.

The establishment of the veterans' hospital in 1959 gave new purpose to the former Fort Walla Walla, one still embodied in today's Jonathan M. Wainwright Memorial VA Medical Center (renamed in 1996).

The establishment of Walla Walla Community College in 1966 provided new educational opportunities in the valley. From its modest beginnings in the old high school building, the college graduated to its own campus in 1974.

Walla Walla, which came out of the postwar period with a strong foundation for growth and quality of life, now faced the same challenges as many communities—an aging infrastructure and a need for economic diversification and expansion. The founding of manufacturing companies and new small businesses showed continuing promise for the Walla Walla Valley. The first commercial wineries got their start in the 1970s and 1980s, led by Leonetti Cellar, Woodward Canyon, and L'Ecole No. 41. By 1984, the Walla Walla Valley was designated as an American Viticultural Area (AVA). Legendary locals led the way.

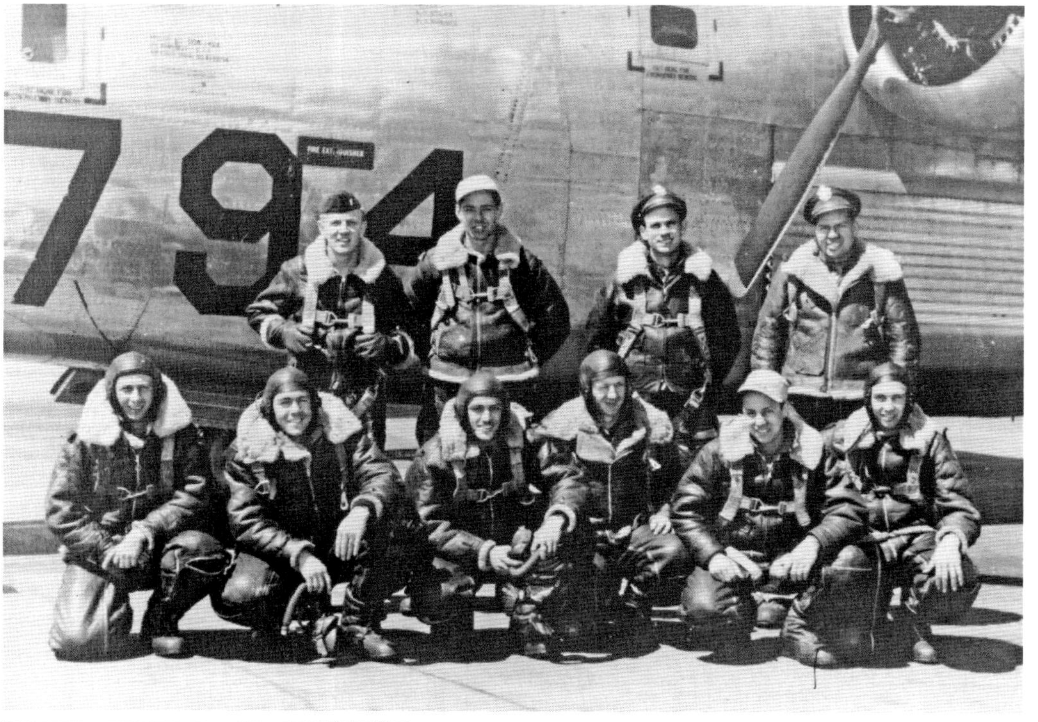

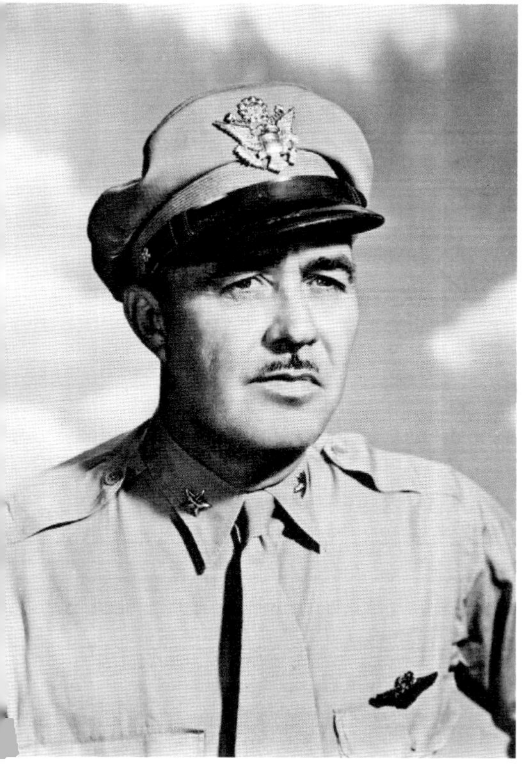

91st Bombardment Group, USAAF

The 91st Bombardment Group (Heavy) was activated at Harding Field, Baton Rouge, Louisiana, on April 15, 1942. It accomplished first-phase training at MacDill Field, Tampa, Florida, under the auspices of the Third Air Force and completed second- and third-phase training on B-17 Flying Fortress bombers at Walla Walla Army Air Base under the direction of the Second Air Force. The 91st saw its first action on November 7, 1942, attacking U-boat pens at Brest. The unit flew throughout Europe during the course of the war, bombing Berlin and supporting the Normandy invasion. After the end of the war in Europe, the 91st evacuated Allied prisoners from German prisoner of war camps. The unit returned to the United States in June–July 1945 and was inactivated on November 7, 1945. Pictured above on May 11, 1945, is Combat Crew No. 207, USAAF, Walla Walla from left to right are (first row) engineer Sgt. Willie Campen, radio operator Sgt. Jack Himmelberger, armor gunner Sgt. Harry Lauer, nose gunner Cpl. John Rogers, ball gunner Cpl. Albert Saucier, and tail gunner Cpl. John Gould; (second row) pilot 2nd Lt. Ed Wilson, copilot 2nd Lt. Bruce Suthergreen, navigator 2nd Lt. Percy Sanders, and bombardier 2nd Lt. Carl Strbenac. Pictured at left in 1943 is Brig. Gen. Walter R. Peck, commander at Walla Walla Army Air Base. (Both, courtesy of Whitman College and Northwest Archives.)

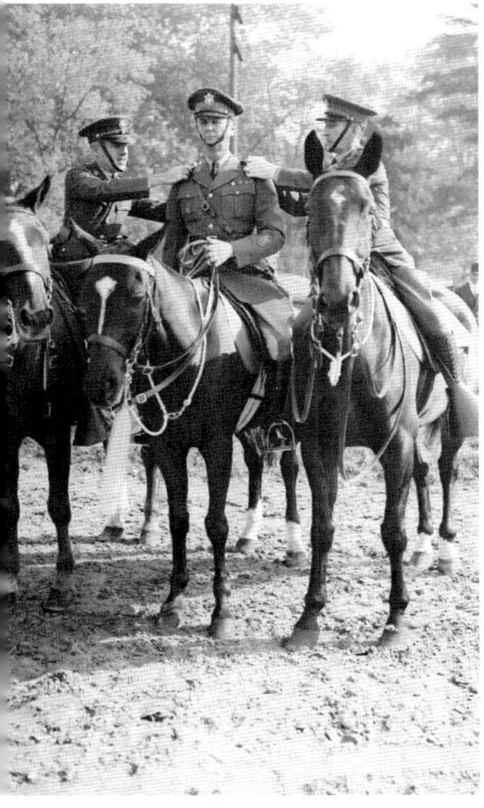

Gen. Jonathan Mayhew Wainwright, Native Son

Jonathan M. Wainwright was born in 1883 at Fort Walla Walla, where his father, Lt. Robert Page Wainwright, was serving. A 1906 West Point graduate, Wainwright served in World War I in Europe, becoming brigadier general in 1938 (left). During World War II, he became the commander of Allied Forces in the Philippines after Gen. Douglas MacArthur departed. Forced to surrender the Allied troops to Japan, he spent three years in captivity. He was liberated from a Manchurian prisoner of war camp by the Russians. After his release, he attended the Japanese surrender ceremony aboard the USS *Missouri* on September 2, 1945, and returned to the Philippines to accept the formal surrender of the Japanese commander, Gen. Tomoyuki Yamashita. Wainwright received a hero's welcome on his return to the United States. He was promoted to four-star general and received the Congressional Medal of Honor. Wainwright returned to Walla Walla in November 1945. The city welcomed its native son home with a parade and ceremonies (below). Fort Walla Walla closed in 1910 and became a veterans' hospital in 1959. In 1996, the facility was renamed the Jonathan M. Wainwright Memorial VA Medical Center. (Left, courtesy of Library of Congress; below, courtesy of Joe Drazan.)

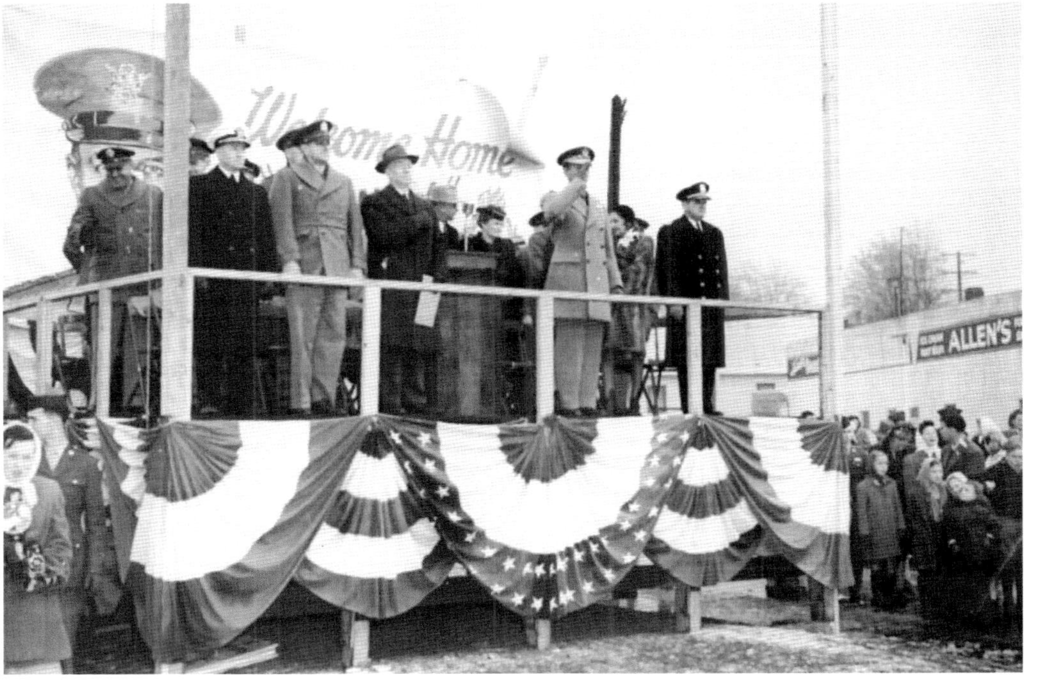

Kajita Family, From Adversity to Achievement
In 1917, Hatsutaro Kajita came to America at age 17 from Japan, returning briefly in 1922 to marry his wife, Kinuyo. The family farmed in Mosier, Oregon, until they were forcibly relocated during World War II. In May 1942, the Kajita family and 450 other Japanese from Mosier and Hood River were sent to Pinedale Assembly Camp near Fresno, California, where they lived in tar paper barracks. In July 1942, the family, including daughters Mary and Frances and son Haruo (Gus), were sent to an internment camp at Tule Lake, California, and later to the camp at Topaz, Utah. At right are Hatsutaro and Kinuyo with children Mary and Gus. After the war, the Kajitas came to Walla Walla. Gus spent his senior year at Walla Walla High School. After high school, he worked on the family farm, then served in the Army during the Korean War. The Kajita and Shinbo families were united (below) when Gus married Patty Shinbo in 1963. Gus retired as a computer systems analyst after 37 years with the US Army Corps of Engineers. The Kajitas' son Mark is president of Baker Boyer Bank in Walla Walla, and their daughters Julie and Carol work for Boeing. (Both, courtesy of Gus and Patty Kajita.)

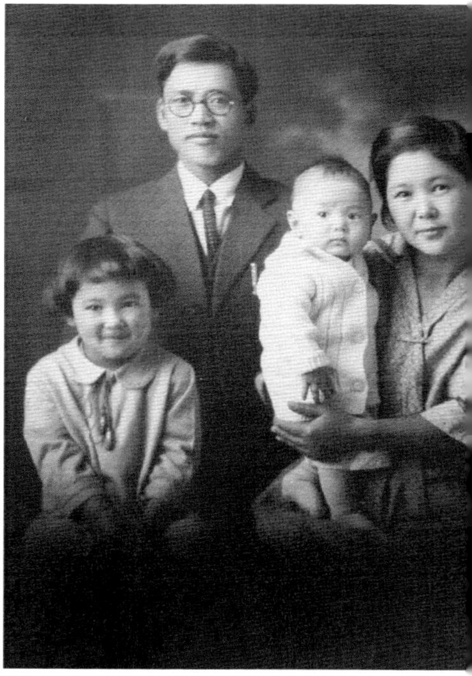

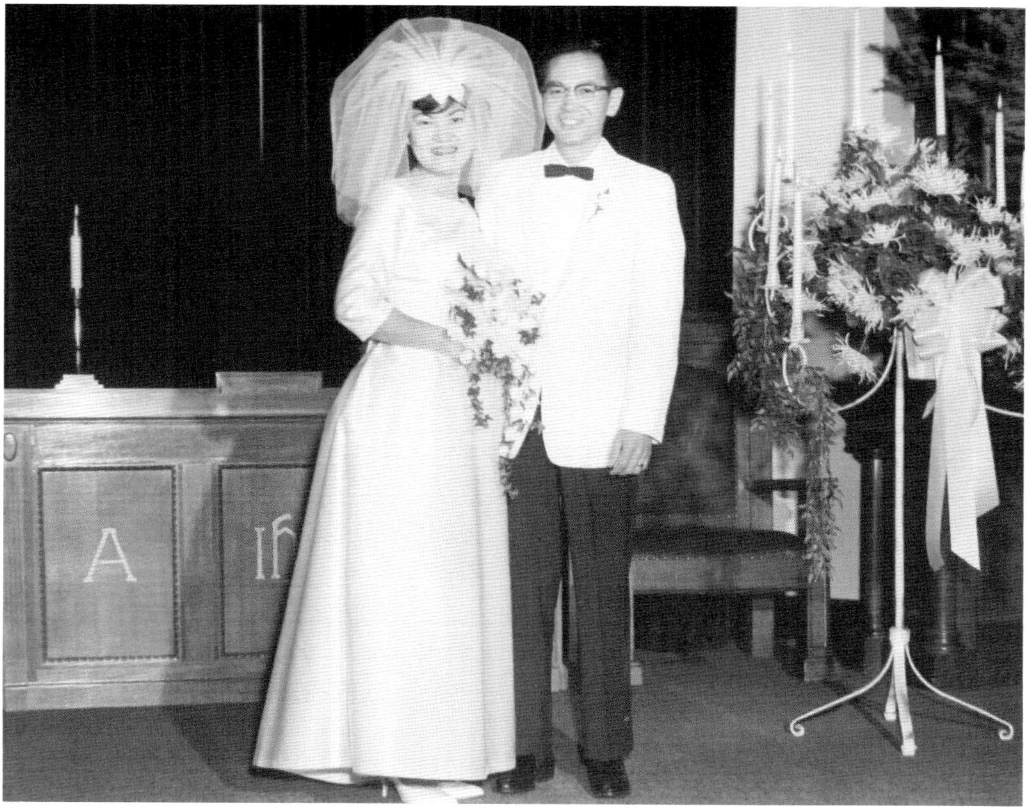

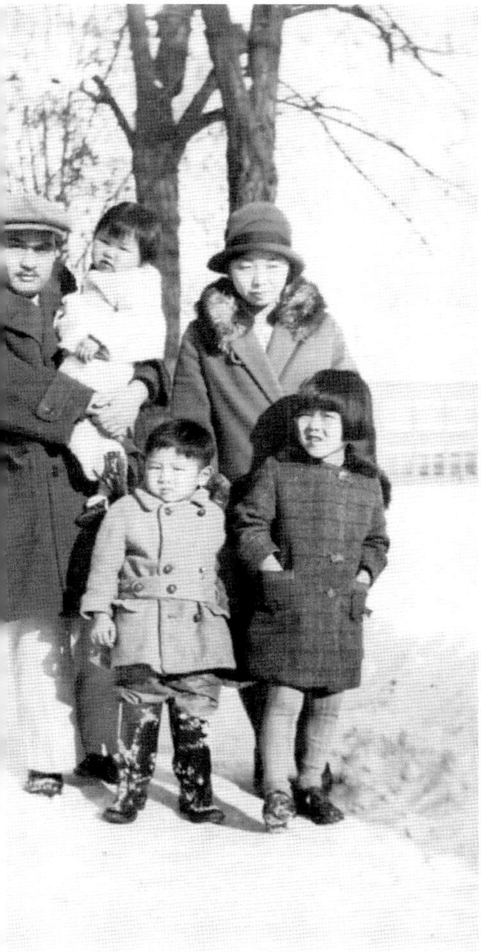

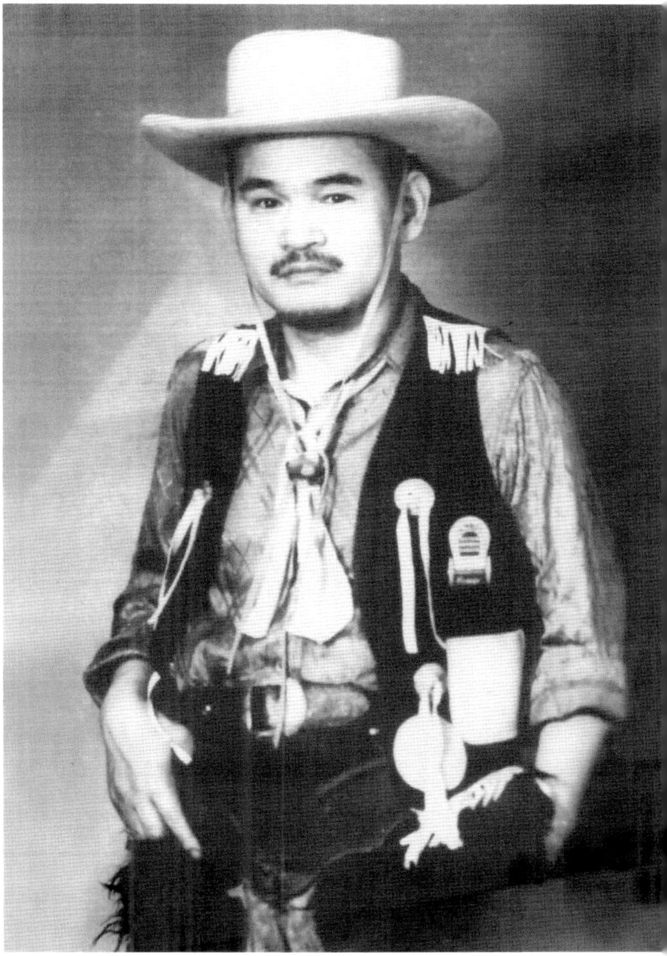

Yuso Shinbo, Japanese Pioneer

Yuso Shinbo emigrated from Japan to Portland, Oregon, in 1907 to join his older brother Takisaku. When Takisaku settled in Walla Walla in 1918 and opened the Japanese Curio store, he asked Yuso to join him as a partner. Yuso went back to his family village in Japan to marry Tomiko Miyamura. When they returned, they opened the Boston Restaurant in Walla Walla. In 1930, they opened the larger Imperial Café, a popular hangout for students. After the attack on Pearl Harbor, the West Coast states were divided into Military Zones 1 and 2. In Washington State, everyone west of the Columbia River was in Zone 1. All Japanese—US citizens included—from Zone 1 were moved from their homes to internment camps. Fortunately for the Shinbos, Walla Walla was in Zone 2, where the Japanese did not have to leave. However, the curfew imposed on the Japanese forced the Shinbos to sell their restaurant at a bargain price. In 1944, Whitman College asked Shinbo to cook at Lyman Hall. After the war, he cooked for the US Army Corps of Engineers. Always active in the community, Shinbo was a member of the Walla Walla Wagon Wheelers (as shown by his regalia). Pictured at left are Yuso and Tomiko and their children, Patty, Art, and June. (Both, courtesy of Shinbo family.)

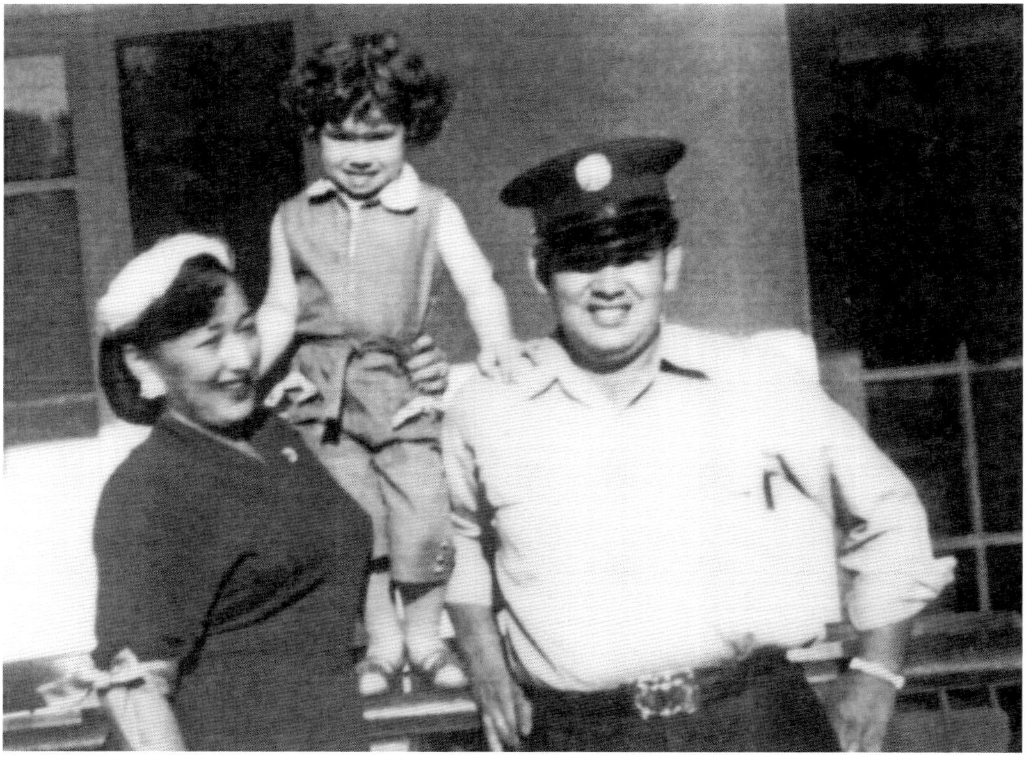

Roger Martinez Rojo, Early Latino Fireman
Roger Rojo was one of the first Latino firemen in Walla Walla and served the Walla Walla Fire Department for 25 years, beginning around 1955 or 1956. He married Joanne M. Schell, who passed away in 2008. This photograph shows three generations: his mother, Dolores Martinez Rojo; daughter Sally Rojo; and Roger in his fireman's uniform. Rojo taught weightlifting, karate, and judo at the YMCA. A competitive pistol shooter, he built a 50-foot concrete tunnel in his house to practice shooting. He was also a member of the Blue Mountain Boat Club. (Courtesy of Sally Rojo Buchanan.)

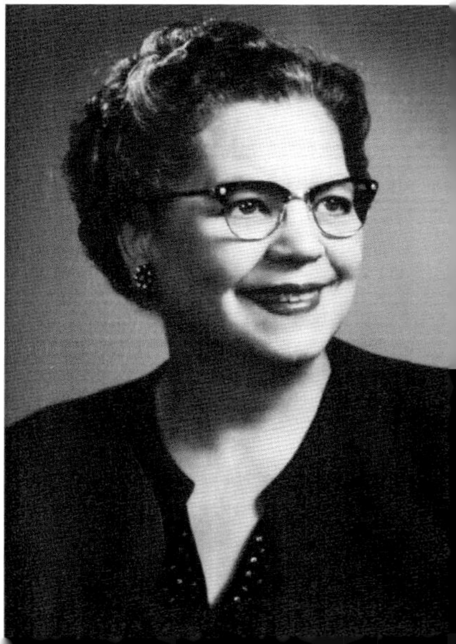

Ruth Reynolds, Longtime Whitman College Librarian
Ruth Sarah Reynolds was born in 1901 to Allen and Fanny Kirkman Reynolds. She graduated from Whitman College in 1922 and then studied at the New York State Library School and served an internship at the New York Public Library. Reynolds completed her graduate work at the University of Chicago. When she returned to Walla Walla, she became assistant librarian at Whitman College, and in 1932, she was named librarian, a position she held until 1966. When she retired, she was named librarian emerita. Even after her retirement, Reynolds volunteered at the library. She died in 1985. (Courtesy of Whitman College and Northwest Archives.)

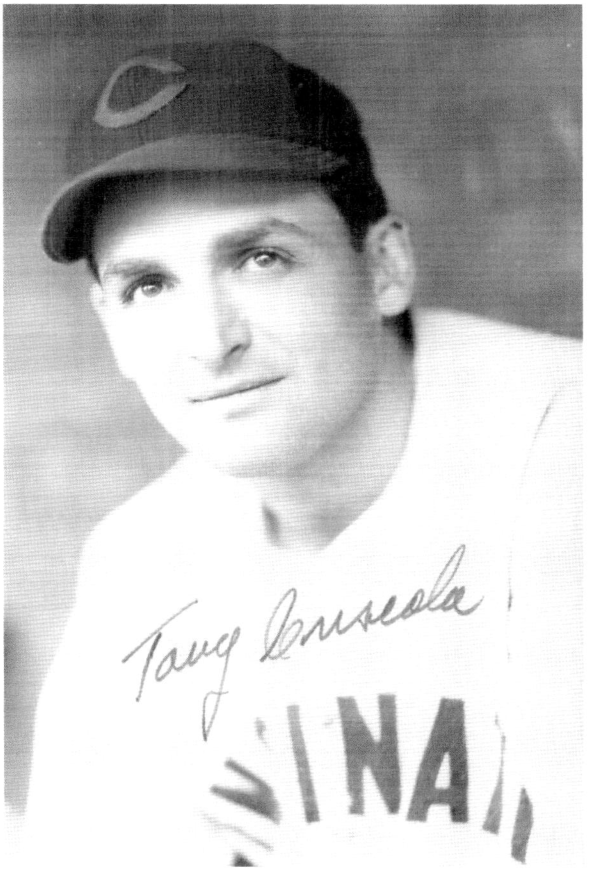

Tony Criscola, Big-League Baseball Player

Anthony Paul Criscola was born in Walla Walla in 1915 to Pasquale and Rosaria Criscola. He graduated from Walla Walla High School and attended Whitman College. He was a major-league baseball outfielder during World War II, playing with the Toledo Mud Hens in 1940, 1941, and 1943. He debuted as a center fielder with the St. Louis Browns in 1942, when he played 97 games and hit .297. Criscola played for the Cincinnati Reds in 1944 and hit .229 in 64 games. After World War II ended, Criscola's baseball career waned. He retired after the 1944 season. (Author's collection.)

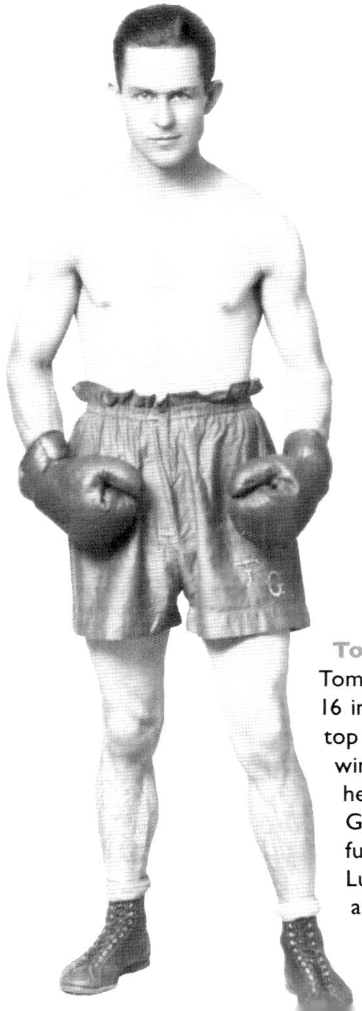

Tommy Gardner, Boxer

Tommy Gardner began bantamweight boxing professionally at age 16 in 1923, winning more than 33 bouts. When he could not get any top contenders to fight him in the Northwest, he went to California, winning all but one of his bouts. Tragically, he contracted polio while he was there and was brought home paralyzed from the neck down. Gardner fought his way back to health, though he still did not have full use of his left arm. After his recovery, he opened Tommy's Dutch Lunch in 1934. The family sold the business in 1971, but it still operates as Tommy's Dutch Lunch. (Courtesy of Fort Walla Walla Museum.)

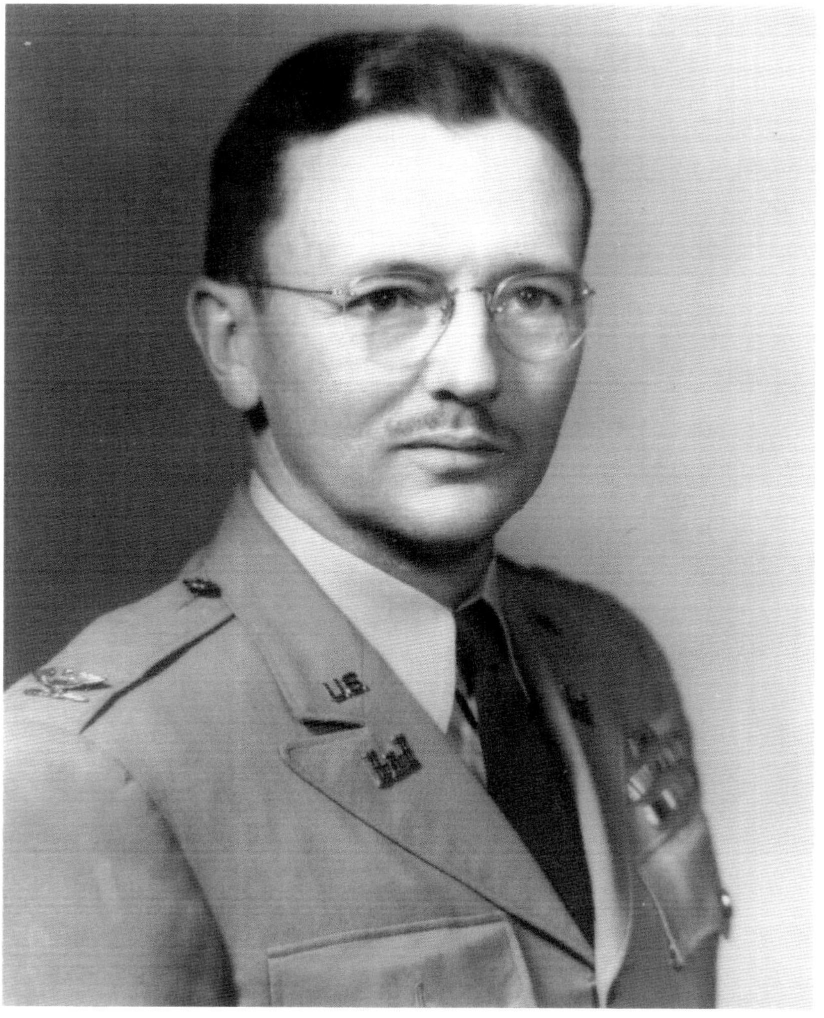

Col. William Whipple, First Commander of Walla Walla District, US Army Corps of Engineers

William Whipple, the son of an engineer, was born in 1909 in Cinclare, Louisiana. Whipple graduated from West Point in 1930 and studied economics and philosophy at Oxford University in England as a Rhodes Scholar. He later studied engineering at Princeton University. During World War II, he served as a member of Gen. Dwight D. Eisenhower's Allied Headquarters staff and later served under Gen. Lucius Clay's headquarters in Berlin. After the war, he returned to the United States and, having achieved the rank of colonel, became the first commander of the newly formed Walla Walla District of the US Army Corps of Engineers (USACE). He served in this capacity from October 1948 to July 1950, leading the planning for water resources development in the Columbia River Basin. Promoted to brigadier general, Whipple later served as division engineer for the Southwestern Division of USACE, and he retired from the Army in 1960. From 1964 to 1965, he served as the chief engineer for the construction of the New York World's Fair. He stayed active, working for the New Jersey Department of Environmental Protection on implementing a statewide water supply master plan. Whipple wrote more than 100 books on water supply, navigation, flood control, and power generation. He died in 2007 and is buried at Arlington National Cemetery. (Courtesy of US Army Corps of Engineers, Walla Walla District.)

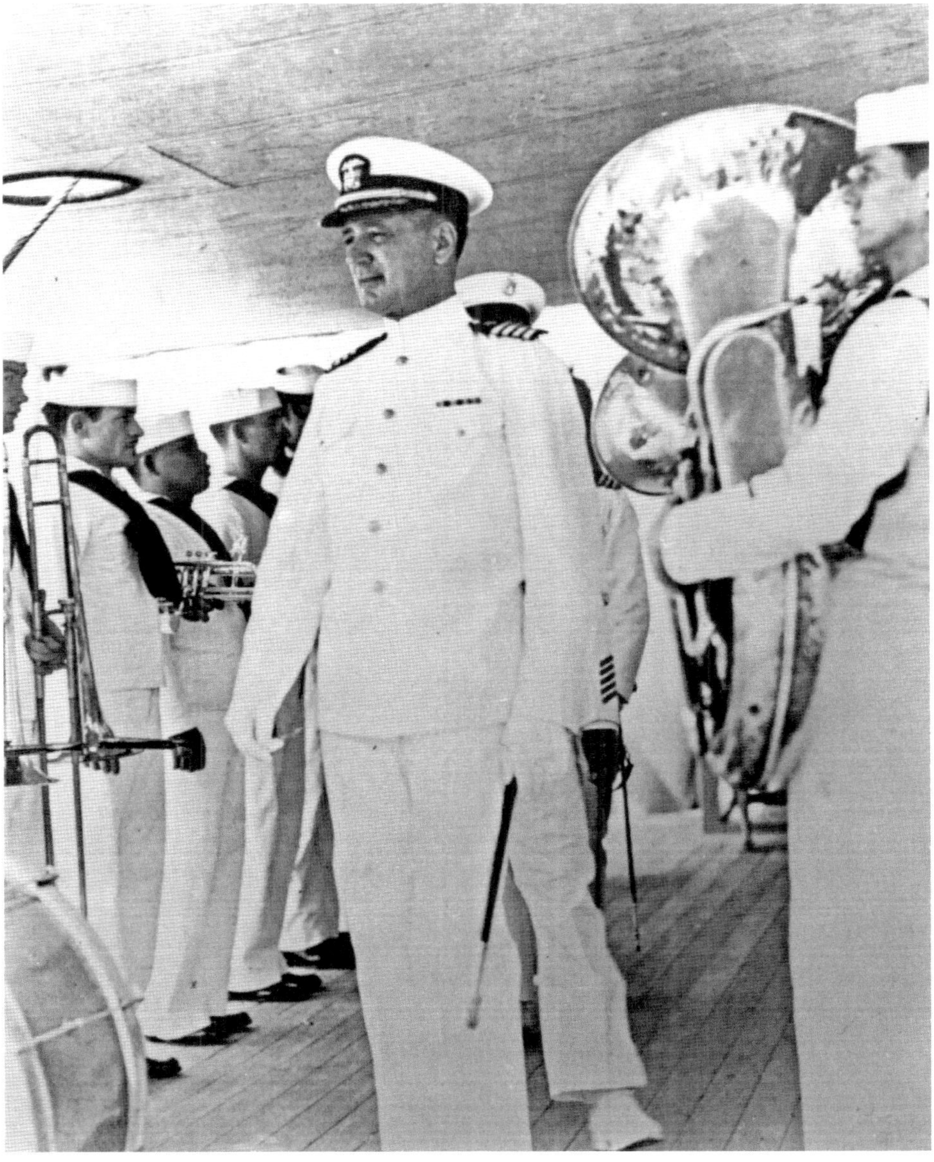

Capt. Albert H. Rooks, Medal of Honor Winner

Albert Rooks was born in Colton, Washington, in 1891, but grew up in Walla Walla. A 1914 graduate of the US Naval Academy, he became a career Naval officer. During World War II, Captain Rooks was in command of the heavy cruiser USS *Houston*, which came under attack in the Battle of Sunda Strait. He was posthumously awarded the Medal of Honor for "extraordinary heroism, outstanding courage, gallantry in action and distinguished service in the line of his profession as Commanding Officer of the USS *Houston* during the period of 4 to 27 February, 1942, while in action with superior Japanese enemy aerial and surface forces." Unfortunately, Japanese forces sank the ship on March 1, and Captain Rooks went down with the ship. This photograph shows Captain Rooks inspecting the band on the USS *Houston* around 1940 or 1941. In 1965, the US Army Corps of Engineers honored him by naming Rooks Park, east of Walla Walla, after him. (Courtesy of Otto Schwartz, collection of the Naval Historical Foundation.)

Virgil Bennington, Chamber of Commerce Leader

Virgil Bennington, a 1913 graduate of Whitman College, was a successful farmer and businessman. An avid sportsman and conservationist, he served on the Washington State Game Commission for 23 years. In 1931 and 1933, floods devastated the city of Walla Walla. Bennington, president of the Walla Walla Chamber of Commerce, went to Washington, DC, in 1937 and successfully lobbied the US Congress for a flood-control project to protect the city from future flooding (the photograph below was taken by Harris & Ewing on that trip). In 1942, the Mill Creek Project was completed by the US Army Corps of Engineers. The project created Mill Creek Reservoir, which would store runoff during flood events. In 1965, the Corps of Engineers added recreation to its mission, and the lake was partially filled for recreational purposes, including fishing. Today, the lake area includes about 20 miles of trails for multiple uses. After Bennington's death in 1983, longtime friend Vance Orchard led a movement to rename the reservoir after him. In 1992, the Mill Creek Reservoir was renamed Virgil B. Bennington Lake in his honor. (Courtesy of Bill Bennington.)

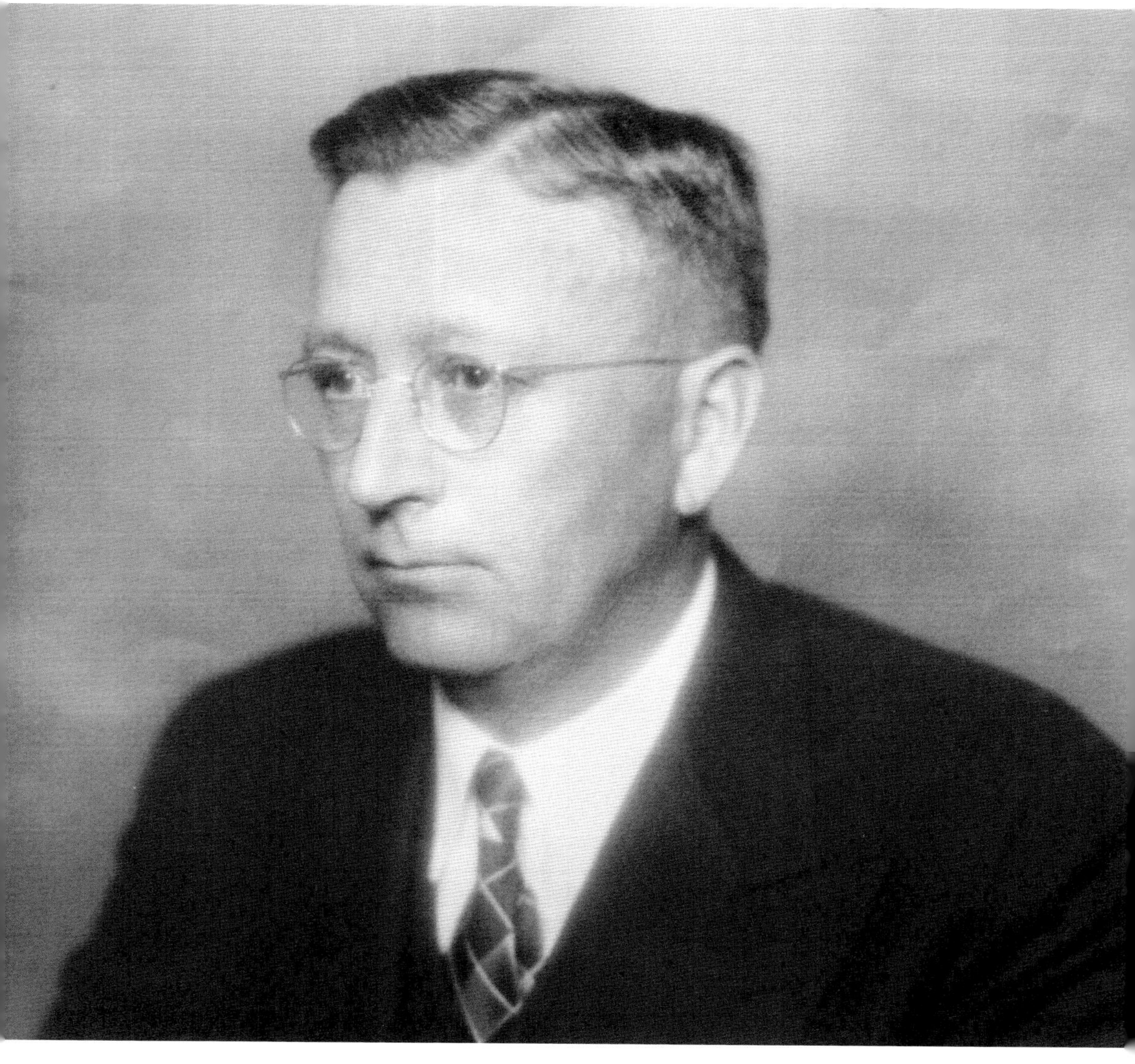

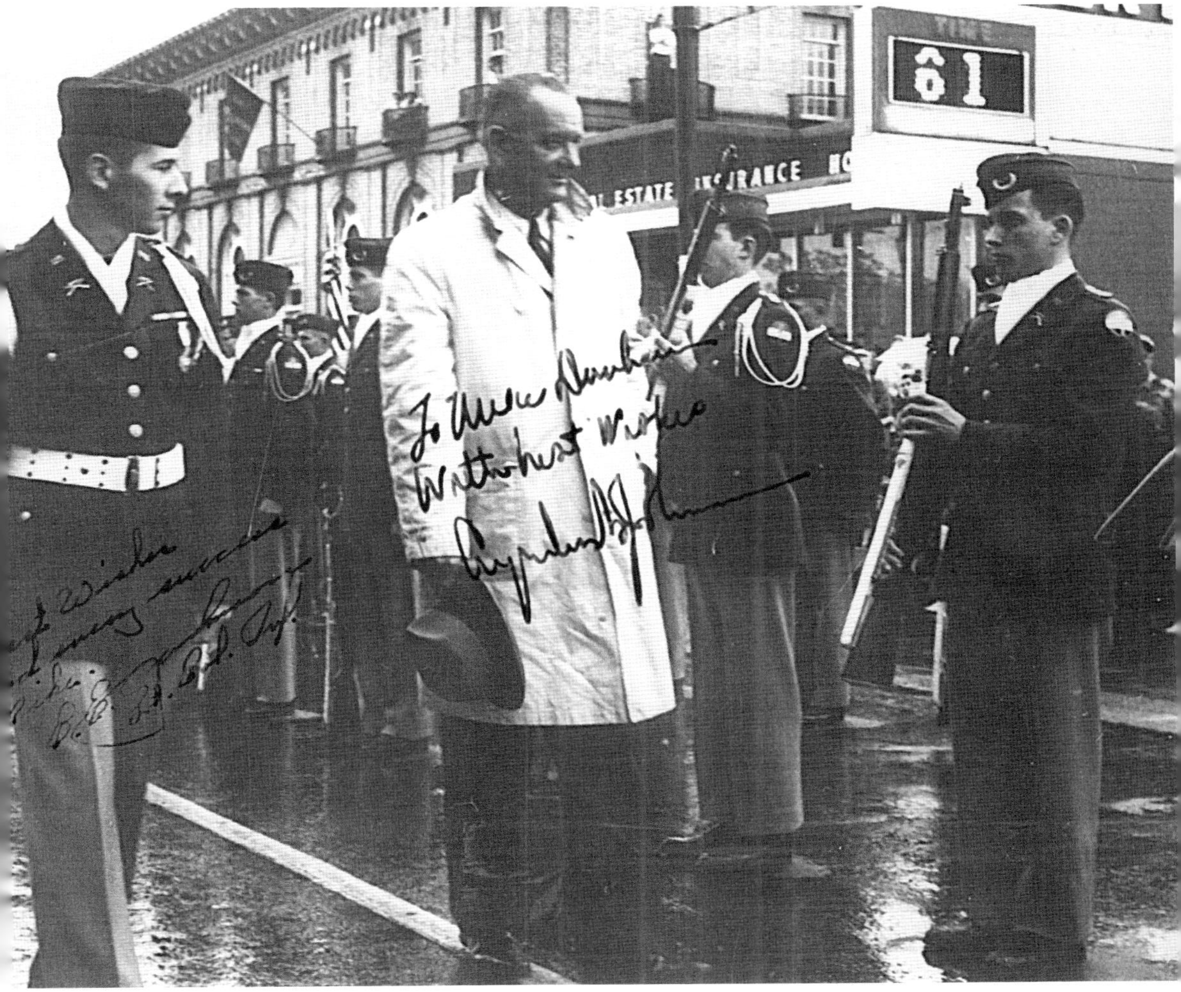

Mike Dunham, Businessman, Winery Owner, and Host

On May 9, 1962, Mike Dunham was a young cadet colonel in the Walla Walla High School Junior Reserve Officer Training Corps Brigade. After Vice Pres. Lyndon B. Johnson dedicated Ice Harbor Lock and Dam near Burbank, Dunham was given the honor of escorting the vice president as he reviewed the brigade's color guard in downtown Walla Walla (as seen in this picture). The high school Junior ROTC program was led by Lt. Col. Clark E. Johnson, a decorated war hero who Dunham said "left an unforgettable memory with me." Dunham went on to Oregon State University, where he majored in marketing. While there, he played in the 1964 NCAA golf championships—competing in a sport that he enjoyed throughout his lifetime and was good at. After a successful career with Standard Oil, Dunham went into the insurance business, returning to Walla Walla to start Dunham Cellars with his wife, Joanne, and his son Eric. In 2001, he retired from Northwestern Mutual Life to concentrate on the winery, especially sales and marketing. As senior winemaker, Eric Dunham has earned many accolades and awards for Dunham Cellars wines. Mike Dunham was an accomplished host—there was always a crowd around him at winery events. Walla Walla and the wine community lost Mike Dunham on May 18, 2013. (Courtesy of Dunham family.)

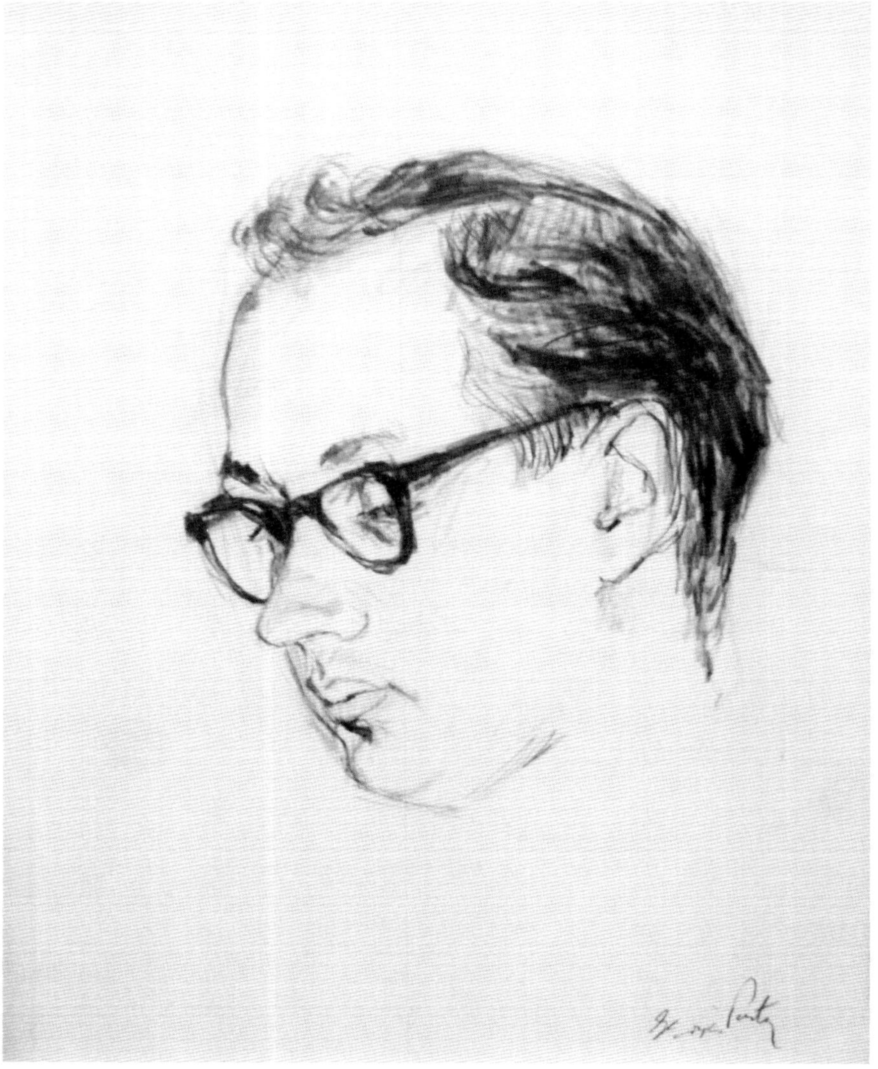

Norman Adams, Artist and Illustrator

Norman Adams, born in Walla Walla in 1933, began painting and drawing at an early age. In the early 1950s, he studied at the Los Angeles Art Center. Adams, who specialized in trompe l'oeil, moved to New York to work for the Charles E. Cooper Studio. Adams's illustrations appeared in a number of periodicals, including *Reader's Digest*, *Harpers*, *National Geographic*, and *Field and Stream*. Adams also authored a textbook, *Drawing Animals*, still available in its 30th-anniversary edition. His illustrations range from historic subjects to animals. In 1988, he won Best of Show at the Minnesota Wildlife Art Show for a life-size painting of a golden eagle at the Grand Canyon. Working in oil, watercolor, and pencil, Adams's attention to detail brought him wide recognition for his realistic depictions, particularly of animals. His photographic memory for visual images earned him acclaim for his illustrations and paintings of historic and natural subject matter. Adams's illustrations can also be found on a number of book covers, Lenox commemorative plates, and a United Nations endangered species stamp. The Norman Adams Collection, including this self-portrait, is housed at Fort Walla Walla Museum. (Courtesy of Fort Walla Walla Museum.)

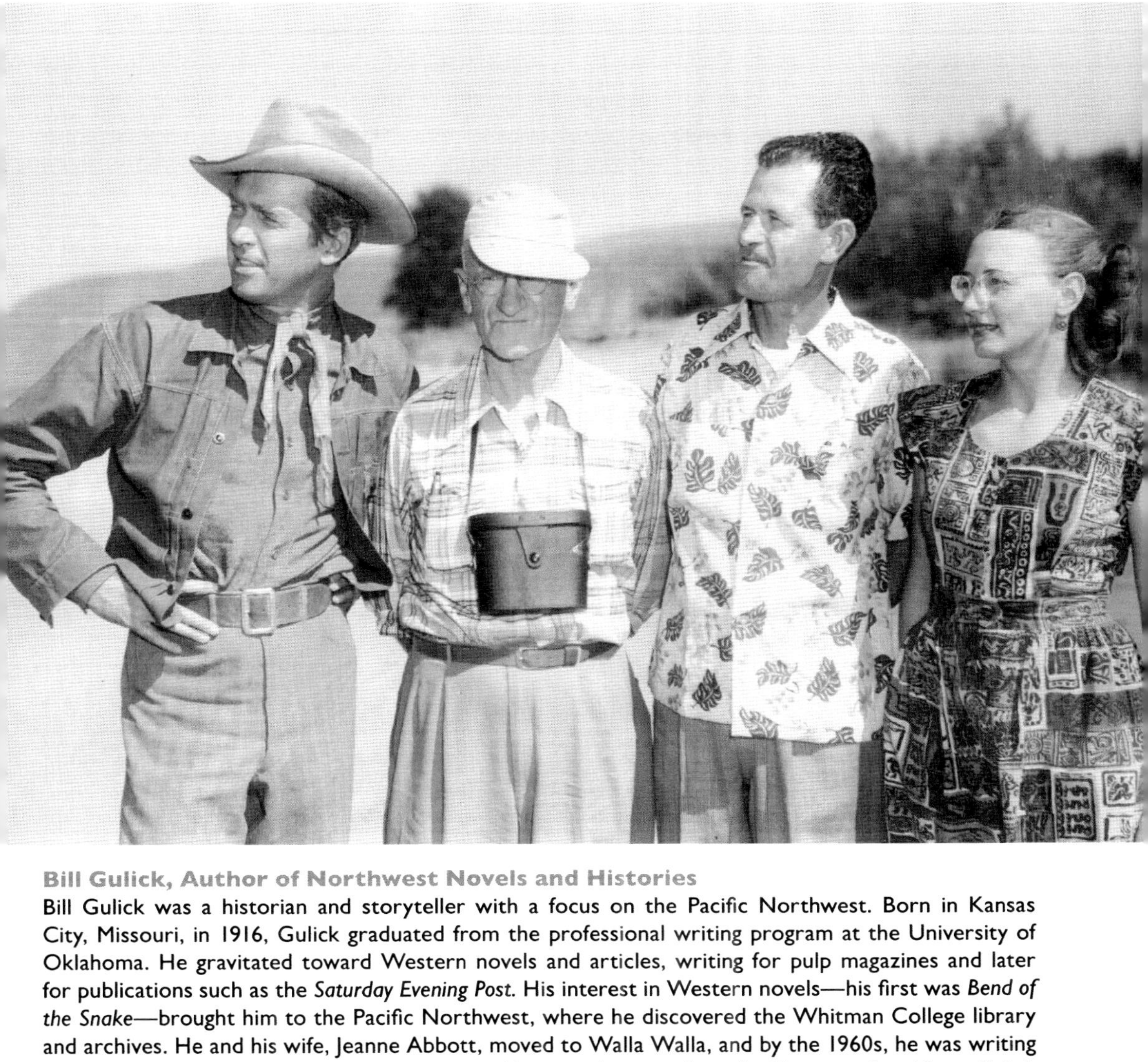

Bill Gulick, Author of Northwest Novels and Histories
Bill Gulick was a historian and storyteller with a focus on the Pacific Northwest. Born in Kansas City, Missouri, in 1916, Gulick graduated from the professional writing program at the University of Oklahoma. He gravitated toward Western novels and articles, writing for pulp magazines and later for publications such as the *Saturday Evening Post*. His interest in Western novels—his first was *Bend of the Snake*—brought him to the Pacific Northwest, where he discovered the Whitman College library and archives. He and his wife, Jeanne Abbott, moved to Walla Walla, and by the 1960s, he was writing historical novels based on the treasure trove of historical materials at the library and archives. Gulick is the author of 20 novels. He wrote books about the Nez Perce, including *Northwest Destiny* (1988), and a series on the Columbia River, Roll on Columbia (1997–2008). Several of his novels were made into movies. *Bend of the Snake* was made into the movie *Bend of the River* (1952) starring James Stewart, Julie Adams, and Rock Hudson. The movie *Hallelujah Trail* (1965), adapted from the book of the same name, starred Burt Lancaster and Lee Remick. This photograph, taken on the set of *Bend of the River* at Rooster Rock Park on the Columbia River, shows, from left to right, James Stewart, Dr. Grover Gulick (Bill Gulick's father), Bill Gulick, and Jeanne Gulick. Bill Gulick passed away in 2013. (Courtesy of Fort Walla Walla Museum.)

Donald and Virginia Sherwood, Philanthropists

Donald Sherwood graduated from Whitman College in 1922 and maintained a lifelong association with the college (he is often credited with saving Whitman from bankruptcy during the Depression). Sherwood worked for Standard Oil after graduation, and in 1932 founded Sherwood & Roberts, a full-service real estate and finance firm. In 1929, he married Walla Walla native Virginia Kelly, daughter of *Union-Bulletin* publisher John Kelly and his wife, Martha (see page 72). Virginia graduated from the University of Washington with a degree in history. Always community minded, the Sherwoods were instrumental in the construction of the new Walla Walla Public Library in the 1960s, loaning the money for construction and holding the debt until the library could pay it off. In 1991, Donald and Virginia (below, left and center) founded the Sherwood Trust, dedicated to the highest sustainable quality of life for everyone in the Walla Walla area. The organization's approach is not based on charity; rather, it makes grants in the form of long-term investments in the Walla Walla Valley and surrounding communities. Organization, community, and community-leadership grants are designed to support on multiple levels individuals, nonprofit organizations, communities, and, ultimately, local economies. Donald and Virginia Sherwood's legacy has been far-reaching, providing funding for a wide variety of initiatives including capital projects, grassroots neighborhood projects, and program grants. (Courtesy of Whitman College and Northwest Archives.)

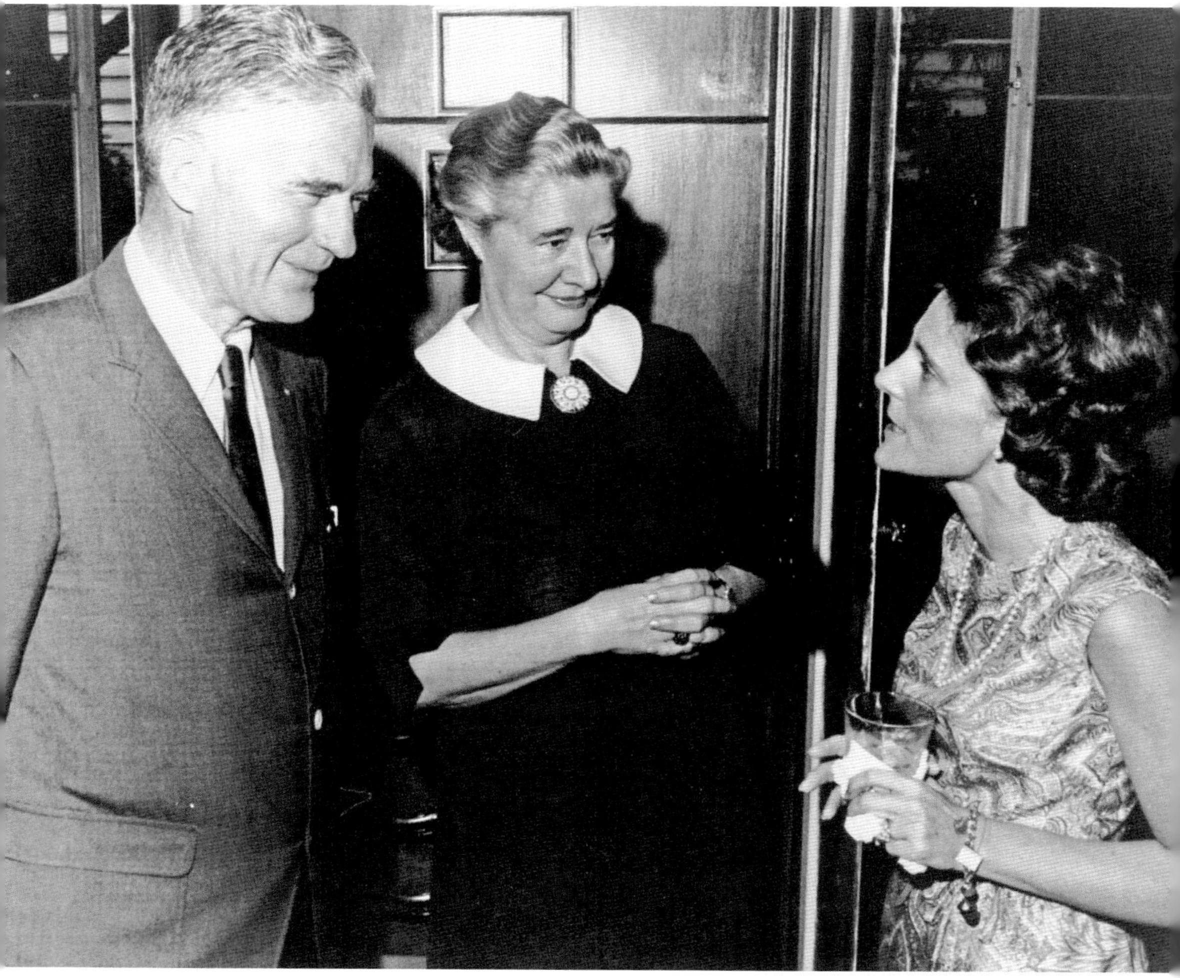

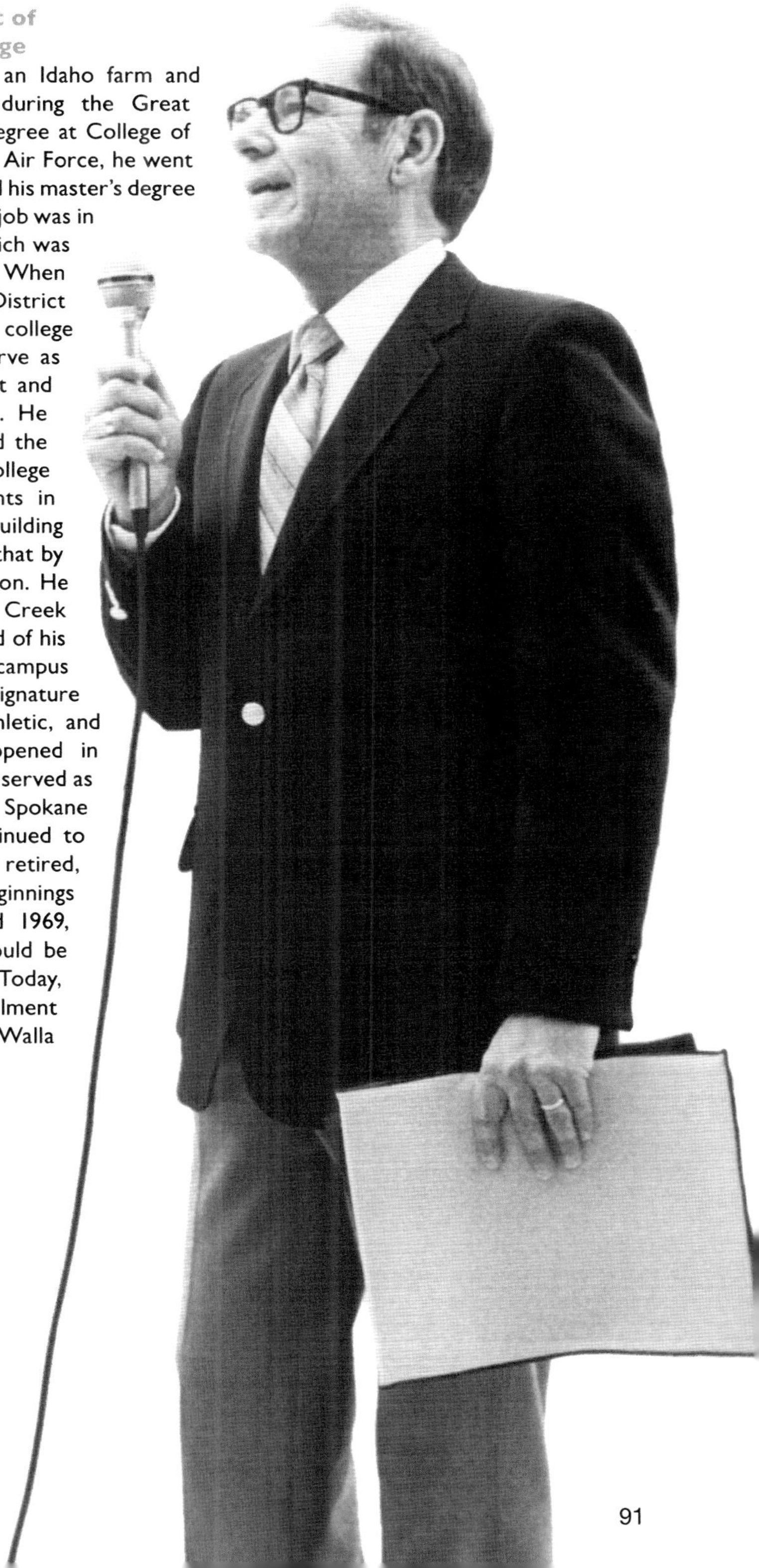

Eldon Dietrich, First President of Walla Walla Community College

Eldon "Pete" Dietrich grew up on an Idaho farm and worked his way through college during the Great Depression, earning his bachelor's degree at College of Idaho. After serving four years in the Air Force, he went to the University of Idaho and received his master's degree in English literature. His first teaching job was in Wapato, Washington. By 1965, Dietrich was principal at Kennewick High School. When Dietrich heard Walla Walla School District had decided to start a community college to serve the area, he applied to serve as superintendent of the school district and as president of the new institution. He began his new positions in 1966, and the new Walla Walla Community College (WWCC) opened with 500 students in the old Walla Walla High School building in 1967. The college grew so quickly that by 1969 it was looking for a new location. He found land near Mill Creek and Titus Creek east of town and convinced the board of his vision for a new campus. The new campus opened in 1974, and WWCC's signature geodesic dome—housing health, athletic, and physical education departments—opened in 1977. The "Dietrich Dome" originally served as the Chinese Pavilion at Expo 74, the Spokane World's Fair. The campus has continued to expand rapidly. In 1982, Dietrich retired, having seen the college from its beginnings to a growing success. In 1968 and 1969, consultants projected that there would be 1,200 students at WWCC by 2012. Today, there are more than 13,000, and enrollment continues to grow. (Courtesy of Walla Walla Community College Media.)

Adam West (Bill Anderson), Actor

Adam West (William "Bill" West Anderson) was born in Walla Walla in 1928 to Otto West Anderson, a third-generation wheat farmer, and Audrey Speer. The family's farm was outside Walla Walla, where Bill lived out his Western fantasies riding his American Saddlebred horse Champ through the fields. He also acquired a comic book collection, and Batman in particular made a big impression on him. As a young man, his one foray into acting was filling in for one of the actors in a Little Theatre of Walla Walla production of *Ladies in Retirement*. Bill attended Walla Walla High School for his freshman and sophomore years and graduated from Lakeside School in Seattle. He returned to Walla Walla for college, earning his bachelor's degree in literature with a minor in psychology from Whitman College in 1951. At Whitman, he was active in debate and sang in the college's choir, but he surprisingly did not do any acting. After college and a stint in the Army, Anderson worked on a children's show in Hawaii. In 1959, he moved to Hollywood and took the stage name Adam West. His first national appearance was in the film *The Young Philadelphians* (1959), which starred Paul Newman and Barbara Rush. He acted in a number of Westerns and in 1966 was cast in the ABC television series *Batman*. A subsequent *Batman* feature film (also in 1966) solidified West's association with the role of the masked crusader. His portrayal of the comic book character was so compelling that the creator of Batman, Bob Kane, inscribed a drawing to him, "To my buddy, Adam, who breathed life into my pen and ink creation." Despite his extensive film and television acting credits, his portrayal of Batman is his best-remembered role. (Author's collection.)

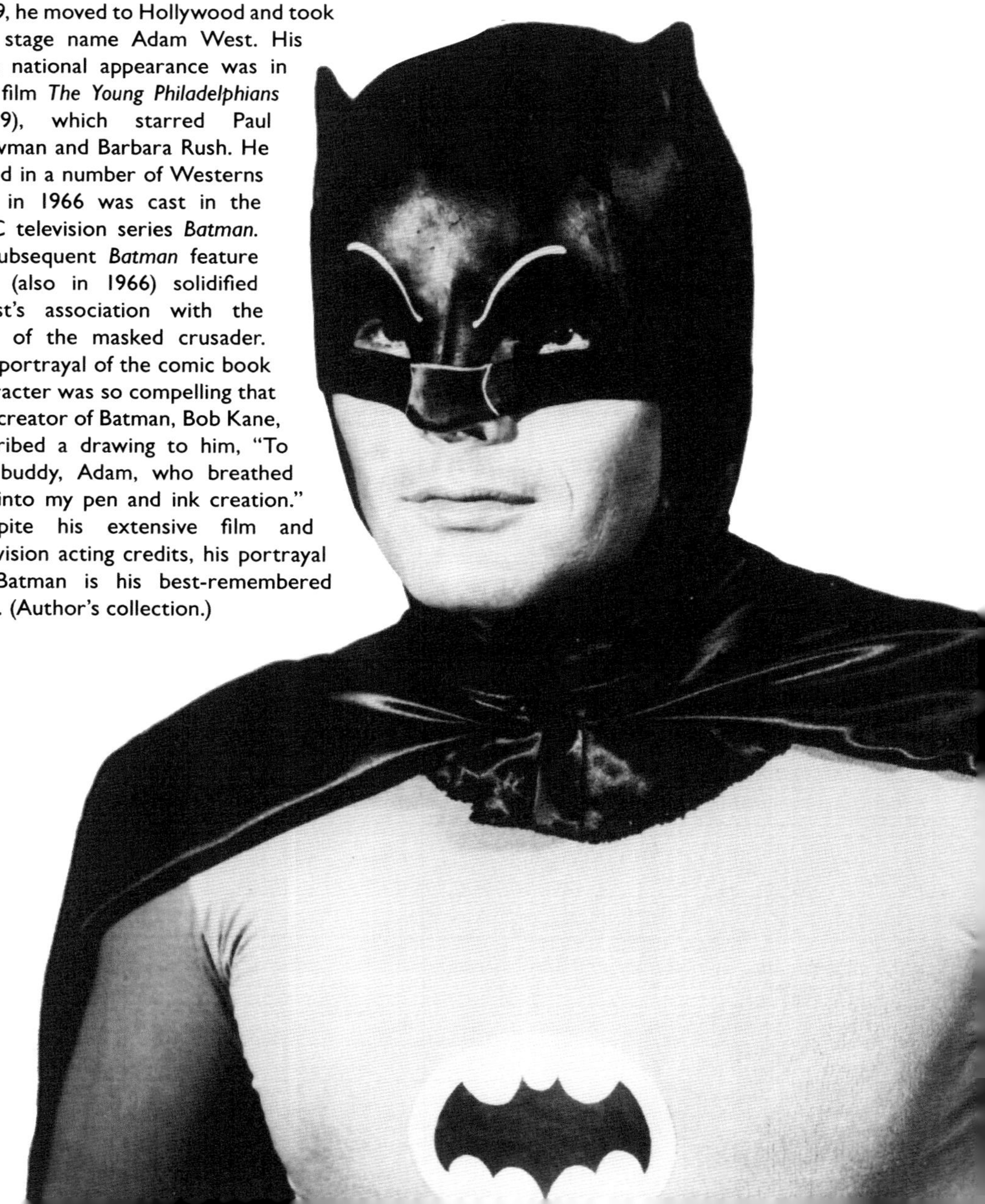

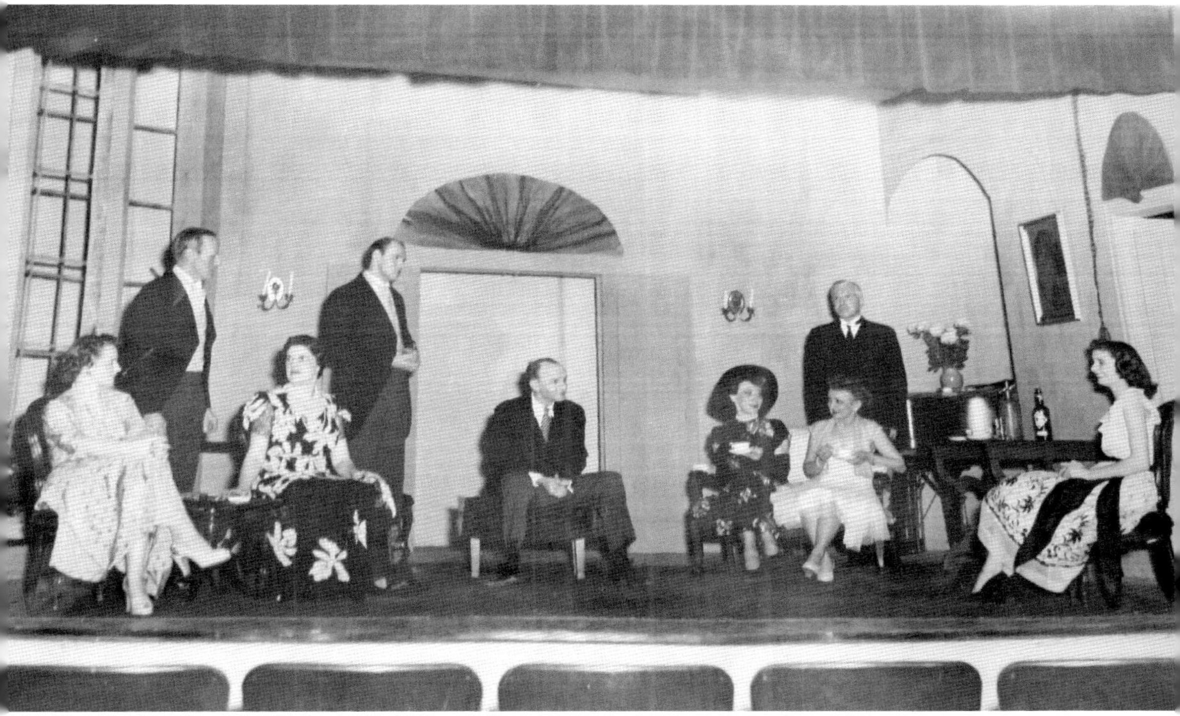

Paul Jackson, Founder of the Little Theatre of Walla Walla
Paul Jackson came to Walla Walla in the spring of 1934 for a temporary teaching position in the English department at Whitman College. In 1936, he came to the college to stay, bringing a love for arts and theater with him. In July 1944, Jackson directed performances of *Yes, My Darling Daughter* for personnel at the Army air base (now the Walla Walla airport). Following the success of the play, the troupe put on performances at the Marcus Whitman Hotel. By September 10, Jackson had called together a group of 40 like-minded citizens, and the Little Theatre was born. Members chipped in $15 each to get the organization started, and they cleaned up an unused space on Main Street. The play *The Old War Horse* became the first of many performances during the 70-year history of the Little Theatre. Forced to give up its downtown location, in 1948, the group bought the World War Veterans Building. After adding a stage and tower, the theater opened in its new location October 15, 1948. The popular theater continues in that venue today. Pictured from left to right, the cast of *The Last of Mrs. Cheney* (performed in the 1951–1952 season) included (first row, seated) Laura Peterson, Grace Heath, Paul Jackson, Mary McMurtry, Lois Walker, and Shirley Dorn; (second row, standing) Otto Anderson, George Grieve, and Richard Eubanks. (Courtesy of the Little Theatre of Walla Walla.)

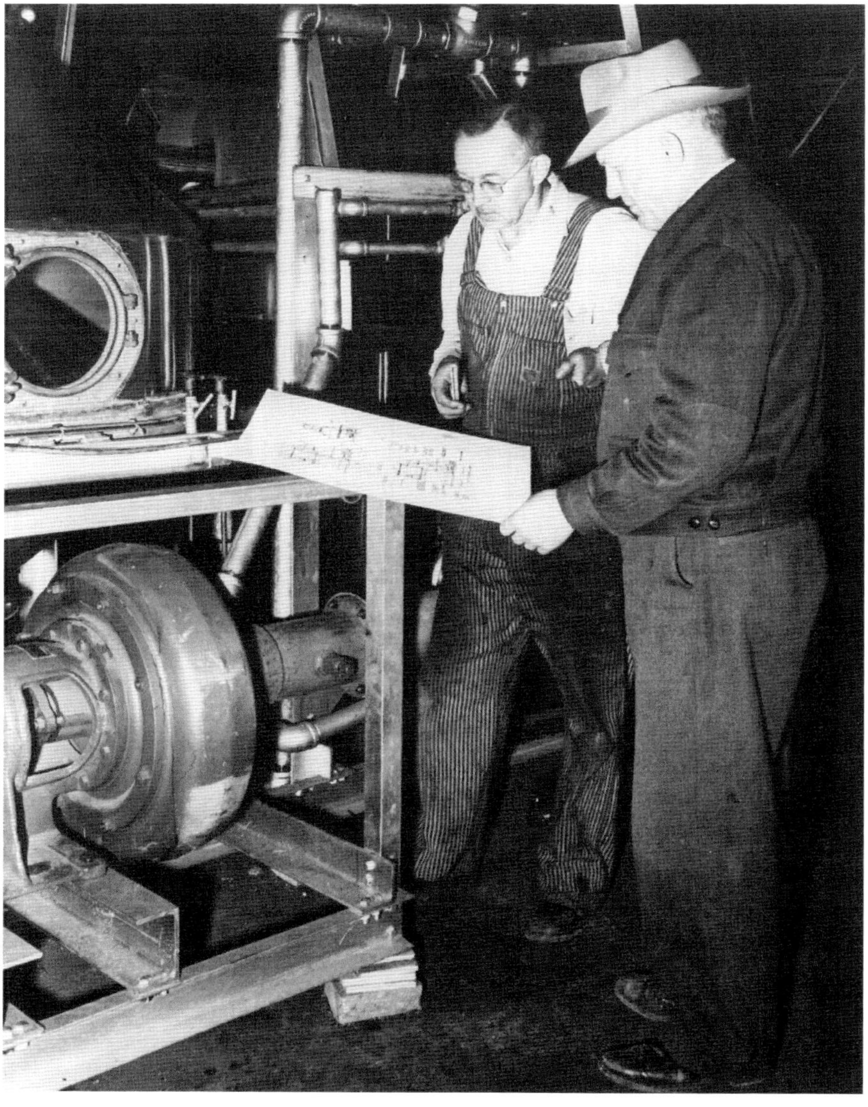

Claude Key, Cofounder of Key Technology

In 1948, a small Milton-Freewater, Oregon, business—Umatilla Canning Company—began its transformation into a worldwide leader in food-processing equipment, Key Equipment Company. In their first year, founders Claude and Lloyd Key (brothers) and Francis Miller built food-processing and agricultural machinery for the green pea–processing industry, including the Froth Flotation Cleaner. Pictured above are Harley Johnson, left, and Claude Key, right, during construction of the earliest Froth Flotation Cleaner in 1948. Renamed Key Technology in 1982, the company moved its operations to Walla Walla in 1990. Today, Key Technology is an international company headquartered in Walla Walla with facilities in the Netherlands, Belgium, Australia, and Mexico. Key designs, manufactures, and integrates automation systems for food-processing and other industries. Its technology includes automated optical inspection systems, specialized conveying systems, and processing and preparation systems. The company is heavily involved in research, development, and engineering. (Courtesy of Key Technology, Inc.)

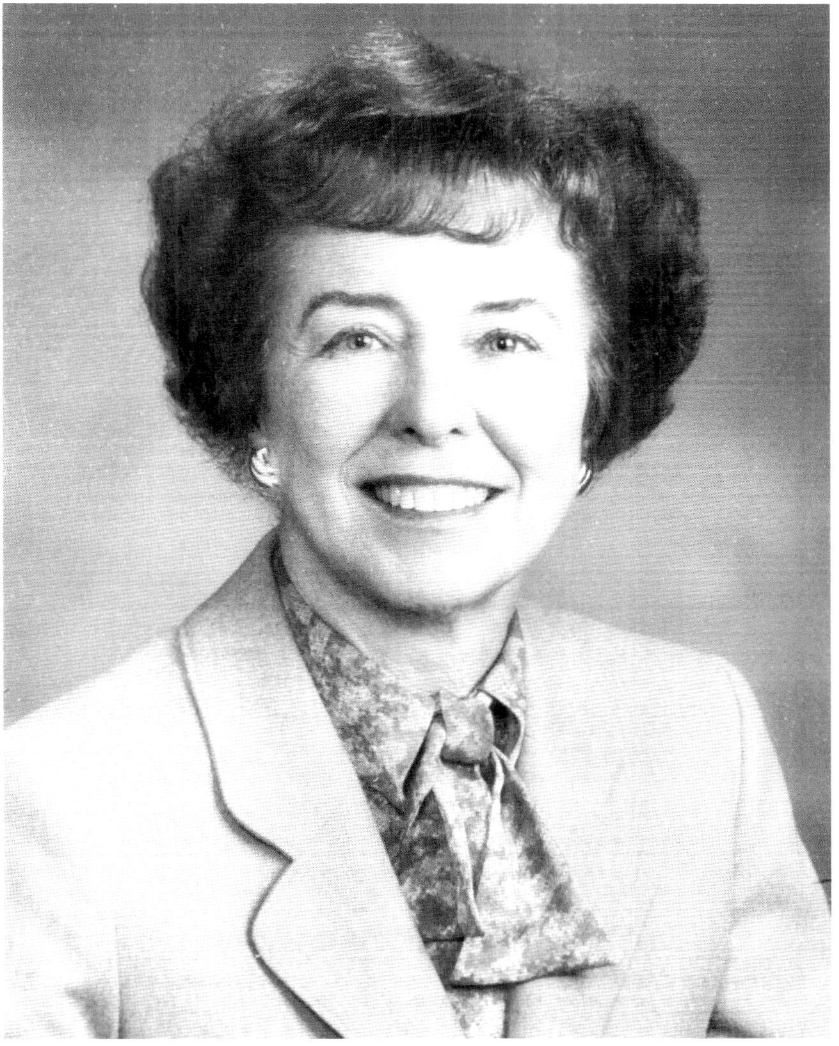

Jeannette Hayner, Walla Walla School Board, State Legislator, Senate Majority Leader
Jeannette Hayner was a woman who knew how to break barriers and build consensus. A native of Portland, she was born in 1919, the year before women were given the right to vote. She graduated from the University of Oregon with a degree in business administration and met her husband at the University of Oregon law school, where she earned her degree in 1942. She and husband Herman "Dutch" Hayner (originally spelled "Hahner") moved to Walla Walla in 1947. Jeannette was active in the community, serving as president of the Walla Walla School Board and participating in the Republican Party. In 1972, she ran for the open 16th District seat in the Washington State House and won. When she took her seat in 1973, there were only seven other women in the house, and no women in the senate. After four years in the house, she was asked to run for the senate seat vacated by Democrat Dan Jolly. She agreed, was elected, and would be reelected every four years until her retirement in 1992. In 1981, she served as majority leader in the state senate, becoming the first woman to serve in that capacity in senate history. Throughout her career, she was known for her problem-solving style, working effectively with the entire political spectrum. Hayner passed away in 2010. (Courtesy of Washington State Archives.)

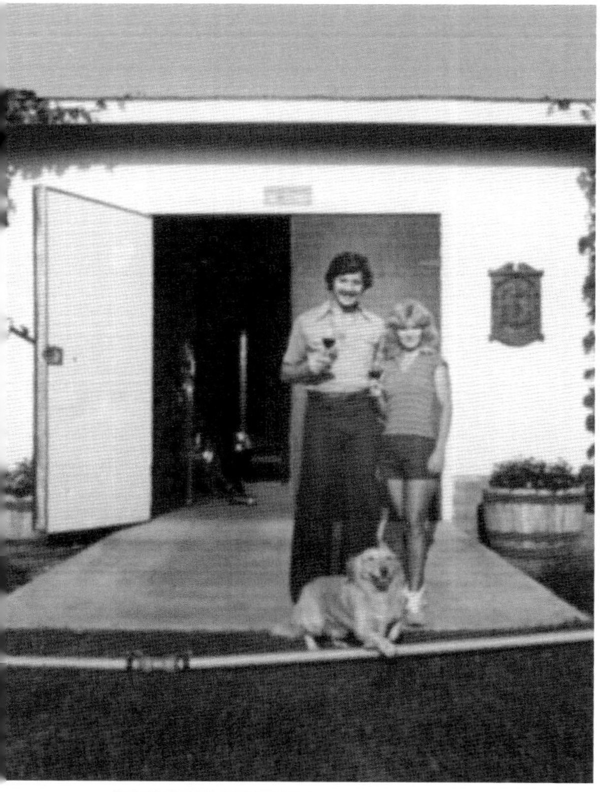

Gary and Nancy Figgins, Leonetti Cellar, Walla Walla's First Commercial Winery

When Gary and Nancy Figgins founded Leonetti Cellar in 1977, the winery's name paid homage to Gary's deep roots in Walla Walla. His grandparents Francesco and Rosa Leonetti, having left their hometown of Serra Pedace, Italy, to find a new life in America, founded their farm in 1906. Little could they have known that in 1974, a one-and-a-half-acre, south-facing hillside on that farm would become the birthplace of the modern wine industry in the Walla Walla Valley. That year, Gary and Nancy Figgins (left) planted a few hundred cuttings of Cabernet Sauvignon and Riesling bare-root grapes. In 1977, the new winery opened, and Leonetti Cellar quickly gained a reputation for making sought-after premium wines and sparked a renaissance of winemaking in the Walla Walla Valley. Carrying on the family tradition, son Chris Figgins (below, left, with, from left to right, Nancy, daughter Amy, and Gary Figgins) became president and winemaking director of the Figgins Family Wine Estates, which includes Leonetti Cellar, Figgins Walla Walla Valley, Toil Oregon Pinot Noir, and the Lostine Cattle Company's grass-fed beef. (Left, courtesy of Figgins Family Wine Estates; below, Andrea Johnson photograph.)

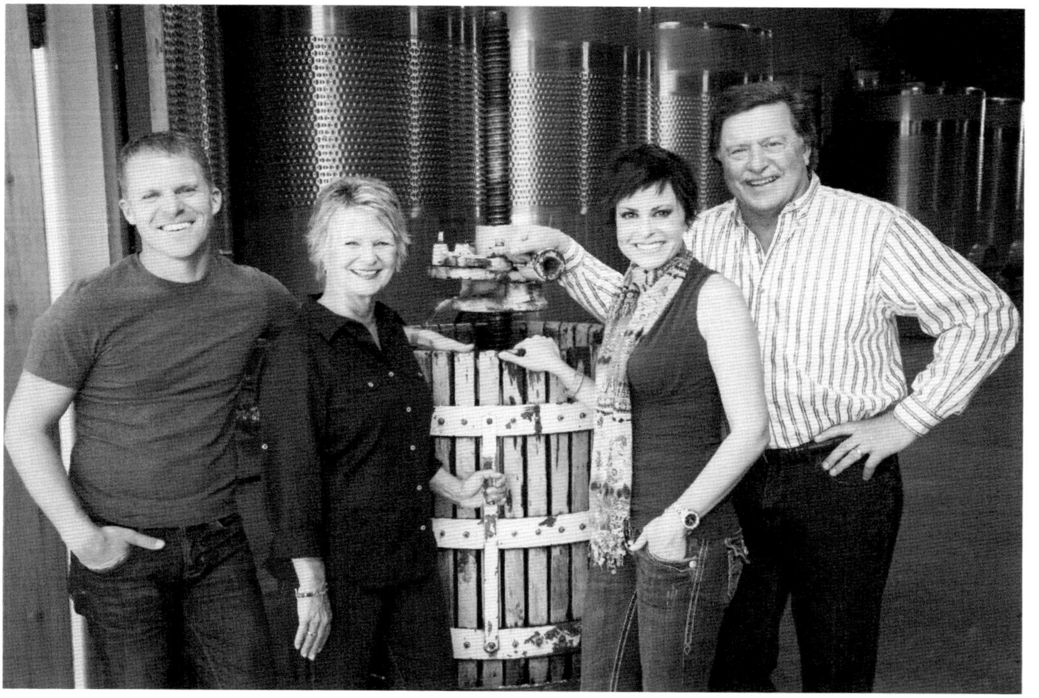

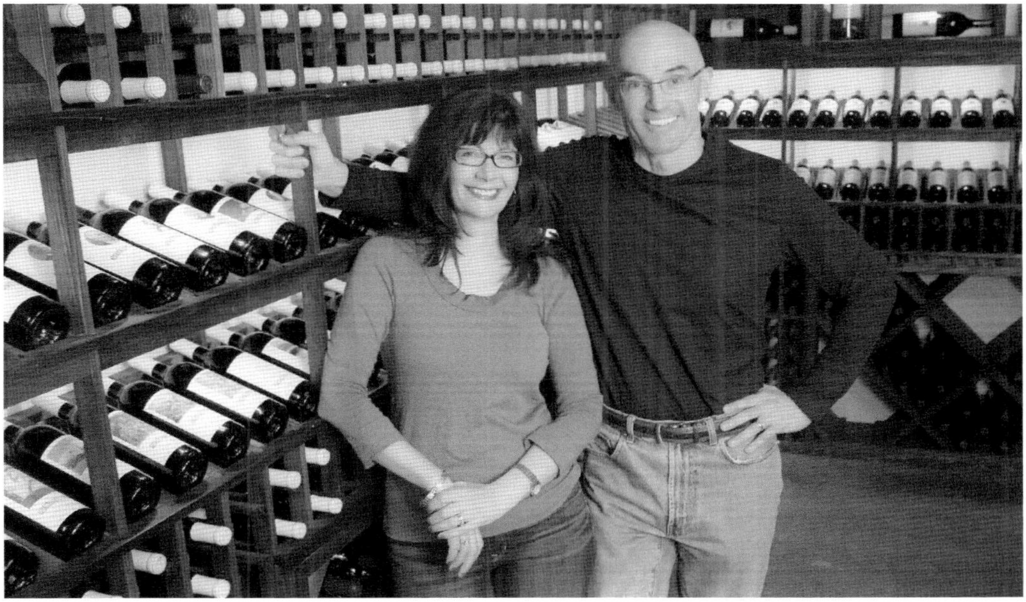

Rick Small and Darcey Fugman-Small, Woodward Canyon Winery
Rick Small's family had a long history in wheat farming and livestock on the Lazy S Arrow Ranch near Lowden, west of Walla Walla. Small returned to the valley after graduating from the University of Washington with a degree in agriculture. He and friend Gary Figgins developed an interest in winemaking, so the crop Small planted in his native Woodward Canyon in 1976 was not wheat, it was wine grapes. In 1978, Darcey Fugman came for a job at the Walla Walla County Regional Planning Department. On her second date with Rick, she helped him bottle Chardonnay. The couple married in 1980; in 1981, Woodward Canyon Winery opened. Although their production has grown from 1,200 cases in 1981 to its current 15,000 cases a year, the winery is committed to quality over quantity. Rick was chair of the Walla Walla Winegrowers when they applied for the Walla Walla Valley AVA (American Viticultural Area); Darcey wrote the application with the assistance of Becky Hendricks, and the new AVA was granted in 1984. In 2000, the Smalls moved the building shown below (left) from its original location in Lowden to the winery, restored it, and opened it as the winery's tasting room. (Both, courtesy of Woodward Canyon.)

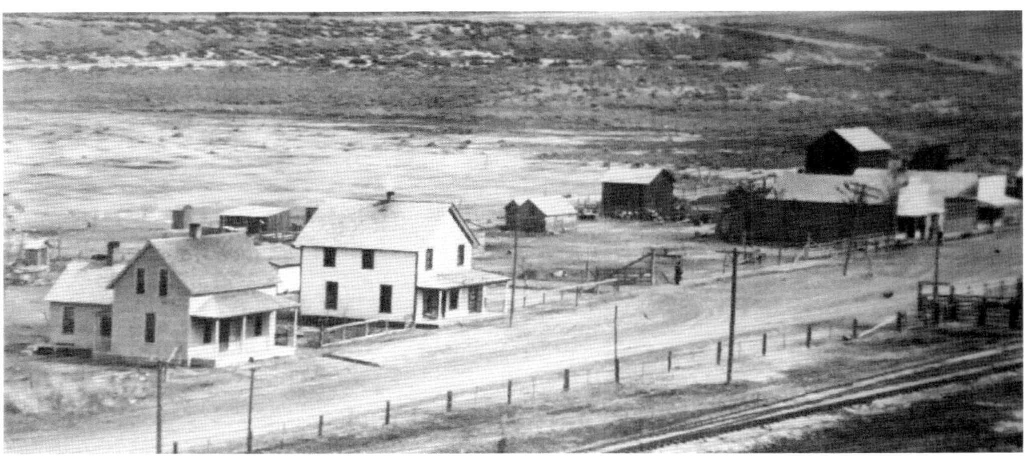

Walter and DeLaine Anderson, Founders of Andy's Market

Andy's Market is a landmark in College Place, which neighbors Walla Walla. The Andersons, Walter and DeLaine (or "Mr. and Mrs. A"), were the market's ambassadors. Andy's, established in 1968 as a corner grocery store, expanded in 1974 to its current location and quickly became a destination for health-conscious shoppers. The Andersons' initial goal was to provide healthy options for customers by offering bulk foods, fresh produce, specialty items, and dietary supplements. The market's reputation for good customer service, fair pricing, and quality attracts a broad range of customers from all over the valley. DeLaine and Walt both passed away, but Andy's Market—still in the family—continues to serve health- and quality-conscious shoppers. (Courtesy of Andy's Market.)

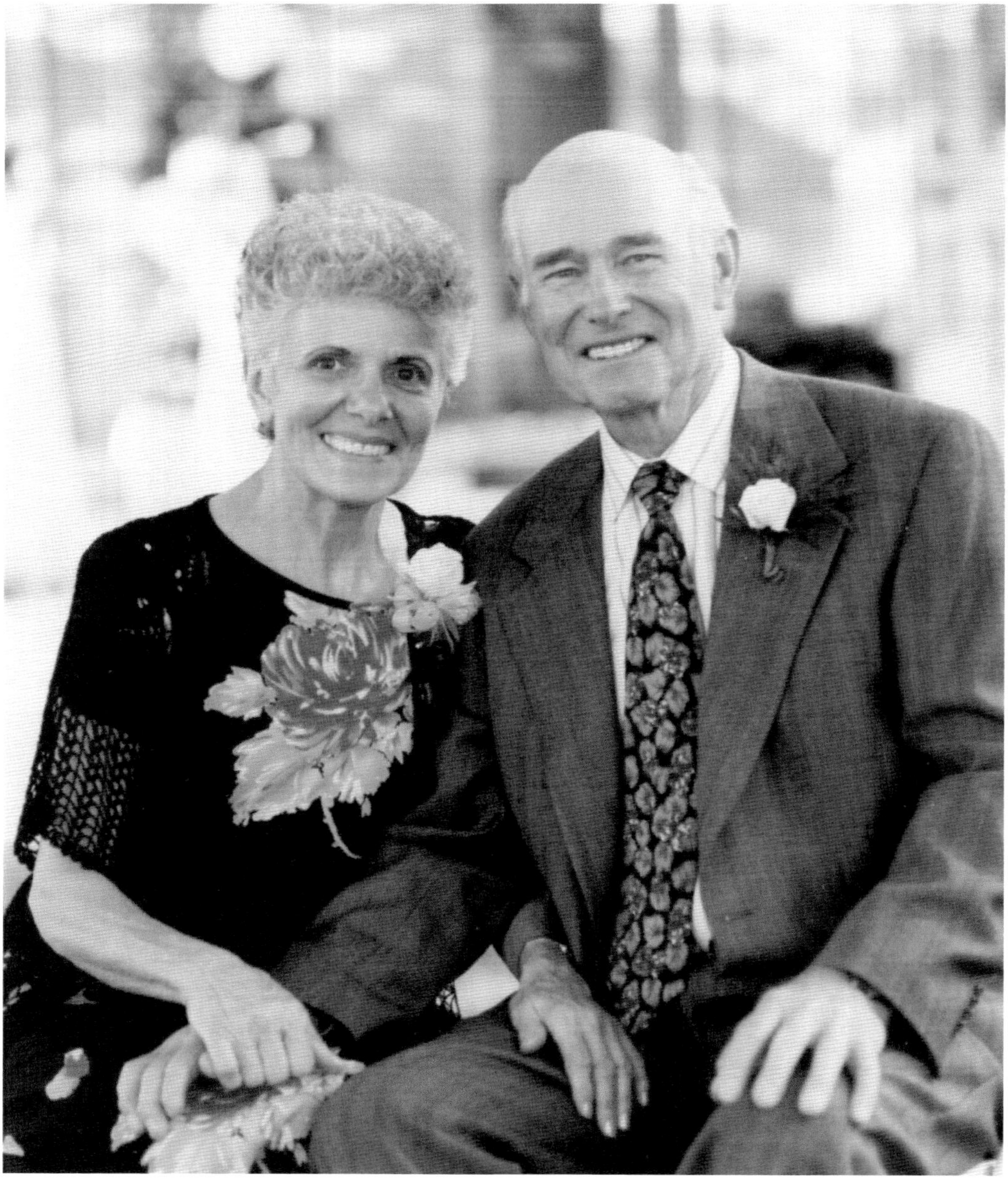

CHAPTER SIX

Building a Bright Future

By the mid-20th century, it was clear that Walla Walla's location, tucked away in the southeast corner of Washington, worked against it economically. Its rich architectural heritage was seen by some as a liability, and a push for a more up-to-date downtown led to the addition of "modern" facades. By the 1980s, these facades looked tired, and downtown vacancies were rising. The opening of a suburban shopping mall in 1989 sparked downtown revitalization, including facade restoration, streetscape improvements, and public art. The Downtown Walla Walla Foundation coordinates events, parades, and community gatherings.

From its first commercial winery, Leonetti Cellar, in 1977 to today's more than 100 wineries, the wine industry has become a significant economic force and attraction to visitors. The industry also led to the establishment of the enology and viticulture program and the Wine Country Culinary Institute at Walla Walla Community College, two of the many programs at this progressive school.

Fueling economic development, the Port of Walla Walla, founded in 1952, turned the old military airfield into today's modern airport and business incubator. Wineries, manufacturers, and high-tech companies are just a few of the businesses taking advantage of the port's facilities at the airport and across the county.

Historic sites add to the appeal of the Walla Walla Valley for residents and visitors alike. Whitman Mission National Historic Site, Fort Walla Walla Museum, and the Kirkman House Museum chronicle the valley's heritage. Fort Walla Walla's living-history program features reenactors who portray historical figures from the valley. Walking tours of the downtown and historic neighborhoods showcase the history, public art, and architecture of Walla Walla.

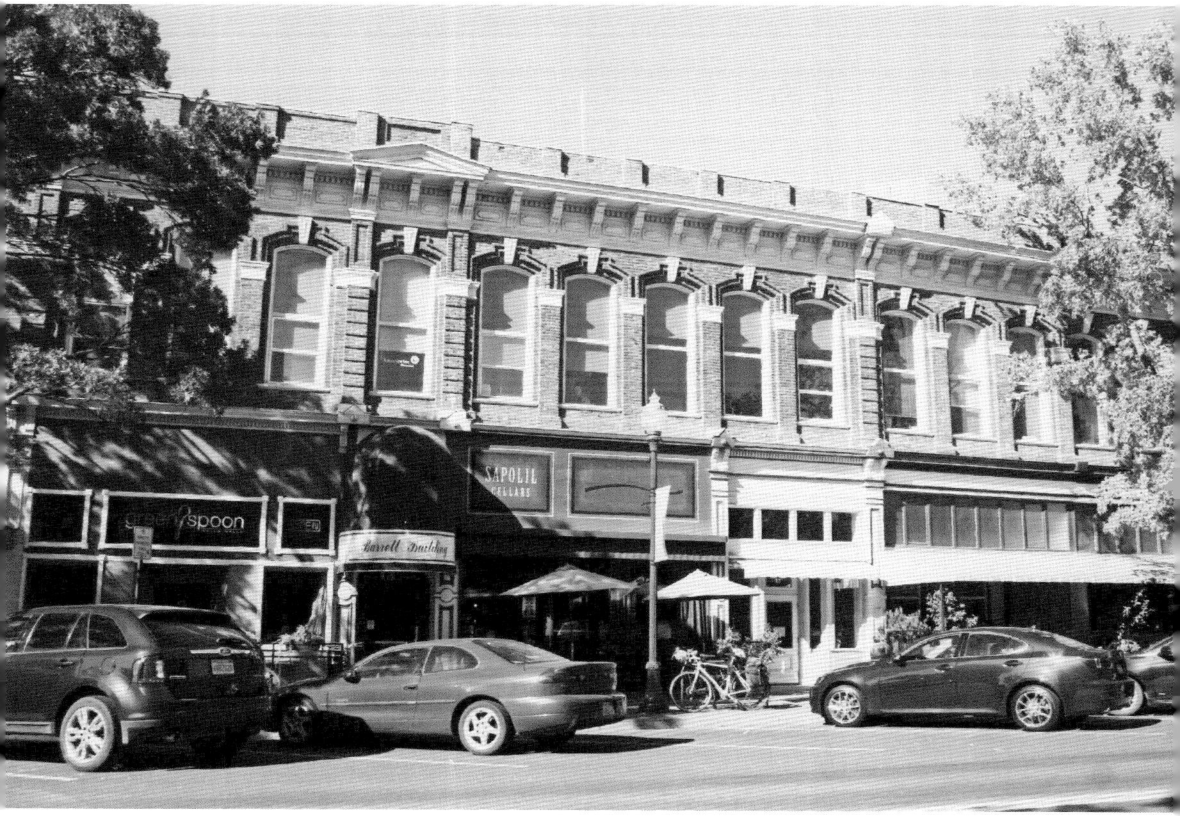

Downtown Walla Walla Foundation

The Walla Walla Main Street Foundation was formed in 1984 to promote the city's downtown. But in the late 1980s, the announcement of the construction of a suburban mall resulted in a wake-up call for the group. With an aging infrastructure and deteriorating properties, the downtown was in no position to compete with the new Blue Mountain Mall. Fortunately, a group of city and grassroots organizations took on the task of revitalizing downtown Walla Walla. The nonprofit Walla Walla Main Street Foundation became the Downtown Walla Walla Foundation and took on the development and implementation of a downtown revitalization plan. The foundation had broad support from across the community. With the support of 65 percent of the downtown property owners, the city council authorized a Local Improvement District (LID), which assessed property owners in order to fund the $2.7 million needed to upgrade the downtown's infrastructure. Among those who made it all possible were Dick Adams, Peter Brooks, Bruce Buchanan, Tom Campbell, Chuck Cochrane, Tim Copeland, Spud Cundiff, Cheri Davis, Dominick Elia, Bill Fleenor, Libby Frazier, Terry Godbout, Adele Goss, Barry Granger, Pat Gregg, Art Griff, Jeannette Hayner, Brian Jones, Linda Kastning, Bob Martin, Dave McClelland, Nanc Murphy, Larry Nelson, Lonnie Ness, Jennifer Northam, Bill Pancake, Pete Reid, Sally Shafer, Keith Soper, Dwight Van Vleet, and Denny Wagaman. Downtown improvements encouraged property owners and investors to undertake major restorations, resulting in an estimated $10-million investment in downtown properties. An influx of new businesses ensured a bright future for the downtown. In 2002, Walla Walla was named *Sunset* magazine's "Best Main Street in the West." Today, downtown Walla Walla features a rich architectural streetscape and is a vibrant retail and business center for the valley, with a major department store, specialty shops, wine-tasting rooms, restaurants, and boutiques. The Downtown Walla Walla Foundation continues to promote and preserve Walla Walla's charming downtown. (Author photograph.)

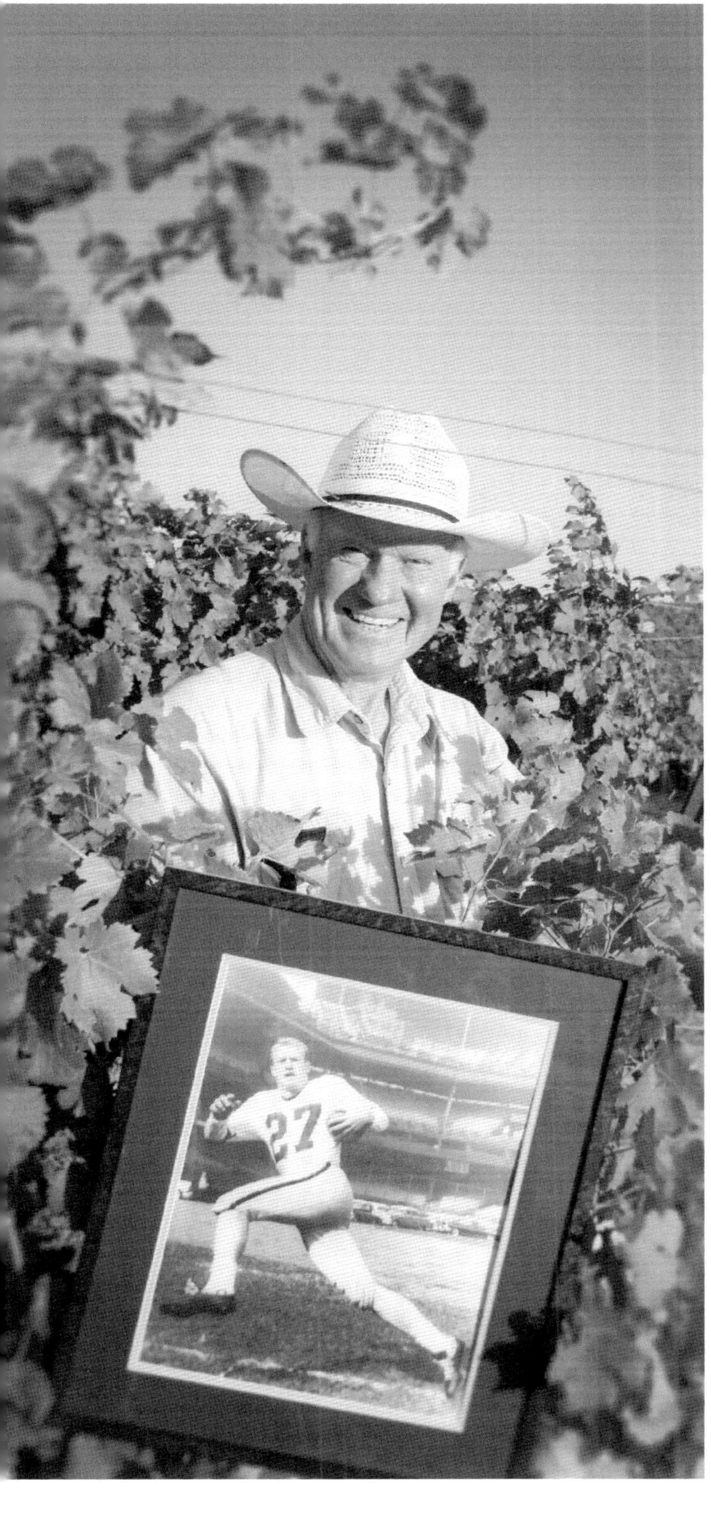

Dean Derby, Walla Walla High School and University of Washington Athlete, NFL Football Player, Spring Valley Wines
Dean Derby and Shari Corkrum met in sixth grade at Sharpstein School in Walla Walla. Derby went on to be an outstanding football player at Walla Walla High School and the University of Washington. He and Shari married in 1954, and in 1956, Derby was drafted into the NFL. He played for the Pittsburgh Steelers (1957–1961) and the Minnesota Vikings (1961–1962). After his football career, Dean and Shari came back to Walla Walla. In 1993, the Derbys planted their first wine grapes on the Corkrum land, which had been in Shari's family since 1910. In 1999, the first wine was produced under the Spring Valley Vineyard label. The Derbys' son Devin Corkrum Derby served as winemaker until his tragic death in 2004. His assistant and friend Serge Laville took over as winemaker, and Spring Valley carried on, winning numerous awards and gaining recognition as a premier Walla Walla Valley winery. (Greg Lehman photograph.)

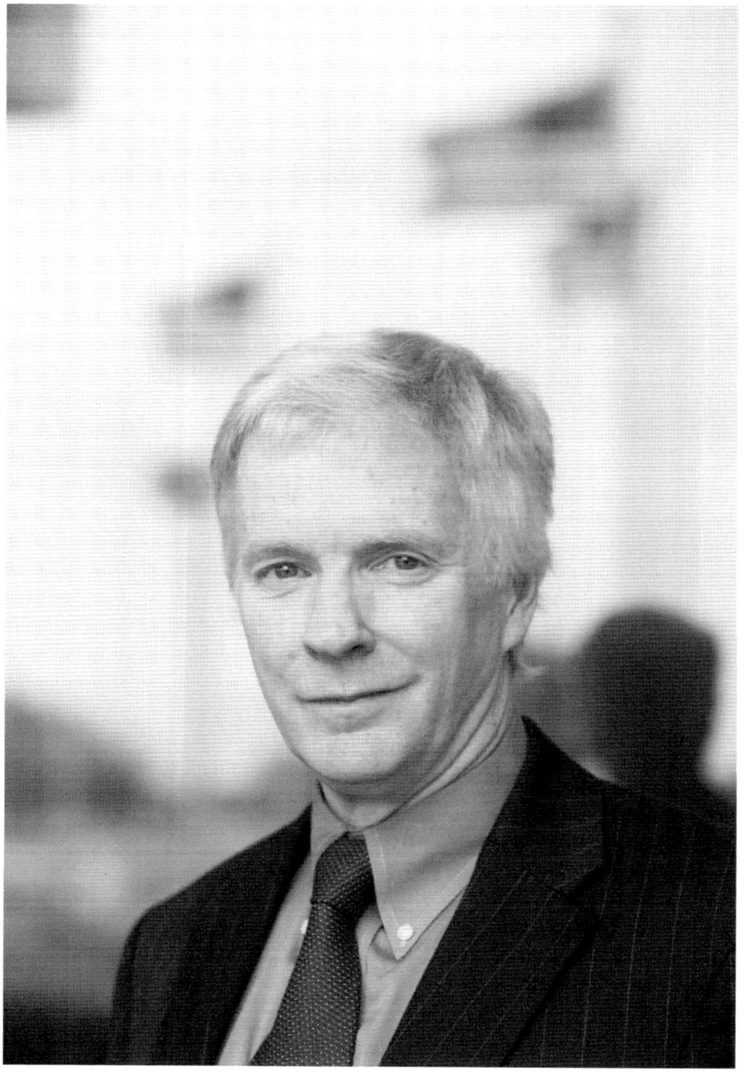

Ryan Crocker, US Ambassador

Ryan Crocker was born in Spokane, Washington, into an Air Force family. He graduated from Whitman College with a bachelor of arts degree in English in 1971 and was awarded an honorary doctor of laws degree from the college in 2001. In 2009, he delivered the commencement address at Whitman. Crocker has maintained an association with the college and currently serves on its board of trustees. He retired in 2009 from a distinguished 37-year career in the US Foreign Service. During his career, he served as ambassador to Lebanon, Kuwait, Syria, Pakistan, and Iraq. He was the deputy assistant secretary of state for Near Eastern affairs from August 2001 to May 2004 and served on the faculty of the National War College from 2003 to 2004. From 2011 to 2012, he served as ambassador to the Islamic Republic of Afghanistan. In 2009, Crocker received the Presidential Medal of Freedom and the State Department's Secretary's Distinguished Service Award. Crocker and his wife, Christine, make their home in Spokane. Crocker is dean and executive professor at the Bush School of Government and Public Service at Texas A&M University and the James Schlesinger Distinguished Visiting Professor at the University of Virginia. He is also a member of the Council on Foreign Relations. (Ian Bradshaw photograph, courtesy of Ryan Crocker.)

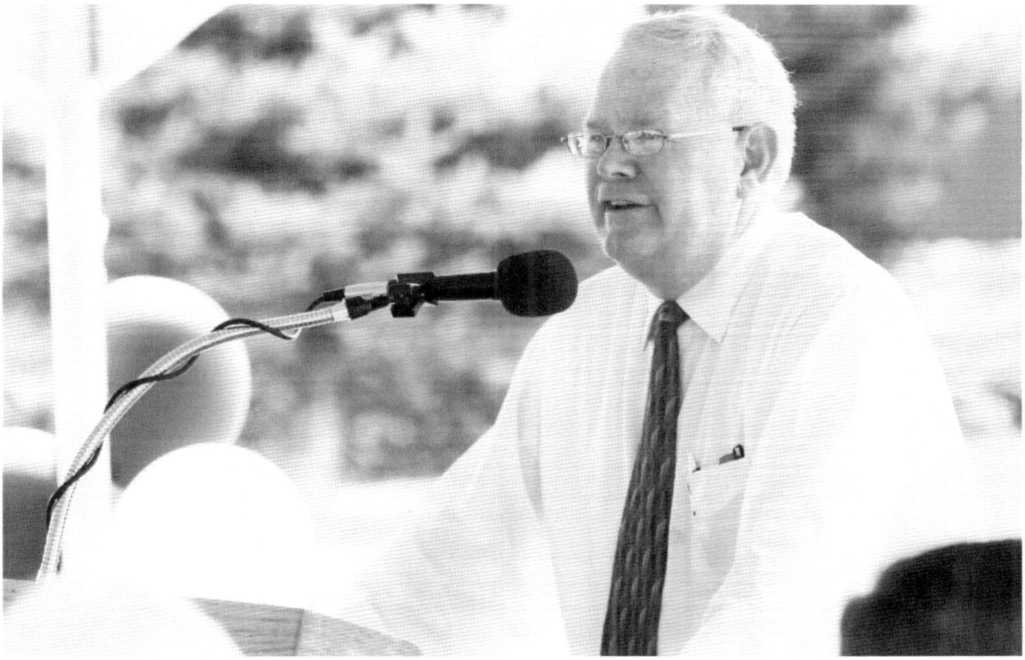

Dr. Steven VanAusdle, Educator and Innovator
Steven VanAusdle is a man of vision. As president of Walla Walla Community College since 1984, he has led a renaissance at the college that earned it the 2013 Aspen Institute College Excellence Award and many other honors. A native of Pomeroy, Washington, VanAusdle has pioneered innovative programs like the college's enology (wine) and viticulture program, energy systems technology (geared toward the wind turbine industry), and the Wine Country Culinary Institute. Partnerships with companies like John Deere provide training that ensures the employability of students. Academic and skills-training programs prepare students for jobs and further education. (Courtesy of Walla Walla Community College Media.)

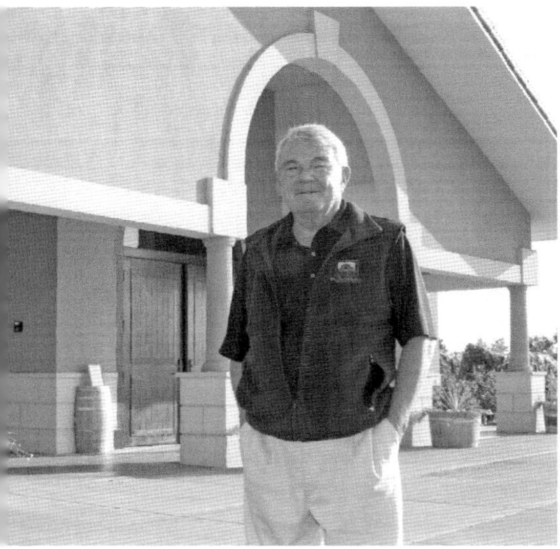

Myles Anderson, Legend of Washington Wine
Myles Anderson was inducted into the Legends of Washington Wine Hall of Fame in 2011, recognizing his role as a winemaker and as the founding director of Walla Walla Community College's Center for Enology and Viticulture. Established in 2000, it was the first official wine school in Washington State. Anderson is also the cofounder and winemaker of Walla Walla Vintners with partner Gordon Venneri. Anderson, who still consults with WWCC's College Cellars, received a Lifetime Achievement Award from the Washington Association of Wine Grape Growers in 2014 for his service to the industry and to the college's enology and viticulture program. (Courtesy of Walla Walla Community College Media.)

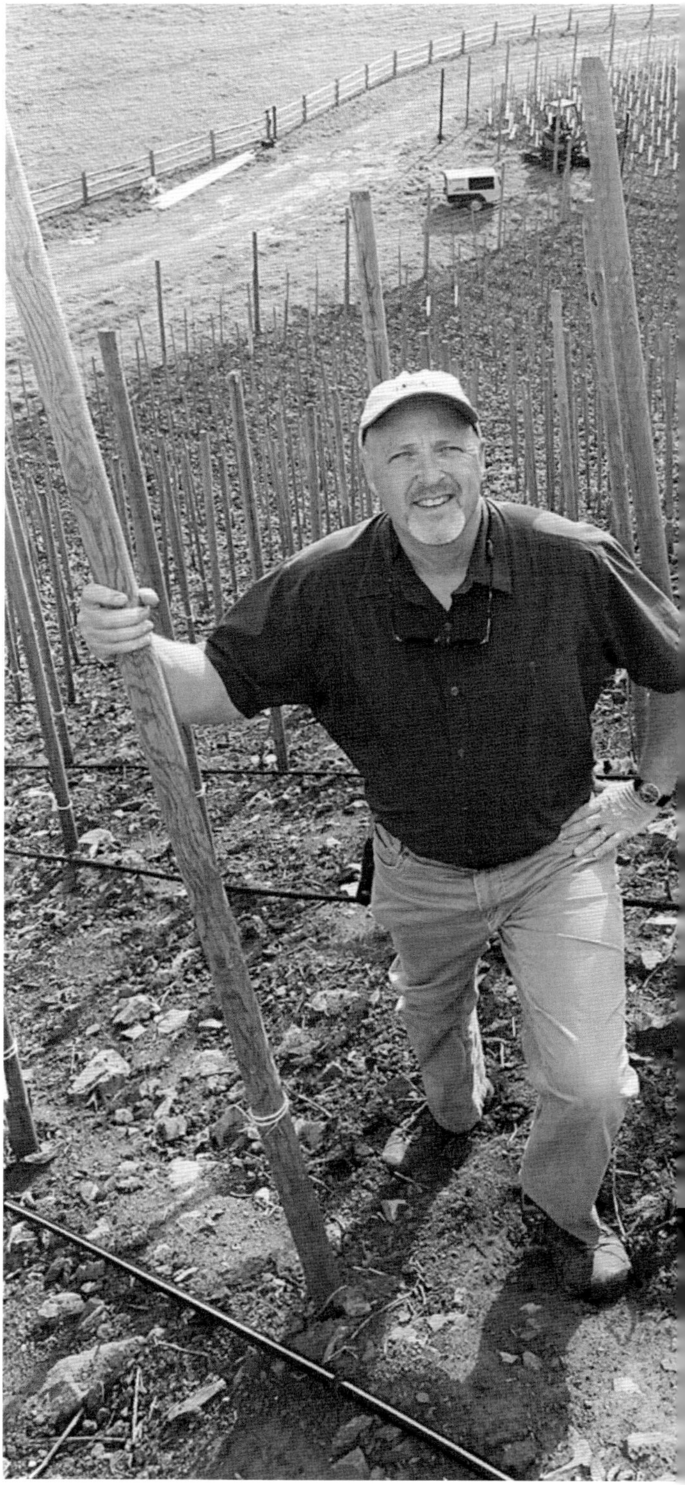

Dr. Kevin Pogue, Whitman Professor and Terroir Specialist

Terroir is an important factor in the production of great wines. Often spoken of in hushed tones, terroir is the combination of soil, altitude, terrain, and climate that can produce the best wines in the hands of a skilled winemaker. Dr. Kevin Pogue, a geology professor at Whitman College, is renowned for his knowledge of the intricate geological peculiarities of the Walla Walla Valley and Columbia Basin. He is sought out for advice on selecting the right location for vineyards—the perfect terroir. Dr. Pogue's research on terroir concentrates on the relationship between topography, vineyard temperature variations, and the influence of basalt—eastern Washington's bedrock—on the climate and soil chemistry of Columbia River Basin vineyards. Working with his students, Pogue also established a network of temperature monitors in the valley, looking for parcels of land that might produce the next great wine. He is often out in the field downloading temperature data or at the bottom of a backhoe trench with trowel and sample bags. Pogue regularly contributes lectures on terroir to the enology and viticulture programs at Washington State University and Walla Walla Community College. He has presented papers at national and international terroir conferences and authored a field trip guide that describes the geological influences on the terroir of the Columbia Basin. His essay on the relationship of the Ice Age Missoula floods to Columbia Basin viticulture appears in the book *Washington: The State of Wine*. (Greg Lehman photograph, courtesy of Whitman College.)

Charles Smith, Winemaker

After nine years managing rock bands in Scandinavia, California native Charles Smith moved back to the United States in 1999. He decided to pursue the passion for wine he had developed while touring, opening a wine shop on Bainbridge Island, Washington. On a road trip later that year, Smith passed through Walla Walla, met a winemaker who shared his love of great Syrahs, and soon took up residence in the valley. In 2001, he released his first wine, a 1999 K Syrah, and launched his winemaking enterprise. In 2004, he initiated his House Wine label (he could not believe no one had trademarked the name), which he sold several years later to Precept Brands. He added a second brand, Charles Smith Wines, which concentrates on wines to fit what today's consumers want—a bottle that they can serve immediately and that is available at an accessible price. His joint venture with Charles Bieler, Charles & Charles, and their signature Rosé and red blend, has added another dimension to his offerings. Smith's wines and his winery have won numerous awards. In 2008, *Wine and Spirits* magazine named K Vintners one of the best new wineries and Winery of the Year in its annual buying guide. Smith was named Winemaker of the Year by *Food and Wine* magazine (2009) and by *Seattle Magazine* (2010). Smith's downtown Walla Walla tasting room, designed by Seattle architects Olson Kundig, and his graphic black-and-white labels, designed by Rikke Korff, show off his edgy style and outside-the-box approach. (Karen Stanton photograph, courtesy of Charles Smith Wines.)

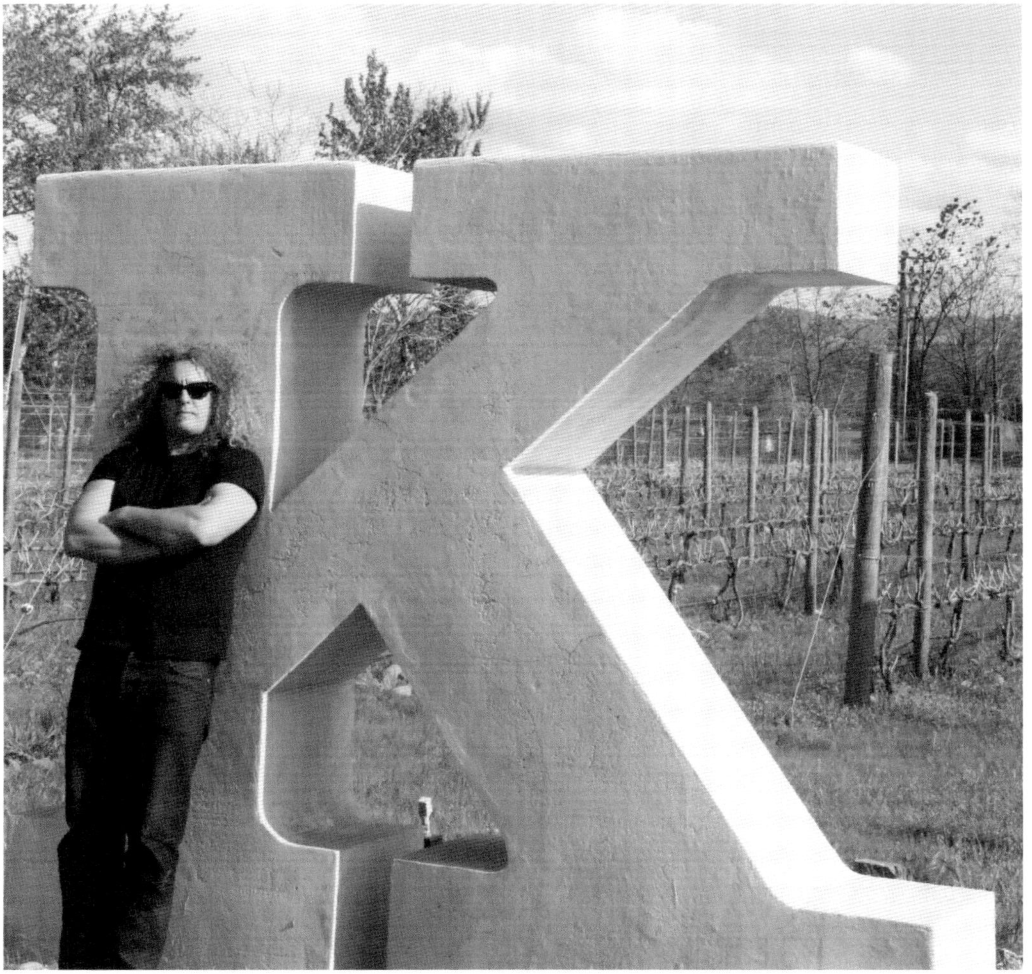

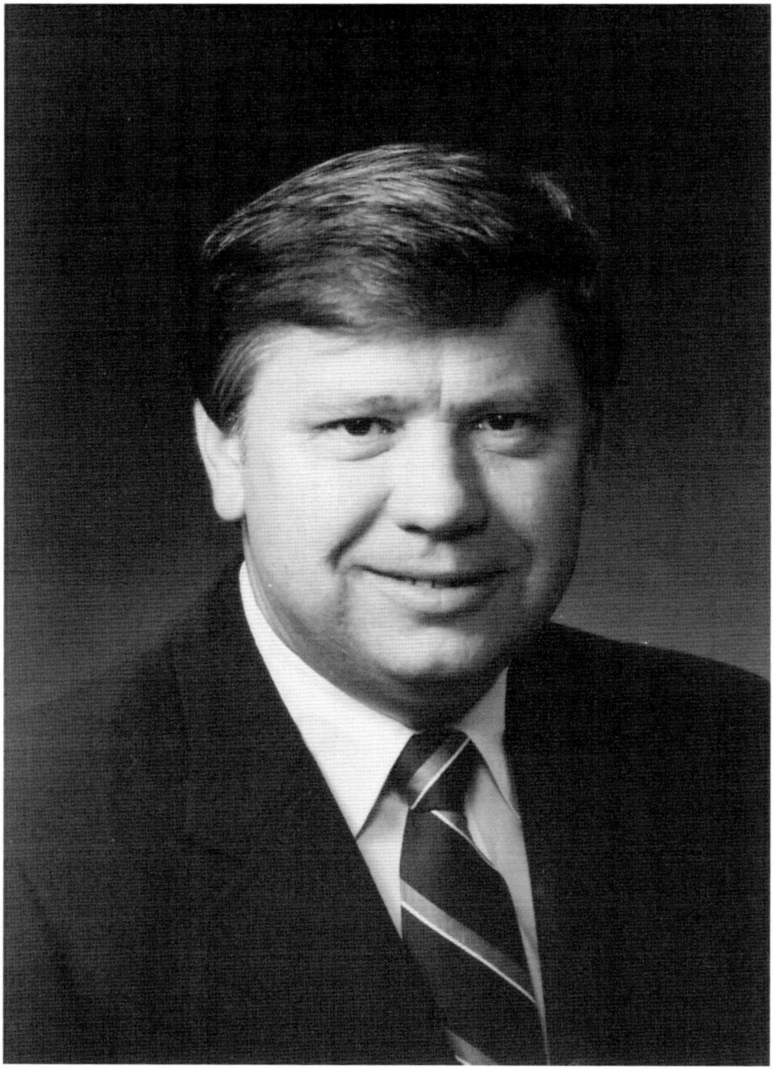

Robert A. Bennett, Businessman, Historian, and Author
Robert Bennett, a native of Walla Walla, is a 1968 graduate of Whitman College with a degree in history. Bennett, owner of Clarette's restaurant, is the founder of Pioneer Press, Inc., which published a number of important historical works under its subsidiary Pioneer Press Books, including J.A. Eckrom's *Remembered Drums: A History of the Puget Sound Indian War*, Charles Convis's *Pioneer Women*, and his own *We'll All Go Home in the Spring: Personal Accounts and Adventures as Told by the Pioneers of the West.* He published a number of books by longtime *Union-Bulletin* journalist Vance Orchard, including *Life on the Dry Side* and *Just Rambling Around Blue Mountain Country.* Bennett has written about Walla Walla's heritage in *Walla Walla: Portrait of a Western Town, 1804–1899*, *Walla Walla: A Town Built to be a City, 1900–1919*, and *Walla Walla: A Nice Place to Raise a Family, 1920–1949.* He also authored a book on the centennial history of the Walla Walla YMCA and *The Bohemians.* Active in the community, Bennett has promoted Walla Walla through the chamber of commerce and is active in the Living History Company at Fort Walla Walla Museum, often portraying Col. Michael McCarthy (see page 19), the Fort Walla Walla soldier who received the Congressional Medal of Honor. (Courtesy of Robert Bennett.)

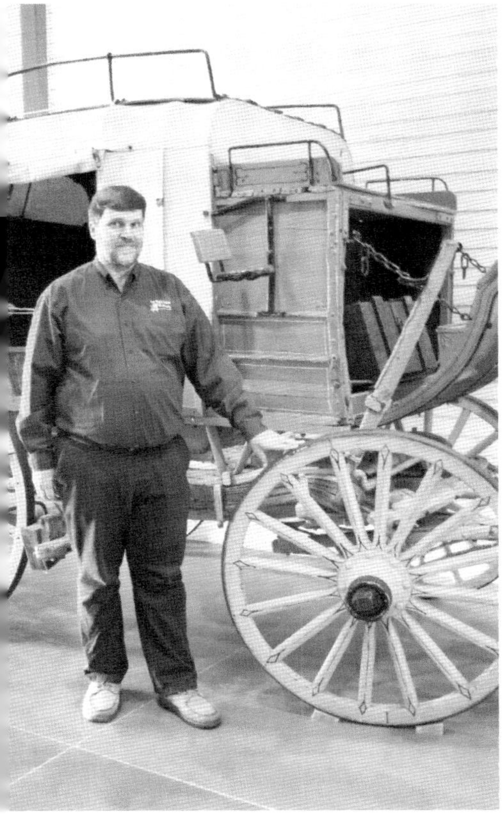

James Payne, Executive Director of Fort Walla Walla Museum

James Payne (left) believes "museum work is a great way to share [his] passion for the discovery, preservation, and sharing of our heritage." He enthusiastically promotes the historical richness of Walla Walla through exhibits, programs, and publications. Since he joined the museum in 1996, it has received over $4 million in grants and community support and has undergone a major expansion in facilities and programs. Payne has also increased its operating revenues by performing cultural resources work for regional development projects. Payne has won numerous awards for his publications, museum initiatives, and wide-ranging community involvement. (Author photograph.)

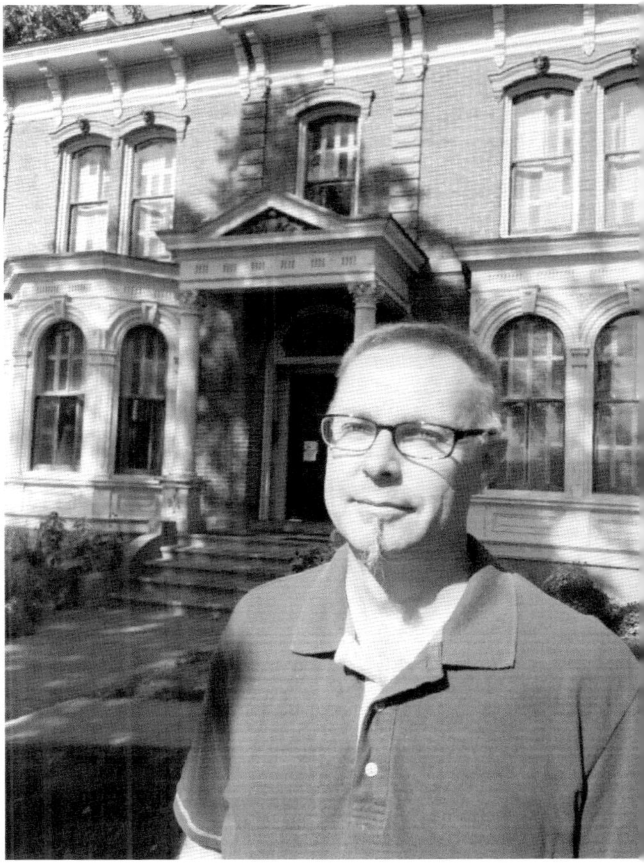

Rick Tuttle, President of Kirkman House Museum

After returning to his hometown in 2001, Rick Tuttle (right) was asked to join the Kirkman House Museum board. He has been a member for 11 of the last 12 years, holding every office at least once. Kirkman House, listed in the National Register of Historic Places, is one of the Northwest's finest Victorian homes, known for its elegant interior. A museum since 1981, Kirkman House holds a number of special events and exhibits, including a Victorian Christmas and a Roaring Twenties exhibit. Tuttle finds sharing Walla Walla's history a great opportunity to meet people from all around the world. (Courtesy of Kirkman House Museum.)

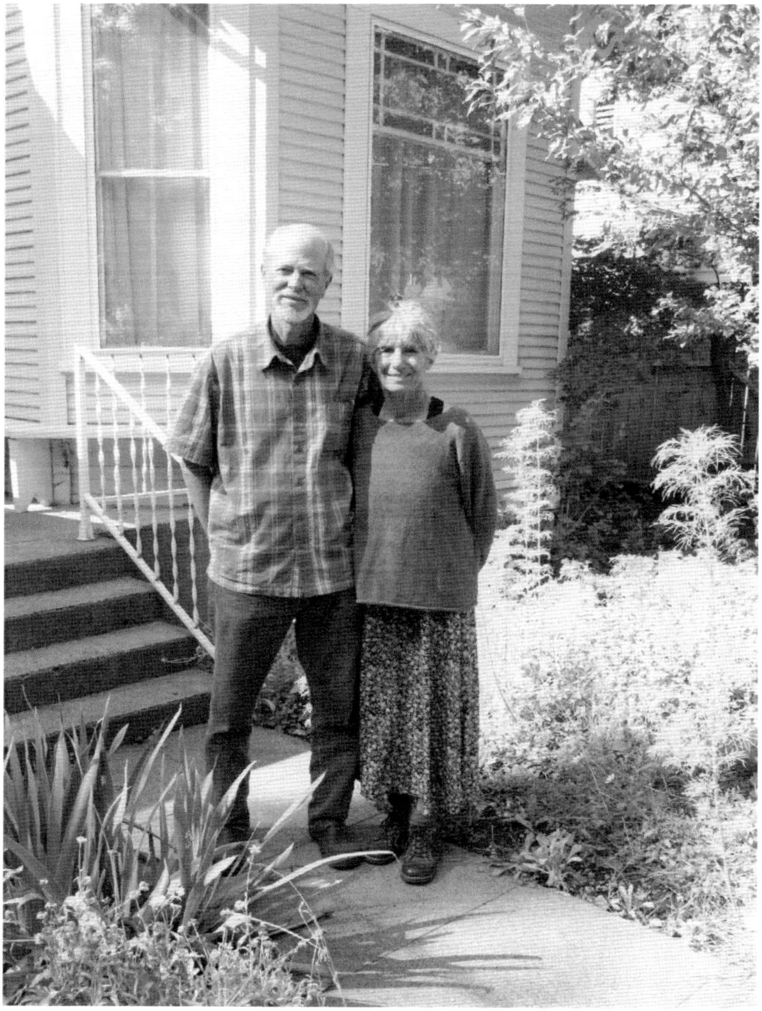

Dan and Barbara Clark, Community Activists

In many communities, there are people who immediately come to mind when one considers community leadership and service. In Walla Walla, Dan and Barbara Clark are two of those people. Barbara, who serves on city council, was first elected in 1997 and also served as mayor from 2010 to 2012. She advocated for tax incentives for owners who restore their buildings, tourism initiatives, the downtown farmers' market, and a small-business development center. Dan, a retired attorney, has a broad range of interests, including "global changes, local history, criminal justice reform, sustainable communities, human rights, peace, contra dancing, and contemplation." He actively served on the Walla Walla Sesquicentennial Committee and is on the board of the Frenchtown Historical Foundation in addition to his involvement in a variety of other local nonprofits. In 1988, Dan and Barbara were instrumental in the formation of Walla Walla 2020, a citizens group that seeks to envision a livable future for the city (in the year 2020 and beyond) and works to realize that vision. Among the group's successes have been a recycling program, bike lanes, historic preservation, landscaping, and economic development. In 1998, the Clarks organized Fort Walla Walla Museum's Living History Company, and they often portray E.B. Whitman, the first mayor of Walla Walla, and his wife, Maria. Callers for the Walla Walla Friends of Acoustic Music, the Clarks also lead and teach contra, square, and circle dancing. (Author photograph.)

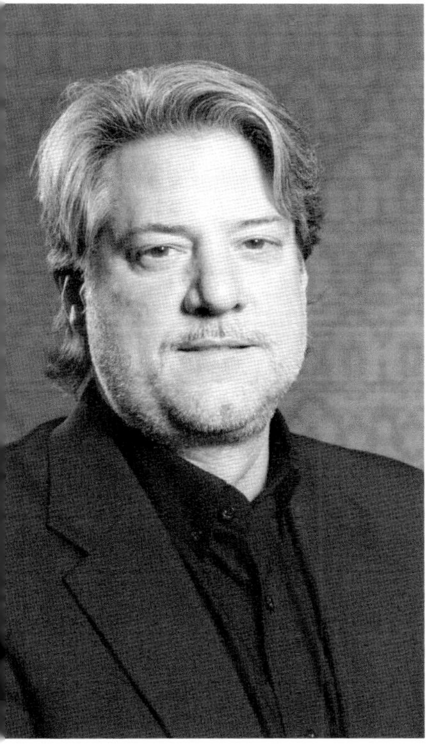

Kyle Mussman, Owner of the Marcus Whitman Hotel
Kyle Mussman, a successful technology entrepreneur, chose to put his resources into restoring the 1927 Marcus Whitman Hotel. The grand hotel, which had fallen on hard times, was returned to its original grandeur and expanded in 1999 at a cost of $35 million. Mussman and project architect Fletcher Farr Ayotte received a 2002 state award for outstanding achievements in historic preservation. With the restoration and the addition of a new conference center and ballroom, the hotel became a premier destination for wine tourists, conferences, and discerning travelers. (Courtesy of Marcus Whitman Hotel.)

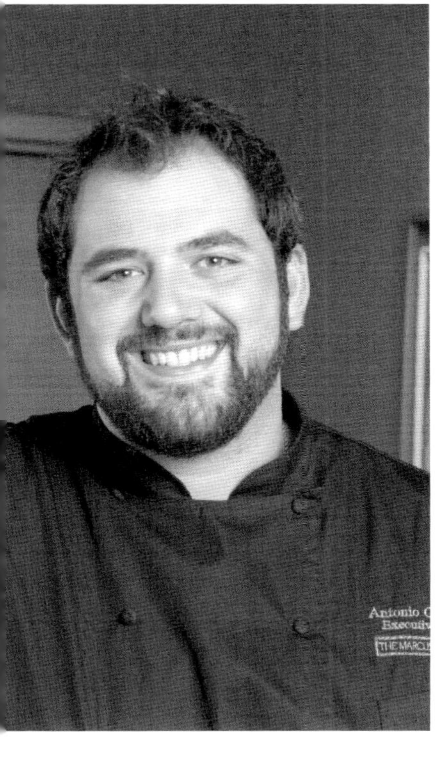

Antonio Campolio, Executive Chef at the Marcus Whitman Hotel
Antonio Campolio, named executive chef at the Marcus Whitman Hotel in 2011, has a long and distinguished résumé. His culinary pursuits began when he worked at his family's restaurant, Tavern 1785, in Fairlea, West Virginia. Subsequently, he was at the Greenbrier Hotel in White Sulphur Springs, West Virginia, and the Broadmoor Hotel in Colorado. Campolio's chef's table dinners, set in the hotel's kitchen so he can interact with guests, are a popular draw. In December 2012, Campolio was asked to create a Walla Walla–themed meal—complete with Walla Walla wines—at the James Beard House in New York. (Courtesy of Marcus Whitman Hotel.)

Jamie Guerin, Chef and Co-Owner of Whitehouse-Crawford Restaurant

Chef Jamie Guerin was a pioneer in the recent culinary renaissance of Walla Walla. In 2000, he became chef of the new Whitehouse-Crawford Restaurant in the old planing mill (see page 65) lovingly restored by Carl and Sonia Schmitt. At the time, Walla Walla's fledgling wine country amounted to less than 30 wineries. Thanks to Guerin and his emphasis on regional cuisine and local wine, Whitehouse-Crawford set an early example for the Walla Walla Valley's reputation for showcasing locally produced food and wines. (Courtesy of Whitehouse-Crawford Restaurant.)

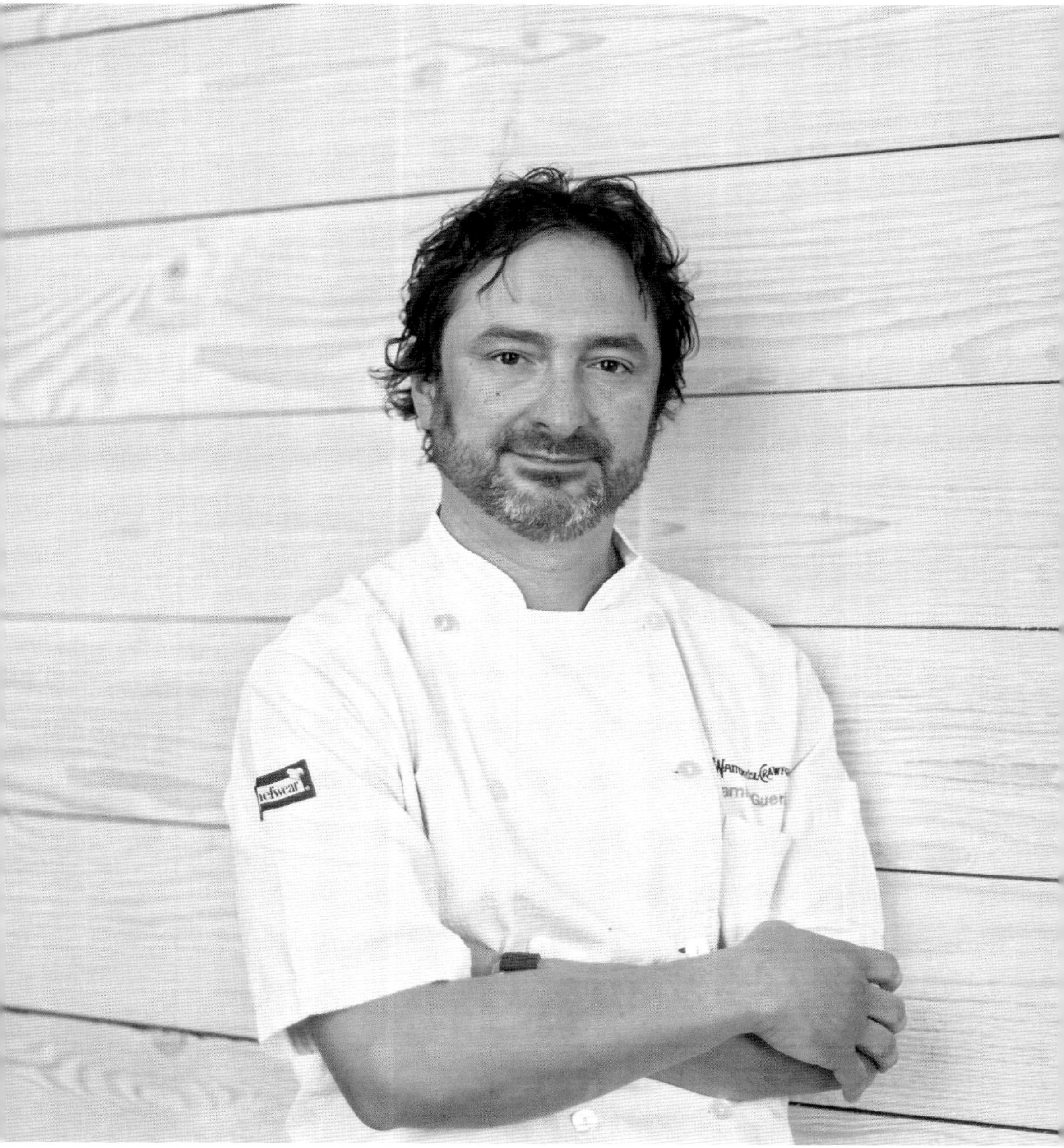

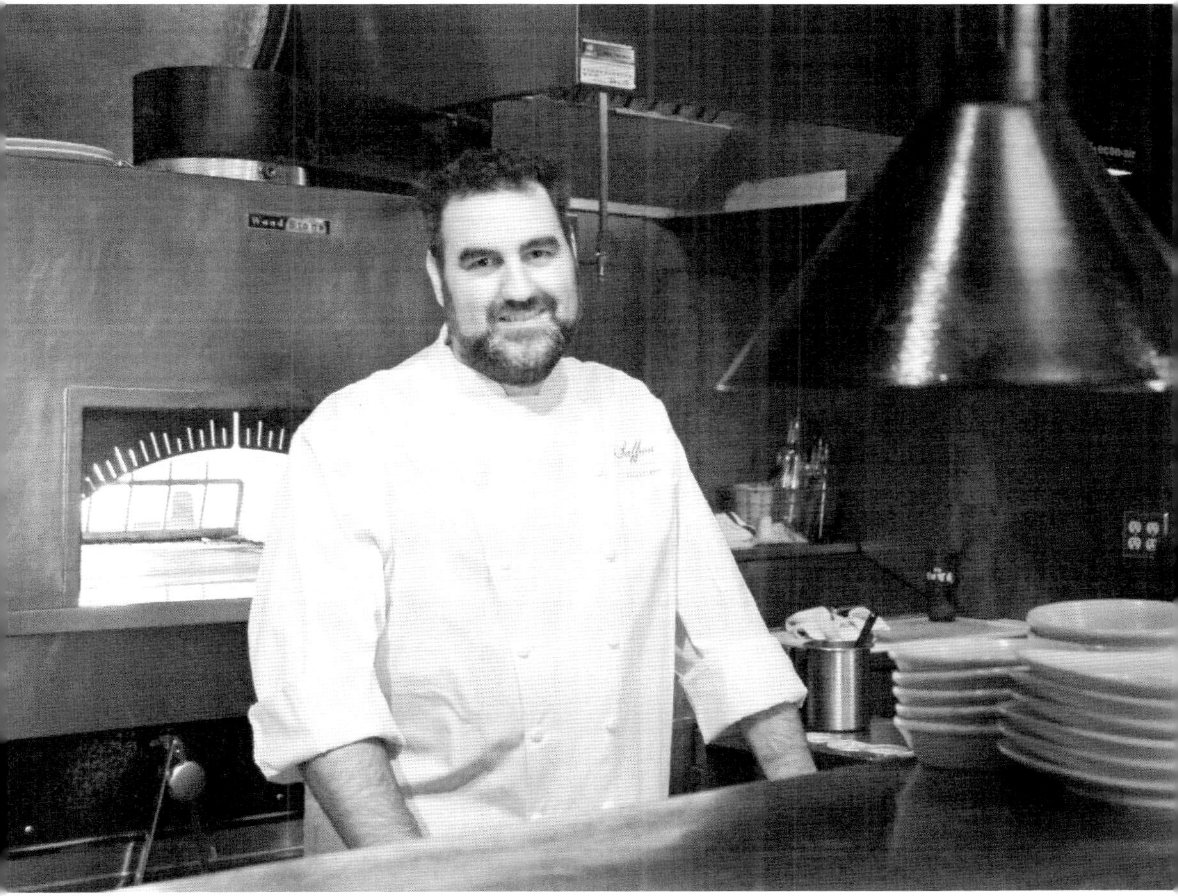

Chris Ainsworth, Chef and Co-Owner at Saffron Mediterranean Kitchen
Chris Ainsworth was introduced to Walla Walla in 2004 and fell in love with Washington Wine Country and the Blue Mountains. Friends who lived in the area encouraged him and his wife, Island, to relocate. The couple opened Saffron Mediterranean Kitchen in 2007 and quickly added a second restaurant next door, Pho Sho Vietnamese Noodles. A graduate of the French Culinary Institute, Ainsworth was also nominated six times for the James Beard Award for Best Chef Northwest. (Author photograph.)

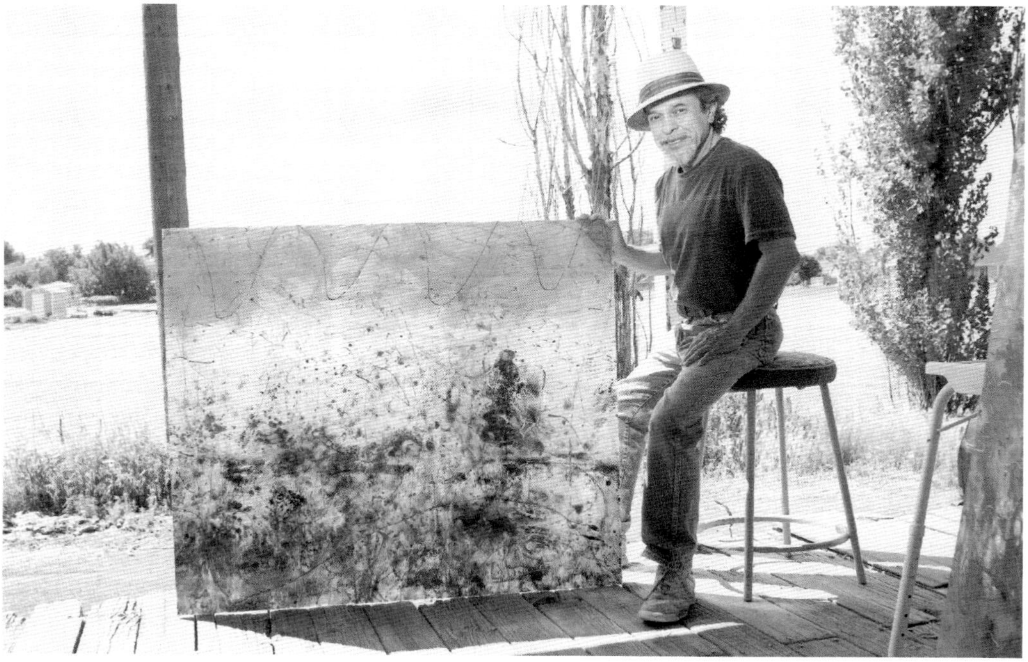

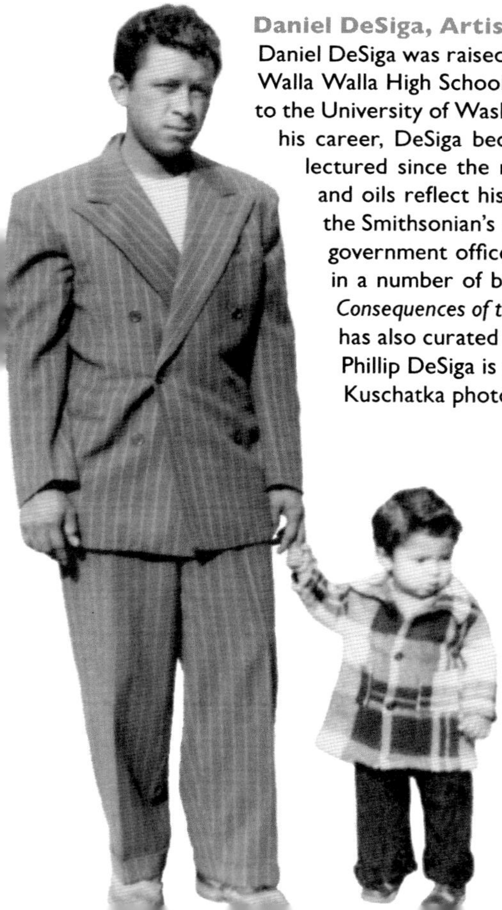

Daniel DeSiga, Artist

Daniel DeSiga was raised in Walla Walla, the son of farmworkers. After graduating from Walla Walla High School in 1967, he spent two years in the Marine Corps before going to the University of Washington, where he earned a bachelor of fine arts degree. During his career, DeSiga became an artist of national importance, and he has taught and lectured since the mid-1970s. Noted for his strong images, his murals, graphics, and oils reflect his Latino and American Indian roots. His works are included in the Smithsonian's National Museum of American Art, and his murals hang in state government offices across Washington State. His paintings have been published in a number of books, and his work appears on the cover of *Culture Y Cultura: Consequences of the U.S.-Mexican War, 1846-1848*. A prolific and diverse artist, he has also curated exhibits in Seattle and designed costumes for operas and plays. Phillip DeSiga is pictured at left with his son, Daniel, about 1951. (Above, Colby Kuschatka photograph; left, courtesy of Daniel DeSiga.)

Jeana Garske, ArtWalla

ArtWalla was founded more than 20 years ago and has been a force in the Walla Walla art scene ever since. Originally known as the Blue Mountain Arts Alliance, the organization changed its name to ArtWalla in 2005. Jeana Garske, one of the founders, also served the organization as executive director from 2001 to 2011. ArtWalla has had a significant impact on the community, starting with the development of a city Arts Collection Management ordinance allowing for public art projects. In 1997, the organization undertook a large public art installation in Heritage Square on Main Street—*Windows on the Past*—utilizing window apertures in the salvaged facade of the former Odd Fellows building to display photographs of cultural groups that enriched Walla Walla throughout its history. Garske is pictured here at the dedication. In 2012, ArtWalla received a grant from the Sherwood Trust to fund an art project for Walla Walla's sesquicentennial. After reviewing proposals and gathering public input, the organization chose a sculpture by local artist Squire Broel titled *Looking Back, Looking Forward* (page 124), which was installed in Heritage Park on Main Street. ArtWalla, which reorganized as an all-volunteer organization in 2012, continues to advocate for a strong local arts community that includes public art, arts education, and vibrant events. (Wayne Chabre photograph.)

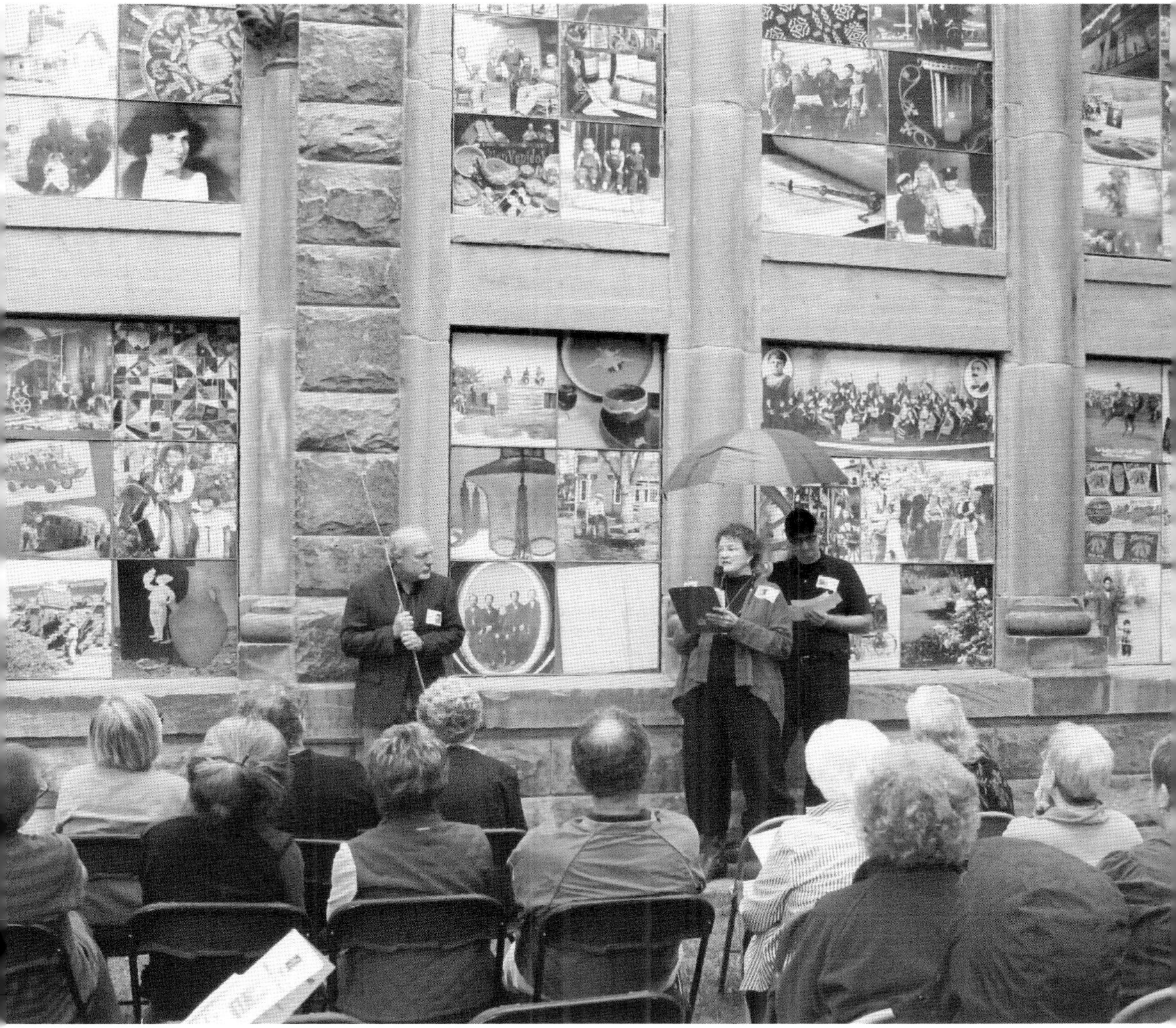

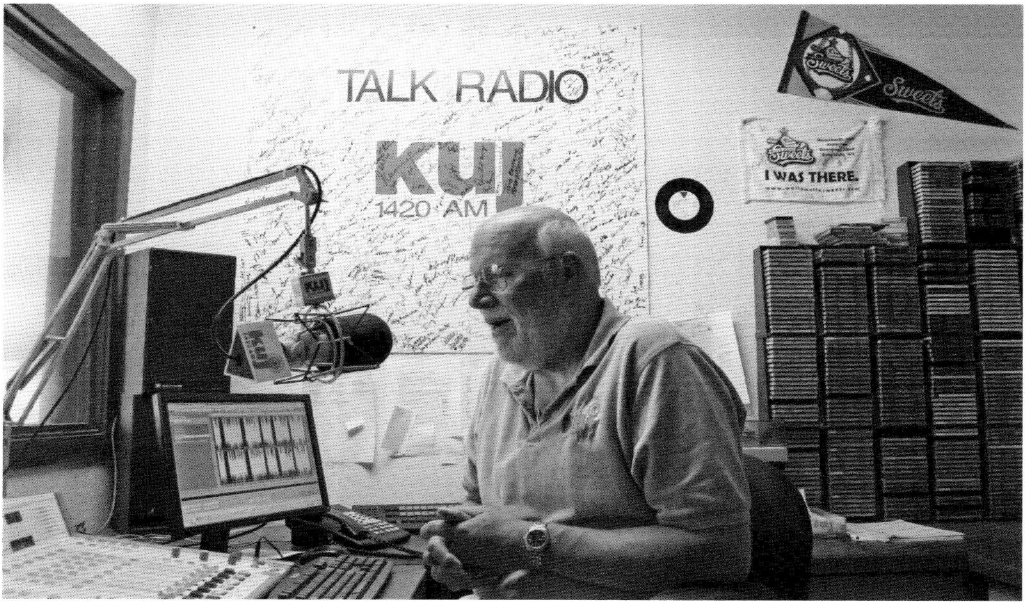

Jim Bock, Local Radio Personality

Local radio personality Jim Bock (above) began his on-air career in 1979. Bock attended Walla Walla University and did advanced studies at San Diego University. He has strong experience in cable television and marketing. His background in communications and drama led Bock to theatrical stages in Walla Walla, Portland, Spokane, and London. He has been active in the Little Theatre of Walla Walla as both actor and director. Known as "the voice of the valley," Bock is noted for his informative and entertaining interviews with locals and visitors to the valley on his KUJ radio show, *Walla Walla Live*. (Author photograph.)

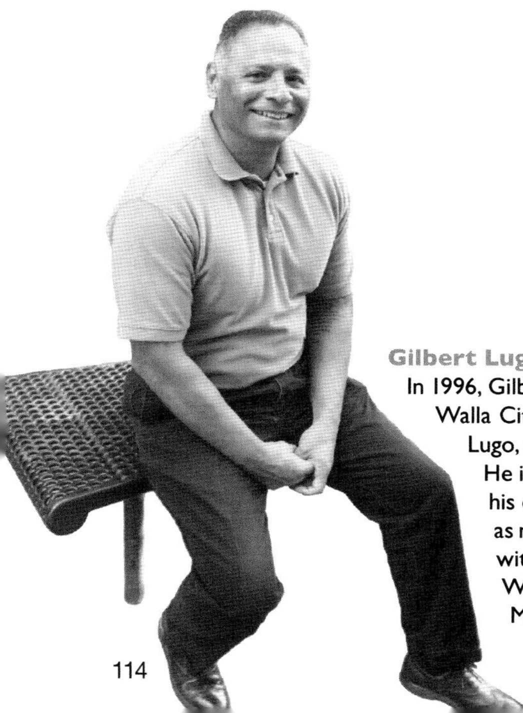

Gilbert Lugo, First Latino City Councilor, Mayor

In 1996, Gilbert Lugo (left) was appointed to a vacant position on the Walla Walla City Council, becoming the first Latino to serve on the council. Lugo, a Coast Guard veteran, was motivated by his sense of civic duty. He is proud of his Latino heritage but was committed to serving all his constituents. He was elected to his seat in 1997, and he served as mayor from 2004 to 2005. During his tenure as mayor, he joined with the city council, city manager, county commissioners, and Washington's US senators to keep the Jonathan M. Wainwright Memorial VA Medical Center open. (Author photograph.)

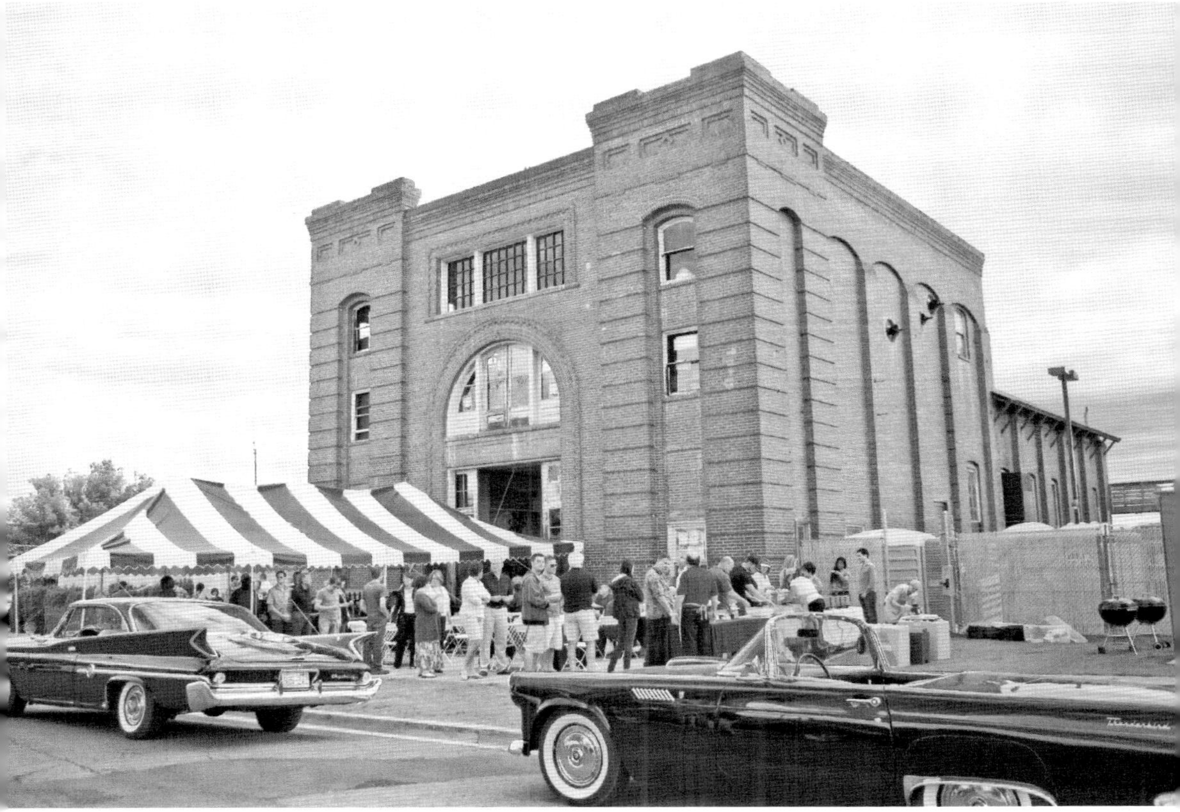

Power House Theatre

The Gesa Power House Theatre is located in the Walla Walla Gas Plant. The 120-year-old building was originally a coal gas plant, producing and piping the gas underground to light Walla Walla. In 1905, the plant was retrofitted with steam-driven dynamos to generate electricity. Current owners Mark Anderson, Dennis Ledford, Ken Harrison, and Harry Hosey converted the imposing vacant building into a theater in 2011. The building's exterior was restored, and the interior was transformed into a 368-seat performing arts center. The owners discovered the building was almost an exact match in size to Shakespeare's Blackfriars Theatre in London, inspiring the new theater's design. The Power House was listed in the National Register of Historic Places in 2012. The theater stages professional theatrical performances, including Shakespeare Walla Walla, as well as concerts and other entertainment and community events. (Courtesy of Gesa Power House Theatre.)

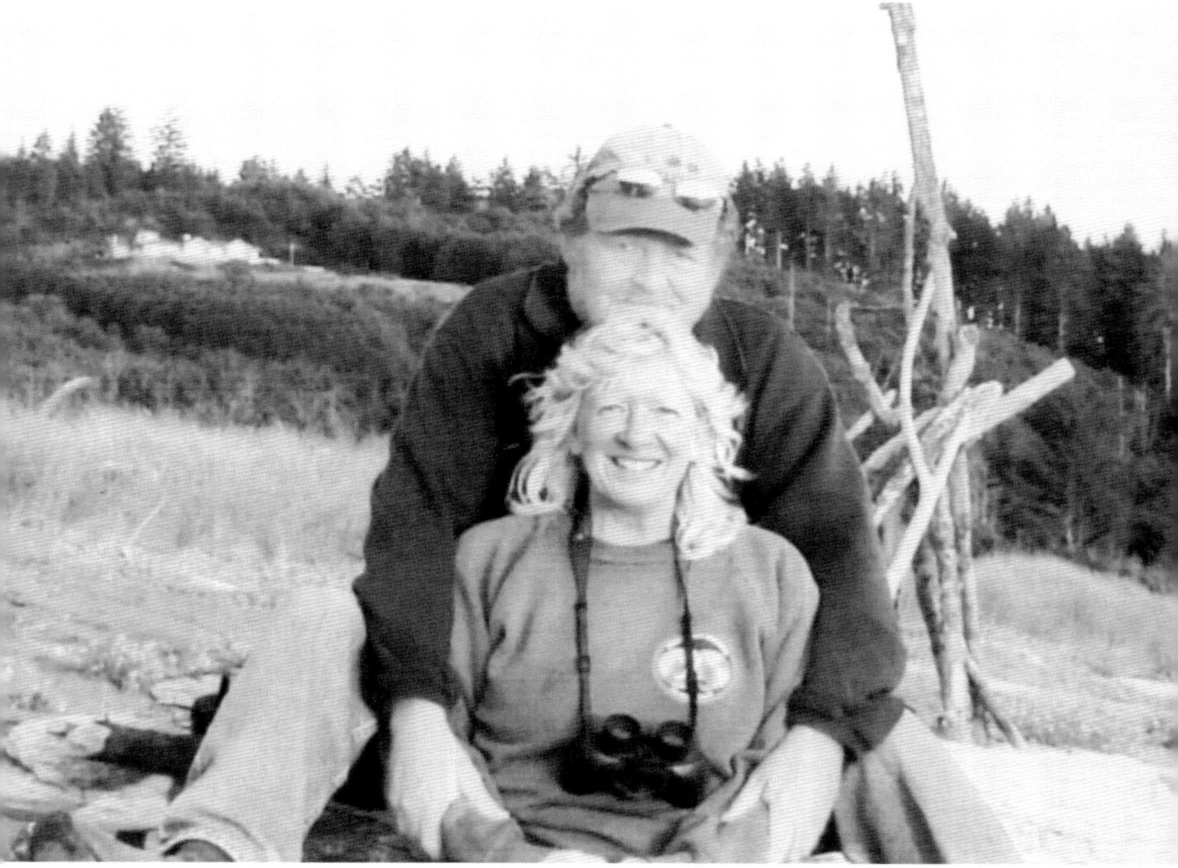

Mike and MerryLynn Denny, Blue Mountain Audubon Society
Walla Walla Valley residents know that upon seeing a rare or unidentifiable bird, Mike and MerryLynn Denny are the people to call. Mike came to the valley in 1979. He worked for the US Forest Service and Walla Walla County Conservation District and currently works for the Pomeroy Conservation District. MerryLynn came to Walla Walla in 1984, and the couple married in 1987. They are active in Blue Mountain Audubon Society (BMAS); Mike served as president several times, MerryLynn has served as treasurer, and the couple have organized the Audubon Christmas Bird Count for the valley for more than 10 years. But they are best known for leading popular field trips for BMAS and the Washington Ornithological Society in search of a wide variety of bird species—both rare and common. Mike has taught popular classes on birding and natural history at Walla Walla Community College's Quest program for 15 years, coauthored *Birds of the Inland Northwest and Northern Rockies*, and writes a monthly wildlife column for the Walla Walla *Union-Bulletin*. (Courtesy of Mike and MerryLynn Denny.)

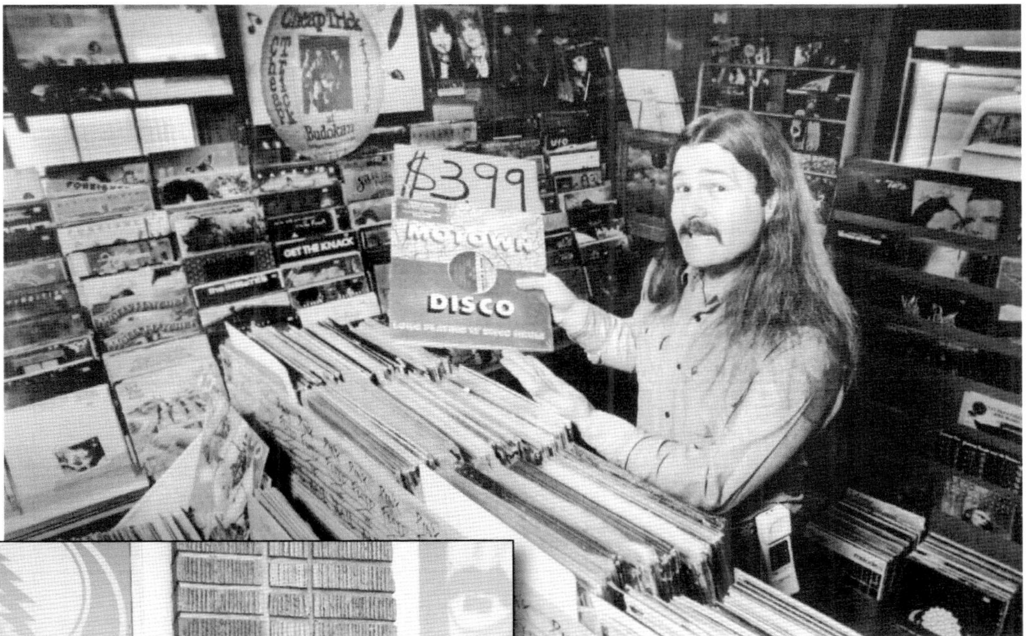

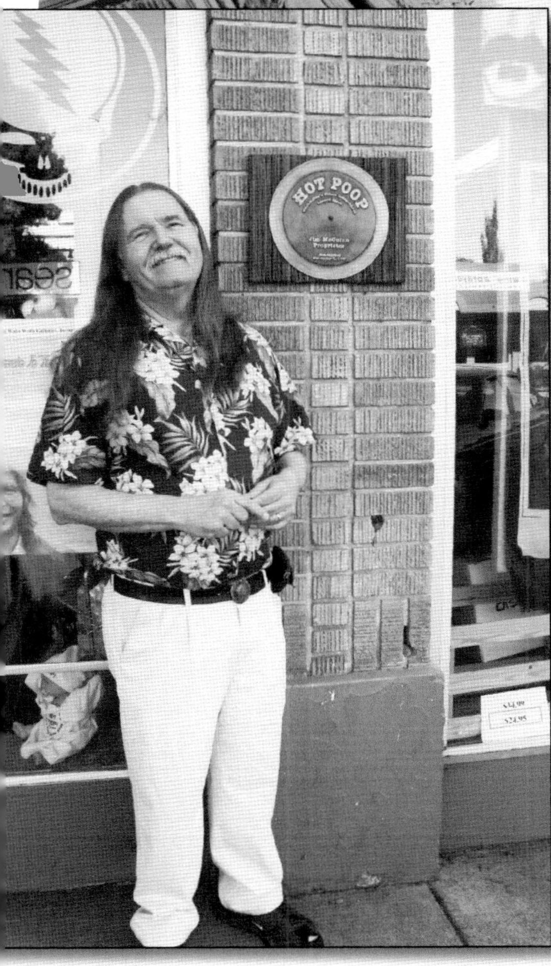

Jim McGuinn, Hot Poop, Washington's Oldest Independent Record Store
Jim McGuinn hardly thought of becoming an institution when he opened his record store in Walla Walla on November 5, 1973. Now, Hot Poop is the oldest independent record store in Washington State. McGuinn, born in Guam, started out in business in San Diego before moving to Walla Walla. Although the store's name (a riff on "Hot Pop") did not go over well with some of the locals in the beginning, it and its proprietor have become a downtown mainstay. Hot Poop evolved over the years and now sells vinyl, CDs, DVDs, televisions, and music memorabilia. Band posters, T-shirts, banners, and ephemera round out the store's eclectic mix. Music greets visitors from the sidewalk and ranges from classic pop to cutting-edge rock. McGuinn confesses that there is very little that he does not like musically. He is also a strong supporter of local musicians. McGuinn is a treasure trove of knowledge about music and musicians, and his stories detailing the early days of the store keep visitors fascinated. After almost 40 years of business, he has not lost his enthusiasm for music and everything related to it. (Above, courtesy of Jim McGuinn; left, author photograph.)

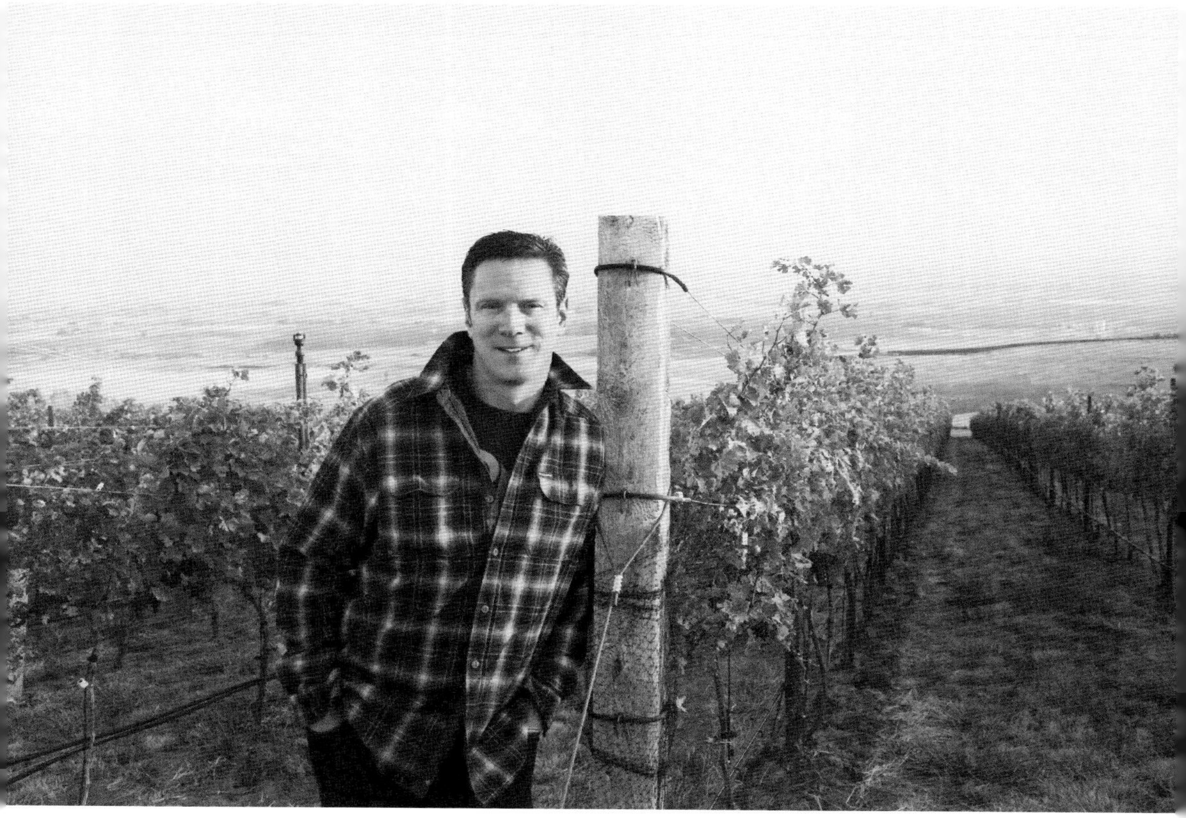

Drew Bledsoe, Quarterback and Winery Owner

Drew Bledsoe attended Walla Walla High School, where he lettered in football and basketball. He was an outstanding quarterback during his three years (1990–1992) at Washington State University. He was picked as an All-American and was named the 1992 PAC-10 offensive player of the year. Forgoing his senior year, Bledsoe was drafted by the New England Patriots, where he played quarterback until 2001. He later played for the Buffalo Bills and Dallas Cowboys before retiring in 2007. Bledsoe continued his ties to the Walla Walla Valley through his wine project, Doubleback. The name pays homage to his return to his roots. He has teamed up with local winemaker and childhood friend Chris Figgins of Figgins Family Wine Estates and Leonetti Cellar to make exceptional Cabernet Sauvignon. Doubleback's first release, a 2007 Cabernet Sauvignon, made the *Wine Spectator* Top 100 list. (Andrea Johnson photograph, courtesy of Doubleback Winery.)

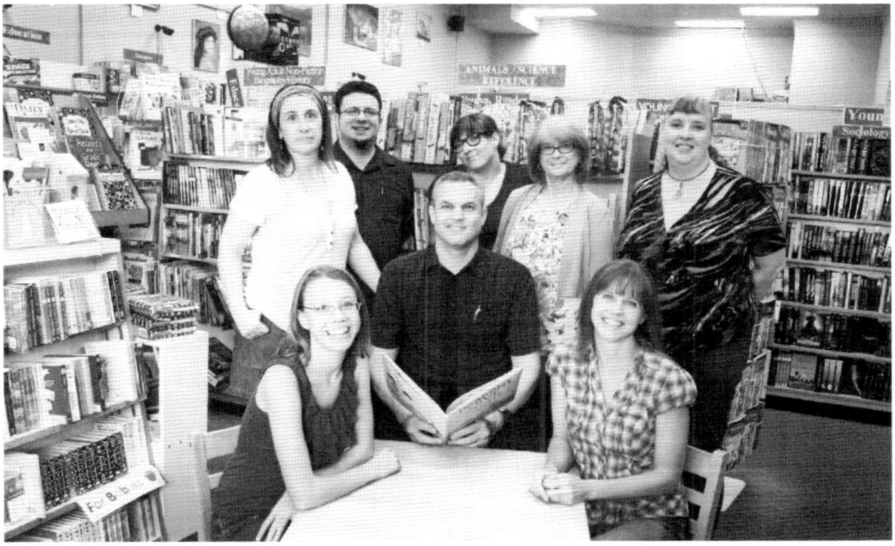

Book and Game, Book Nook Successor

Book and Game bookstore occupies a prominent corner downtown in the 1903 Die Brucke Building, the location of the historic Book Nook (below), which operated on that corner from around 1903 until 1993. The Book Nook sold paperbacks, magazines, and office supplies. Book and Game, which opened in the Blue Mountain Mall in Walla Walla in 1989, moved into the restored Die Brucke building in 1999. Locals Gene, Mike, and Jannelle Bruns bought the store on May 1, 2003. Book and Game features a large selection of books, games, and magazines. The store regularly hosts readings, book signings, and special events, and it has become a gathering place in Walla Walla. Staff members, pictured above from left to right, are (first row) Bethany Loe, Benjamin Fenton, and owner Jannelle Bruns; (second row) Julie Harper, Ben MacSpadden, Amber Delph, Dianne Moser, and manager Becky Hatley. (Above, author photograph; below, courtesy of Joe Drazan.)

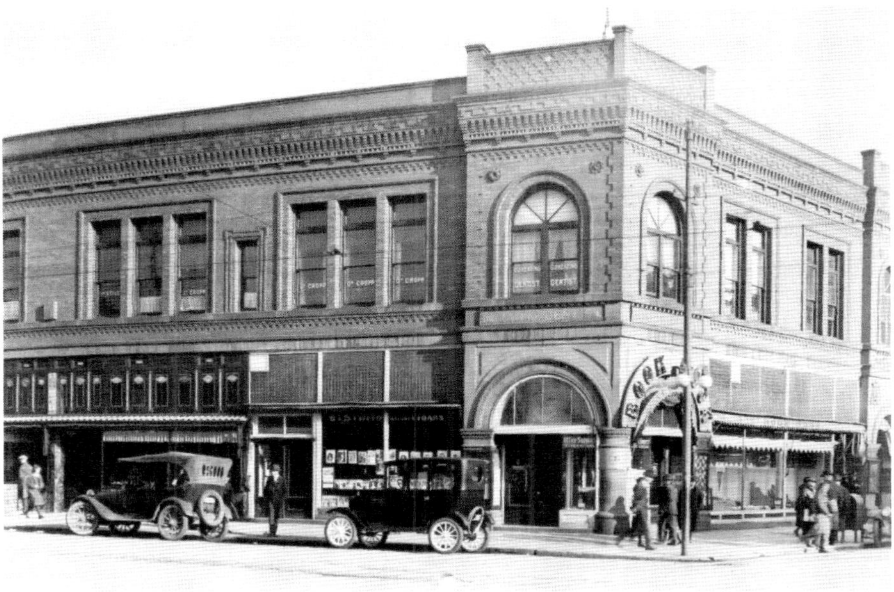

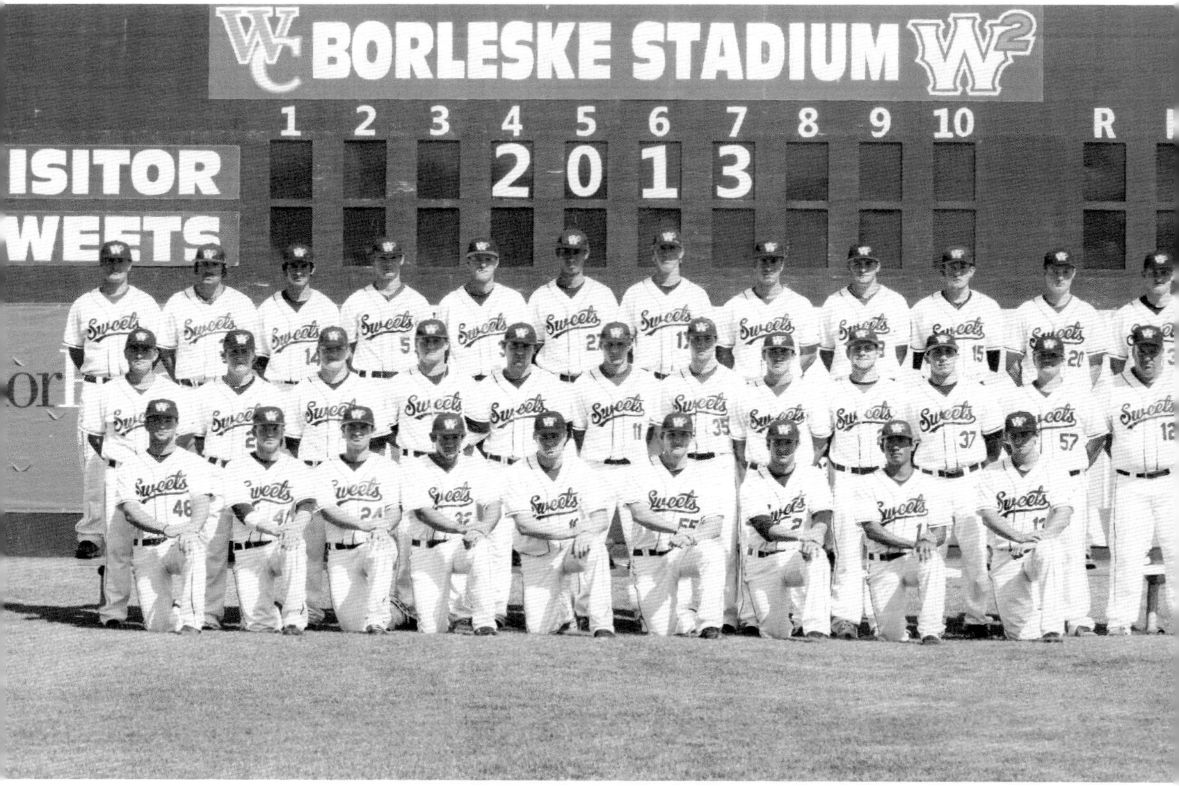

Walla Walla Sweets Baseball Team

Walla Walla has always had a strong baseball tradition, but when minor-league baseball left the city in 1984, things looked bleak. Fortunately, in 2009 a civic-minded group formed the Walla Walla Sweets Baseball Club under the West Coast League (WCL). Not only did the group invest in improvements to Borleske Stadium, the team attracted a large fan base, drawing 40,000 people each season. In an era of high-priced sporting events, the family-friendly ticket prices and cozy stadium provide an old-fashioned experience that recaptures the real thrill of baseball. Local families play host to the players during the season, further enhancing the team's strong community bonds. The Sweets also go out of their way to provide a platform for nonprofits, helping them raise thousands of dollars. The club secured two playoff berths in its first four seasons and in 2013 won its first WCL North pennant. Since the team's establishment, 11 players have signed contracts with major-league baseball teams. (Courtesy of Walla Walla Sweets.)

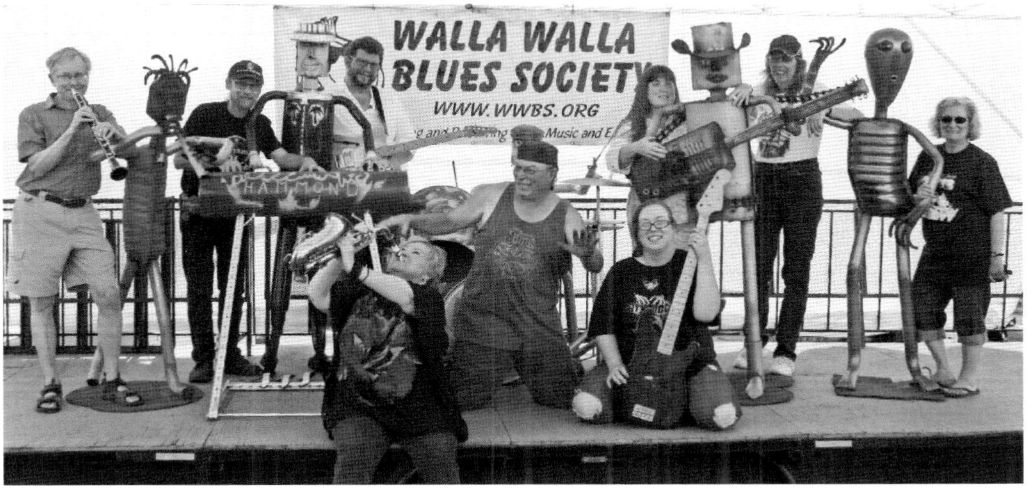

Walla Walla Blues Society

The Walla Walla Blues Society, which celebrated its 20th anniversary in 2013, is dedicated to the preservation of the blues as a traditional American art form. The society's Blues in the Schools program, started in 2000, brings a series of presentations and performances by local, regional, and national blues musicians plus historians to entertain and enlighten students. They also started Instruments for Kids, which pairs donated instruments with children who want to pursue music but cannot afford an instrument. Pictured from left to right are Rich Smith, George Copeland, Phil Lynch, Patty Keyes, Mike Hammond, Kat Adkins, Laura Hall, Donna Johnson, and Verna Reesman. (Author photograph.)

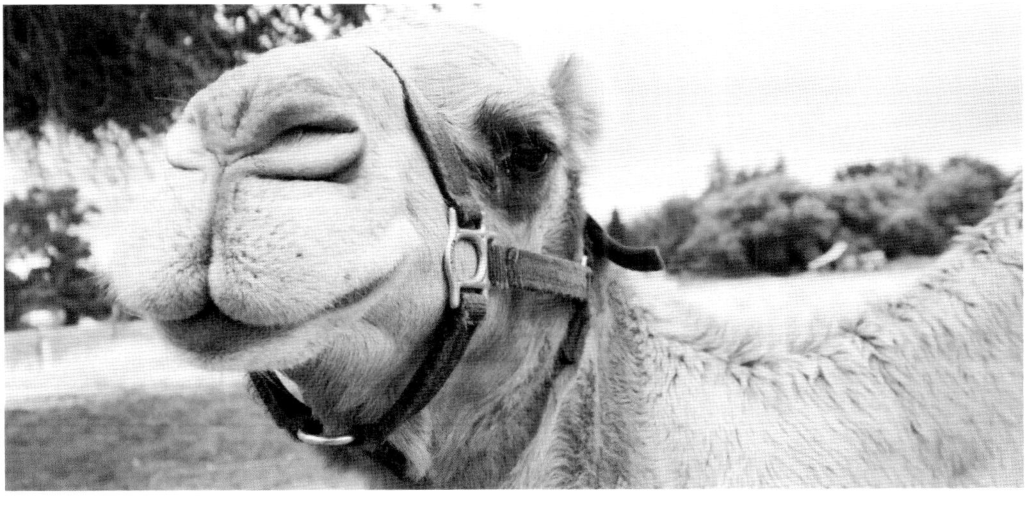

Izzy the Camel

Folks traveling through nearby Waitsburg may think they are seeing a mirage on their way into town. But it is just Izzy the camel, perhaps Waitsburg's best-known celebrity. Izzy, a Texas native, is a dromedary with personality—he thinks he is a person. This camel superstar just loves people, particularly those with apples and carrots. When he is not sharing his pasture with Winny the miniature donkey and owners Mickey and Tawnya Richards's horses, Izzy maintains a busy schedule of events that includes Christmas pageants, birthday parties, parades, and just about any event where he can meet people. (Colby Kuschatka photograph.)

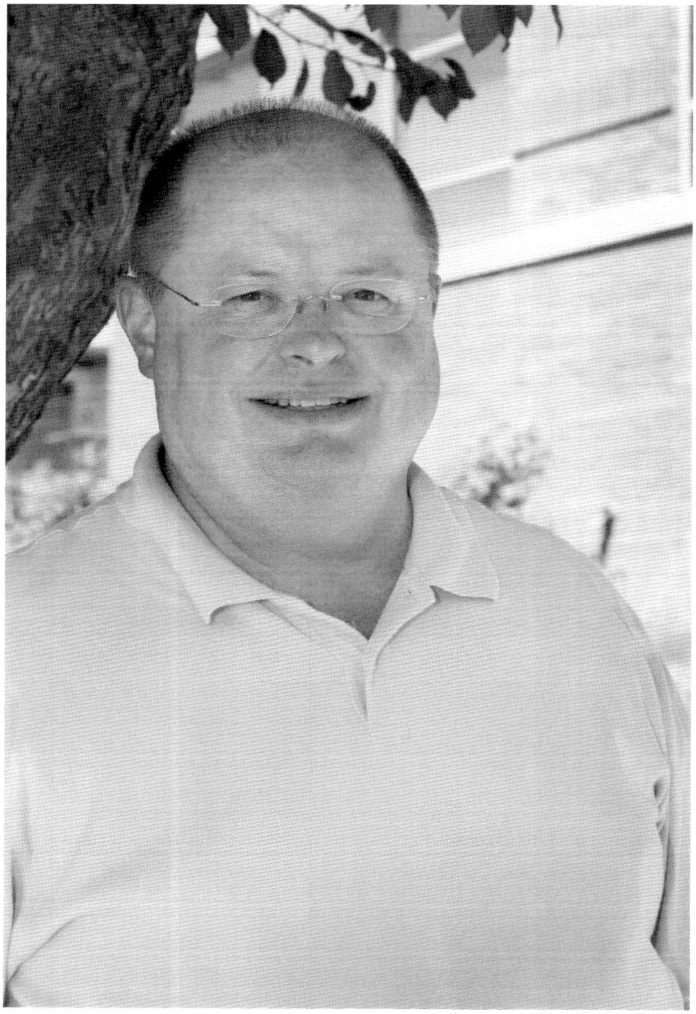

Dr. Richard Simon Jr., Renowned Sleep Specialist and Walla Walla Symphony Stalwart
Dr. Richard Simon Jr. is the medical director of the Kathryn Severyns Dement Sleep Disorders Center at Providence St. Mary Medical Center in Walla Walla. He also serves as clinical associate professor of medicine at the University of Washington School of Medicine and is a nationally recognized sleep specialist known for his clinical work, teaching, and research. Simon, a Walla Walla native, graduated from Whitman College and the University of Chicago Medical School but chose to return to his hometown. He developed an interest in sleep disorders when he met Dr. William "Bill" Dement of the Stanford University School of Medicine, whose research on sleep disorders led to the identification of REM (rapid eye motion) sleep. Simon became one of the first primary care physicians in the nation to treat his patients' sleep disorders, which led to the establishment of the Sleep Disorders Center at Providence St. Mary Medical Center. Simon is equally well known as a musician and a strong supporter of the Walla Walla Symphony. He served on the orchestra's board of directors and performs as its principal bass clarinet player. The symphony was founded in 1907 and is the oldest continuously operating symphony west of the Mississippi River. Under its current music director and conductor, Yaacov Bergman, the symphony is well known for its diverse offerings and its programs for young people, including its youth orchestra, instrument lending program, and the popular summer Rock Camp. (Courtesy of Providence St. Mary Medical Center.)

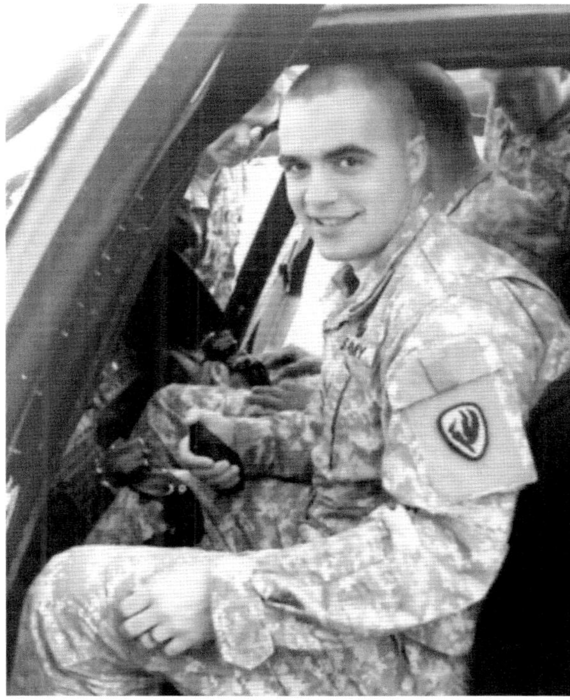

1st Lt. Mathew G. Fazzari, First Walla Walla Soldier to Die in the War in Afghanistan

The war in Afghanistan came home to Walla Walla on June 6, 2012, when native son Matt Fazzari became the first Walla Walla soldier to die in the conflict. He was killed by enemy fire while flying his helicopter out of Bagram Air Base on a surveillance mission. Fazzari, the son of Greg and Susan Fazzari, graduated from Walla Walla's DeSales Catholic High School in 2005. He joined the ROTC program at Gonzaga University and, after graduating with honors, was commissioned as an Army second lieutenant in May 2010. Married to high school sweetheart Tovah Kingman, he was the father of two young boys, Dominic and Samuel. His favorite quote from Gen. Douglas MacArthur included the words, "By profession I am a soldier and take pride in that fact. But I am prouder—infinitely prouder—to be a father." The news hit the Walla Walla community extremely hard, and on June 19, 2012, thousands turned out along the flag-lined route from the airport through downtown under an arch of flag-draped fire department ladder trucks. It was a day of sadness, yet also of pride, love, and community. (Both, courtesy of Fazzari family.)

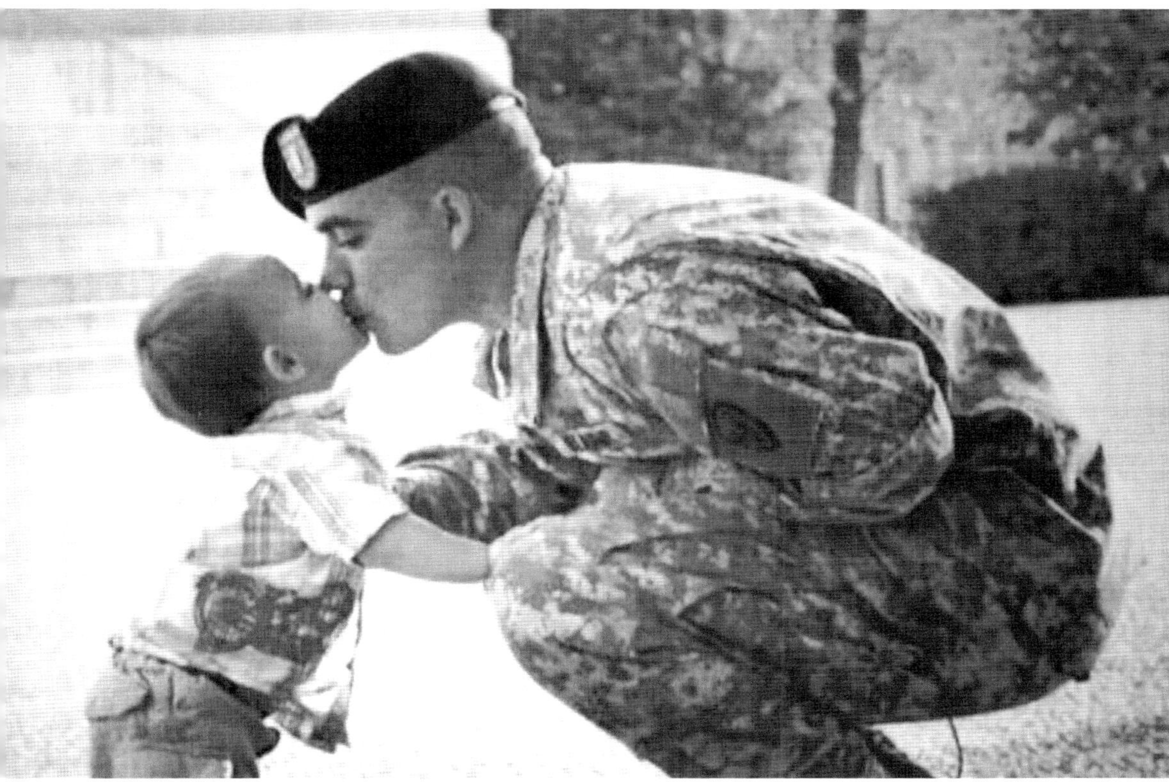

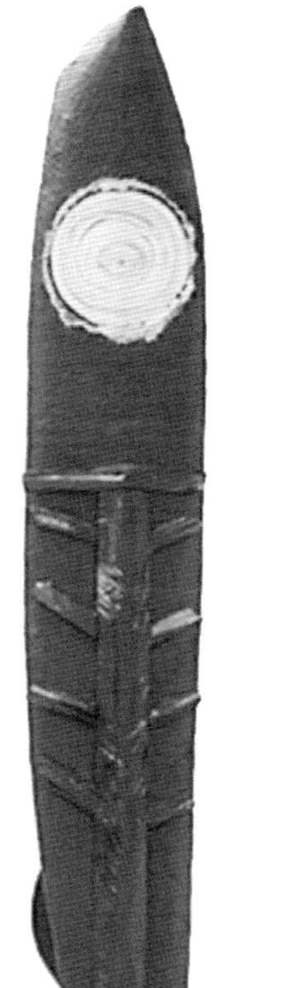

Squire Broel, Artist

Looking Back, Looking Forward was selected as the public art installation commemorating Walla Walla's sesquicentennial in 2012. The cast bronze and cast glass sculpture is described as totemic, paying homage to the spirit of the totem—a Northwest Indian tradition. The piece incorporates elements that contributed to Walla Walla history, including "growth, a pioneering vision, industry, agriculture, commerce, banking, and education." Squire Broel came to Walla Walla in 1993 and worked as the *patineur* (bronze coloration specialist) for Walla Walla Foundry until 1999, when he opened his own studio. In addition to expanding his skills at the foundry, Broel believes that his art—sculpture, painting, and blown glass—is influenced by experiences gained from living in the rural West. Although his work has exhibited internationally, he finds living in Walla Walla has allowed him to develop "his own visual voice that continues to gain attention outside the Northwest." (Melissa Christy photograph, courtesy of Walla Walla Foundry.)

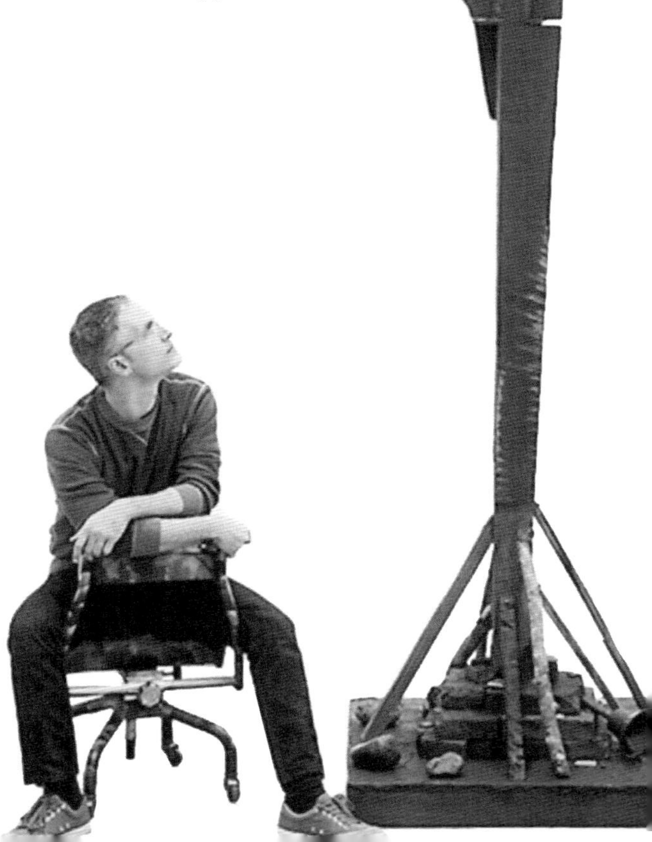

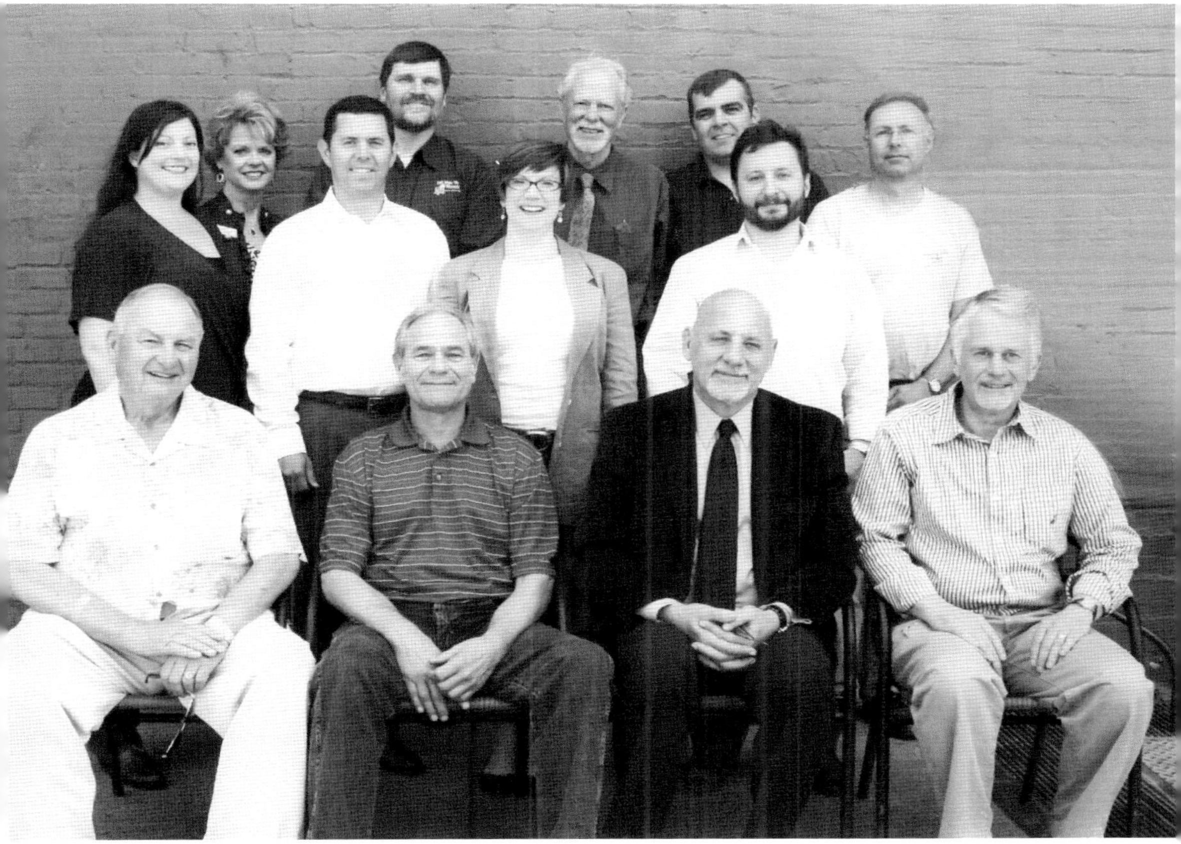

Sesquicentennial Committee

Walla Walla celebrated its sesquicentennial in 2012 with a wide variety of events as well as banners, commemorative coins, and posters. In April, a special conference and commemoration of the Mullan Road included rededicating a monument to this historic route. Fort Walla Walla Museum's Living History Company was featured in performances at the museum and the city council, and it led downtown walking tours. A special Fourth of July commemoration in Pioneer Park included state and local government officials. A Victorian ball was held in September featuring dancing and costumes from the era. The sesquicentennial year wrapped up with the unveiling of the public art installation of Squire Broel's sculpture *Looking Back, Looking Forward* (opposite page). The Sesquicentennial Committee included, from left to right, (first row) Mayor Jim Barrow; cochair Jim Dumont, City of Walla Walla; cochair Elio Agostini, Downtown Walla Walla Foundation; and Doug Saturno, Historic Preservation Commission; (second row) Greer Garske Buchanan, ArtWalla; Rob Blethen, publisher of Walla Walla *Union-Bulletin*; Jennifer Northam, Downtown Walla Walla Foundation; and Alex DeMambro, USKH, Inc.; (third row) Bonnie Bowton, Banner Bank; James Payne, Fort Walla Walla Museum; Dan Clark, Walla Walla 2020; Shane Laib, Walla Walla City Council; and Rick Tuttle, Kirkman House Museum. (Author photograph.)

INDEX

INDEX